D0116955

PL
2677
.L5
A23

Li, Ho

The poems of Li
Ho (791-817)

DATE DUE

COLLEGE OF MARIN LIBRARY
COLLEGE AVENUE
KENTFIELD, CA 94904

THE OXFORD LIBRARY OF
EAST ASIAN LITERATURES

Edited by

DAVID HAWKES

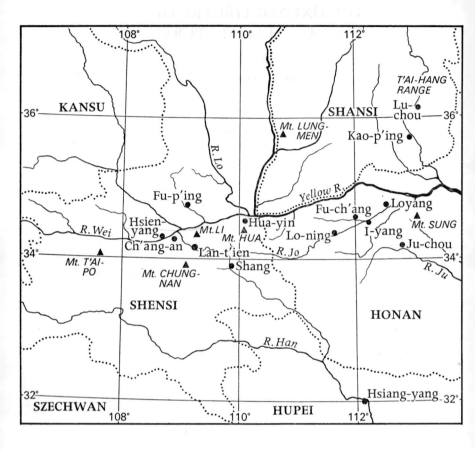

THE POEMS OF
Li Ho

(791–817)

Translated with an Introduction by

J. D. FRODSHAM

READER IN CHINESE
AUSTRALIAN NATIONAL UNIVERSITY

CLARENDON PRESS · OXFORD

1970

Oxford University Press, Ely House, London W1

GLASGOW NEW YORK TORONTO MELBOURNE WELLINGTON
CAPE TOWN SALISBURY IBADAN NAIROBI DAR ES SALAAM LUSAKA ADDIS ABABA
BOMBAY CALCUTTA MADRAS KARACHI LAHORE DACCA
KUALA LUMPUR SINGAPORE HONG KONG TOKYO

© OXFORD UNIVERSITY PRESS 1970

PRINTED IN GREAT BRITAIN BY LUND HUMPHRIES
LONDON AND BRADFORD

FOR

JULIA DERLING FRODSHAM

WORKS BY THE SAME AUTHOR

An Anthology of Chinese Verse: Han Wei Chin and the Northern and Southern Dynasties

The Murmuring Stream: The Life and Works of the Chinese Nature Poet Hsieh Ling-yün (385-433), Duke of K'ang-Lo, 2 vols.

PREFACE

I FIRST became interested in Li Ho as long ago as 1955, when asked to review a couple of Japanese articles about him for the *Revue Bibliographique de Sinologie*. Though his collected poems became my constant companion during the years that followed, it was not until 1965 that I found the leisure to begin the present study. This was originally intended to present only a selection of Ho's poems: but Professor David Hawkes, who was kind enough to read through my original draft, urged me to present an integral translation of the complete poems, a task I should never have dared to undertake without his encouragement. Since many of Ho's poems are so esoteric as to defy translation, I am well aware of my rashness in embarking on such a venture. I can only hope that what this volume lacks in quality it may make up for in quantity and thus convey something of the range and sustained intensity of this extraordinary poet.

I should like to take this opportunity to thank Professor Hawkes for his interest and helpful advice; Miss Matsubara Junko and Mrs. Nobuko Gardiner for their assistance with Japanese materials; Professor Liu Ts'un-yan for devoting his profound scholarship to solving problems that had frequently baffled the commentators. My thanks also go to Dr. Margaret South for sending me a copy of her thesis on Li Ho, though this unfortunately arrived too late for me to benefit from it; to Miss Enid Bishop and Dr. K. H. Gardiner, both of whom kindly lent me books; to Miss Ludmilla Panskaya for reading the proofs and compiling the index, and to Mrs. Audrey Marks for typing most of the manuscript. I should also like to record my indebtedness to the Australian Research Grants Committee for a generous award which enabled me to complete the work without undue delay

Finally I owe a debt of personal gratitude to Anthony Short, Donald Fryer and Ch'eng Hsi for their advice and assistance during the difficult period when this book was first taking shape.

J. D. FRODSHAM.

CONTENTS

CHRONOLOGY

755 – Rebellion of An Lu-shan begins.

791 – Li Ho born.

805 – Emperor Te-tsung dies. Accession of Emperor Shun-tsung.

806 – Accession of Emperor Hsien-tsung. *Yüan-ho* period begins.

807 – Revolt of Li Yi in Eastern China. Wang Ts'an-yüan, Yang Ching-chih and Ch'üan Ch'ü receive *chin-shih* degree.

808 – Li Ho's father died before this date.

809 – Ho meets Han Yü and Huang-fu Shih? Chang Ch'e receives *chin-shih* degree. Campaign launched against rebel Wang Ch'eng-tsung.

810 – Ho rejected as candidate for *chin-shih*

811 – Ho takes up post in Court of Imperial Sacrifices.
Li Chi-fu returns from east and becomes Chief Minister.

813 – Han Yü appointed to Board of History.

814 – Li Chi-fu dies. Ho resigns post at Court.

815 – Po Chü-yi banished to Chiang-chou. Li Chih-tao's troops raid Lo-yang. Wu Yüan-chi rebellion breaks out.
Ho journeys to Lu-chou and stays with Chang Ch'e.

817 – Wu Yüan-chi rebellion defeated. Ho dies.

TRANSLATOR'S NOTE

THE POEMS in this collection are arranged according to the order of their appearance in the *Chung-hua Shu-chü* edition of the *San-chia Li Ch'ang-chi ko-shih* (1760) of Wang Ch'i (Shanghai, 1959.) Thus the rubric Ho, p. 35, means that the original of this poem may be found on that page of the edition mentioned.

Most of the poems translated were originally written in either the five-character or the seven-character line. The former comes over well into English; but the latter tends to produce lines too long to be handled without clumsiness. In the seven-character line, the caesura normally falls after the fourth syllable thus:

Ch'ui yang yeh lao // ying pu erh
Weeping willow leaves old // orioles feed young.

I have therefore tried to resolve this problem by breaking the line into two at the caesura:

In the ageing leaves of weeping willows
Orioles feed their young.

Change of rhyme has been indicated by beginning another stanza wherever a new rhyme occurs. A modified form of the Wade-Giles system of romanization has been used throughout.

'The business is not alone to translate language into language, but poesie into poesie, and poesie is of so subtle a spirit that in the pouring out of one language into another it will all evaporate and if a new spirit is not added in the transfusion there will remain nothing but a *caput mortuum*.'

SIR JOHN DENHAM, *Preface to the Second Book of the Aeneid*

'The work of the translator (and with all humility be it spoken) is one of some self-denial. Often he would avail himself of any special grace of his own idiom and epoch, if only his will belonged to him; often would some cadence serve him but for his author's structure – some structure but for his author's cadence... Now he would slight the matter for the music and now the music for the matter but no, he must deal with each alike. Sometimes too a flaw in the work galls him and he would fain remove it, doing for the poet that which his age denied him; but no, it is not in the bond.'

D. G. ROSSETTI

INTRODUCTION

LI HO 李賀, style Ch'ang-chi 長吉, was born in A.D. 791 to a minor branch of the imperial house of T'ang. Though his connection with the imperial family is well established, we have no precise details about his relationship.[1] Several sources assert that he was a descendant of a certain Prince Cheng 鄭: but since there were no less than three princes of that name in the T'ang royal house we cannot be sure with which one Ho was connected.[2] Though several of his relatives held offices of great distinction in the mid-T'ang period, his immediate family gained very little besides respect from its kinship with royalty, for neither wealth nor honours accrued to it from this connection. Ho's father, Li Chin-su, never rose very high in the official hierarchy, attaining only the magistrateship of a county. His sole claim to fame lies in his friendship with the great poet Tu Fu (712–770), who once wrote a farewell poem to him.[3] He died before Ho was eighteen, leaving the boy to make his own way in the world with nothing but his admittedly extraordinary talents to recommend him. The family's lack of status and consequent neglect by the official histories and local gazetteers, involves the historian in considerable difficulties when it comes to finding out something about Ho himself, since very little information can be obtained from any reliable sources. What we do know is all too often fragmentary and tantalizingly vague. We are aware, for example, that Ho's mother

[1] See *Chiu T'ang-shu, Po-na pen* (hereinafter referred to as *CTS*), CXXXVII, biography of Li Ho; *Hsin T'ang shu, Po-na pen* (referred to as *HTS*) CCIII, biography of Li Ho; *T'ai-p'ing kuang-chi*, XLIX.

[2] Of these three princes, only two, namely Liang 亮 eighth son of T'ai-tsung and Yüan-yi 元懿 thirteenth son of Kao-tsu, can be considered seriously. Commentators are about equally divided as to which of these two was Ho's ancestor. Both Yeh Ts'ung-ch'i and Suzuki Torao come out in favour of Yüan-yi.

[3] *Tu Shao-ling chi hsiang-chu*, XXII. p. 9, *After Seeing off My 29th Younger Brother Li Chin-su at Kung-an on His Way to Shu, I Go down the Mien to Lo.* This poem, written in 768, is held by some commentators to indicate kinship between Tu Fu and Li Ho. I can see no objection to this argument.

née Cheng, came in all probability from the Chengs of Honan, who were one of the most distinguished families of the period. We know also that he had an elder sister who married into the Wang clan as well as a younger brother, whom he mentions several times in his poems. But apart from these, he and his widowed mother, to whom he was devoted, would appear to have had no other immediate family.

Several commentators have maintained however that Ho had several elder brothers and a wife. The first assertion is based merely on a misunderstanding of the term *hsiung* 兄 which is often used in the sense of 'elder kinsman of the same generation' and does not necessarily mean 'elder brother'. If Ho had really had four-teen elder brothers, as some critics would have us believe, it is likely that some of them at least would have survived him. But in fact, his friend, Shen Tzu-ming, writing only fifteen years after Ho's death, says explicitly that Ho had no brothers, sisters or children alive.[4]

The question of whether he had a wife or not is more difficult to resolve. It seems highly unlikely that he would have been mar-ried, since during this period it was unusual for any scholar to take a wife until after he had gained his doctorate and been given an official post. Moreover marriage was an expensive business since the bridegroom had both to provide a dowry and pay for the wedding. Ho could never have afforded to do this. Furthermore, the case for his having had a wife rests on nothing more substantial than his use of the term *ch'ing-ch'ing* ("my dear one") in one of his poems. This is very flimsy evidence indeed. We should note, also, that Li Shang-yin (812–58), one of his earliest biographers, makes no mention of any wife of Ho's being present at his death-bed and has to rely on the testimony of his elder sister. Critics who naïvely insist that Ho must have been married, simply because he wrote numerous love-poems, would seem to be merely over-anxious to assure us that he was a respectable citizen who did not squander his substance on singing-girls. It seems to me that the

[4]See Tu Mu's *Preface*.

Ch'ing commentator, Yao Wen-hsieh, who asserted that Ho's death was brought about by sexual dissipation was possibly nearer the truth of the matter, in the light of evidence provided by the poems, than those who would make our poet into a pillar of domestic sobriety.

Perhaps the main obstacle encountered by the historian is the fact that Ho's collected works, which might have been a valuable source of information about the writer's life, consist only of poems, songs and ballads – some 243 in all – while prose works, invariably a much richer digging-ground for the biographer, are totally lacking.[5] This dearth of biographical material means that Ho is all poet; the man himself has become almost as shadowy a figure as Ch'ü Yüan, reputed author of the *Li Sao* from which Ho drew so much of his own inspiration. The faded picture can at best only be restored a little through a perusal of his poems; the lineaments of that vanished face conjured up again through such brief biographies and anecdotes as have come down to us. Consider for a moment Ho's official biography as recorded in the *New T'ang History* (*Hsin T'ang-shu*), written some 250 years after his death:[6]

Li Ho, styled Ch'ang-chi, was a descendant of Prince Cheng. When

[5]Two of these poems are held to be forgeries, thus reducing the number to 241. Since Tu Fu has some 2,200 poems extant, Po Chü-yi 2,800 and Li Po more than 1,000, this is a very small number indeed. The T'ang writer, Chang Ku, has a story which explains this. He alleges that Li P'an (text mistakenly reads 'Fan'), a Vice-President of the Ministry of Rites, was a great admirer of Ho's work. After Ho's death Li P'an handed over all his songs and poems to an elder cousin of Ho's and asked him to correct them. This cousin, who had often been slighted by Ho, took revenge by throwing the lot down the privy. See *Yu-hsien ku-ch'ui*, in *T'ang-jen shuo-hui*, p. 2a. Li Shang-yin notes in his autobiography that Ho never bothered about what became of his poems once he had written them. See *Li Yi-shan wen-chi*, IV, p. 20b.

[6]*HTS*, CCIII. The biography in *CTS*, CXXXVII, is much shorter: 'Li Ho, style Ch'ang-chi, was a descendant of Prince Cheng of the Imperial House of T'ang. Because his father's name was Chin-su he could not become a *chin-shih*. Han Yü wrote his "Essay on Taboo-names" on his behalf: but Ho was never allowed to sit for the examination. His brush was quick and clever. He

B

only seven years old he could write verse. When Han Yü and Huang-fu Shih first heard of this, they could not believe it, so they called at his house and asked him to write a poem. He picked up his writing brush and dashed one off as though he were merely copying it out, giving it the title: *The Tall Official Carriage Comes on a Visit.* Both men were flabbergasted. From this time on Ho was famous.

Ho was frail and thin, with eyebrows that met together and long fingernails. He wrote at great speed. Every day at dawn he would leave the house riding a colt, followed by a servant-lad with an antique tapestry bag on his back. When inspiration struck him, he would write the verses down and drop them in the bag. He never wrote poems on a given topic, forcing his verses to conform to the theme, as others do. At nightfall he would go home and work these verses into a finished poem. If he was not blind drunk or in mourning, every day was spent like this. Once he had written a poem he did not greatly care what became of it. His mother used to have her maid rummage through the bag and when she saw that he had written so much she would exclaim angrily: 'This boy of mine won't be content until he has vomited out his heart'.

Because his father's name was Chin-su, he was not allowed to sit for the Doctoral examination. Han Yü wrote his 'Essay on Taboo Names' on his behalf; but he was never accepted as a candidate.

His verse delights in the extraordinary. Everything he wrote was startlingly outstanding, breaking with accepted literary tradition. None of his contemporaries could follow him in this. He wrote dozens of ballads, which the Yün-shao musicians set to music. He became a Harmoniser of Pitch-pipes, dying when he was twenty-seven *sui*.

His friends Ch'üan Ch'ü, Yang Ching-chih and Wang Kung-yüan frequently made off with what he wrote. This fact, coupled with his premature death, has resulted in very few of his poems and songs coming down to us.

This account, which is largely based on the short biographies which the poets Tu Mu (803–52) and Li Shang-yin wrote for Ho's

was especially good at writing songs. His thoughts and his style were like towering precipices and lofty mountain-walls, soaring up ten thousand cubits high. Contemporary literary men sought to imitate him, but could not come near him. He wrote several score ballads which were sung by everybody, even by the Yün-shao musicians. He held the rank of Harmoniser of Pitch-pipes in the Court of Imperial Sacrifices. He died at the age of twenty-four.'

collected poems, tells us very little indeed. The lack of a solidly based biography means that Ho has been romanticized more than most Chinese poets of his stature. The Li Ho of literary legend is the demon-talented (*kuei-ts'ai*) poet, tall and cadaverous, his hair white as snow round his haggard face, who on his death-bed is summoned to heaven by a spirit-messenger riding a red dragon. These legends, nevertheless, have their uses, for they direct us to an important truth about the poet; namely, that his verse and his personality alike were considered odd both by his contemporaries and by later critics. Ho is, in fact, close to the western idea of the *poète maudit* – and this is not a stock type of literary man at all in China. Chinese poets were almost invariably members of the bureaucracy, cultivated officials who yet secreted poetry as naturally as oysters produce pearls. For the Chinese, the poetic vocation and the official career have never been at variance. To attain a post at all one had of necessity to be something of a poet, since the passing of the government examinations demanded considerable poetic proficiency of all aspirants to office. This was true of most periods of Chinese history, but never more so than during T'ang, when poetic talent alone could steer one through the examinations.[7] In short, Flaubert's dictum: 'Les honneurs déshonorent, le titre dégrade, la fonction abrutit', would have been quite incomprehensible in China to anyone but a Taoist hermit. The Chinese gentleman sought office, first and foremost: everything else – fame, riches, literary renown – was subordinate to this great aim; could hardly indeed be won without the fulfilment of it.

It was Ho's great misfortune never to have attained high office. His failure to do so was all the more humiliating since he was not only renowned for his literary talents but had for his patron one of the most eminent literary men of the time, the great Confucian scholar, Han Yü (768–824). To understand the importance of this,

[7]The poet Meng Chiao (751–814), however, remarked sardonically:
       'Bad poetry makes you an official,
       Good poetry leaves you on a lonely hill.'

one must realize that to be sure of success in the examination
system of the time, it was not enough to be merely talented. One
had in addition to secure the support of a powerful patron who
would act as a guarantor and later on further one's official career.
To be sure, Han Yü was not as highly esteemed by his contemporaries as he was by later generations, but he was nevertheless an
eminent, if controversial, writer. One story of Ho's first encoun-
ter with Han Yü has already been mentioned in the brief biography given above. Another and rather more likely version has
Ho visiting Yü, not at seven years of age but on the eve of his
sitting for the examinations, when he was nineteen or so: 'Li Ho
went to visit Han Yü, taking with him his songs and poems. Han
Yü at that time held the post of Doctoral Professor at the Lo-yang
branch of the University of Sons of State. He had just returned
home exhausted after seeing somebody off when his retainers
presented the scrolls to him. He loosened his belt and began to
read the first poem: *Ballad of the Grand Warden of Goose Gate*
(p. 27) which begins:

> Black clouds whelm on the city,
> Till it seems the city must yield.
> Our chain-mail glitters under the sun,[7]
> Metal scales agape.

He immediately girded on his belt again and gave orders to invite
Ho in.'[8]

Whatever the truth of these stories, there can be no doubt that
Ho did succeed at an early age in attracting the attention of two
influential patrons, Han Yü and Huang-fu Shih.[9] Ho seems to
have been on especially intimate terms with Huang-fu Shih – a
surprising fact, in view of the latter's notorious irascibility – and
wrote at least four poems in his honour. However, since Shih had
become involved in an examination scandal in 808, Ho found
himself solely dependent on the good offices of Han Yü, whose

[8] *Yu-hsien ku-ch'ui*, p. 2a.
[9] Huang-fu Shih (biography in *HTS*, CLXXVI), a *chin-shih* of 806, was one
of the leading literary men in the circle around Han Yü.

support was especially valuable since practically every candidate who had enlisted his backing had succeeded brilliantly.

It must have been with high hopes, then, that Ho secured Yü's sponsorship for the Honan district examinations of 810.[10] Candidates successful in this examination were eligible to sit for the Doctoral (*chü*) examination held in the capital under the auspices of the Ministry of Rites. There were several types of Doctoral examination in T'ang times varying from law, calligraphy and mathematics to knowledge of the classics (the *ming-ching* degree). However, the most difficult and the most highly regarded was the *chin-shih* examination, which rigorously tested both a candidate's literary abilities and his grounding in the classics. To succeed in this, Ho would have to answer questions on current affairs, write exegetical essays on passages from classical texts and – most important of all – compose long poems of a type called *fu* ('rhymeprose') as well as *shih* ('lyric verse'). Once he had gained his doctorate, he was entitled to sit for the Selection (*hsüan*) examination, which determined whether or not he could be appointed to office. The Selection examination was very like the country-house interviews which are so much a feature of British Civil Service examinations. The candidate was judged by his bearing, ability to express himself, calligraphy and wisdom in making judgements. Only when he had satisfied the examiners in all these qualities was he judged to be a gentleman (*chün-tzu*) and therefore fit to govern.

It is hardly surprising to learn that the road to office was long and weary, with many falling by the wayside. Han Yü once pointed out that of every 3,000 candidates who emerged from the great crowd of aspirants, only 200 finally reached the Selection examination.[11] This means that fourteen out of every fifteen

[10]See his *Twelve Lyrics for Music* . . . (pp. 35–44) which he wrote on this occasion. Since these lyrics include a song for the intercalary month (p. 44), they must have been written in 809, the only year with an intercalary month which will fit the rest of our chronology.

[11]*Han Ch'ang-li ch'üan-chi, Tseng Chang T'ung-tzu hsü, Ssu-pu pei yao* ed., XX, pp. 2a-b.

candidates failed even to reach the last hurdle. Add to this the fact
that only a modest percentage of the final two hundred could be
allotted a post and the heart-breaking nature of the T'ang examination system becomes only too apparent. As Han Yü remarked,
since a candidate might well spend twenty years or more in
reaching the Selection examination, half of those who succeeded
were already grey-haired old men.[12]

With the stakes so high and the course so difficult it is not too
surprising to find that every sort of unscrupulous practice was
adopted to advance oneself and eliminate one's rivals. This was a
free-for-all, with no holds barred as Ho himself was soon to
discover to his cost. To a casual observer, however, his success
must have seemed a foregone conclusion. Dazzlingly talented,
scion of a branch of the royal house, and supported by a prominent literary man, he must have already been marked down as the
most outstanding candidate of his year. Yet it was almost certainly
this very fame which was to prove his undoing, making him too
conspicuous a target to avoid the shafts levelled at him. Shortly
after arriving in Ch'ang-an he was stunned to hear that he was
not even to be allowed to sit for the *chin-shih* examination at
which he should have carried all before him. The excuse put
forward was that since his deceased father's name had been
Chin-su, the word *chin* in the term *chin-shih* violated a family
taboo.

To understand what had occurred, some explanation is neces-
sary. The Chinese have always been scrupulously careful to avoid
using the personal names of certain people – one's father or the
emperor, for example – either in speech or in writing. When such
a word was met it had to be avoided, either by pronouncing it
mou (so-and-so) or by substituting another character in its place.
Now the Chinese spoken during T'ang times, though differing
markedly from the Mandarin (*p'u-t'ung hua*) of today, was similar
to it in that it abounded in homophones. Hence official regula-

---

[12]*Ibid., loc. cit.*

tions concerning these taboos had shown common sense in asserting that only the word itself had to be avoided, while its homophones could be pronounced or written with impunity. Since the *Chin* 晉 of Ho's father's name is quite a different word from the *chin* 進 ("to advance") of the term *chin-shih*, though closely related to it etymologically, it might have been supposed that no taboo was therefore violated. Unfortunately, official regulations have never owned the force in China that they have enjoyed in Europe. What mattered was customary law, not bureaucratic rulings: and customary law insisted that homophones be considered taboo.

Tradition has it that it was Po Chü-yi's friend, the poet Yüan Chen (779–831), who brought this matter to the notice of the authorities because Ho had once insulted him.[13] If this is true, the situation would have been ironic, since Po himself had once been attacked on the ground that he had infringed a taboo by writing poems about a well and plum-blossom, though it was known his mother had died by falling into a well while admiring some blossom.[14] However, Han Yü's account of the affair is less specific designating the informer as simply 'one who was contending with Ho for fame' – a description which leads one to suspect one of Ho's fellow-candidates and rivals. Since Yüan passed his Selection examination in 803, when Ho was only a child, the traditional story is clearly inaccurate. However, one writer has suggested that the informer was in fact Yüan, who at that time held the post of Censor and had made a good many enemies, among them Fang Shih, governor of Lo-yang, the man responsible for authorizing Ho's candidature. So Yüan is held to have acted in this way not so much to obtain revenge on Li Ho as to discomfit Fang Shih, since the authorizer of an unworthy candi-

---

[13]The *Chü t'an lu* of the T'ang writer K'ang Ping alleges that when Yüan Chen went to pay his respects to Li Ho one day Ho refused to see him. See *Chü t'an lu* in *Chin-tai pi-shu* (Shanghai, 1922), XXXIV, p. 35a.

[14]A. Waley, *The Life and Times of Po Chü-yi*, A.D. 772–846 (London, 1951), p. 102.

date was himself liable for severe penalties.[15] To this I would join the conjecture that some faction hostile to Han Yü was also involved in this questionable manoeuvre, since Yü, as guarantor, also stood to lose a great deal by his protégé's disgrace. This would explain why Yü rushed in to intercede for Ho with his famous essay on taboo-names, as Yü himself points out:

> Ho's candidature for the *chin-shih* degree has become a *cause célèbre*. Somebody who was contending with Ho for fame slandered him, saying: 'Ho's father's name was Chin-su. It would be bad form for Ho to sit for the *chin-shih* examination. Those who sponsored him are in the wrong!' . . . Hence Huang-fu Shih said to me: 'If you do not explain matters, both you and Ho will find yourselves in trouble.'[16]

Yü then goes on to ridicule the accusations made against Ho by pointing out that to apply the homophone taboo in this way would result in ridiculous excesses. If, for example, the father bore the personal name Jen (仁) then the son would be unable to call himself a man (*jen* 人)! Yü's essay was successful in so far as it ensured that neither he nor Ho was involved in any further trouble. But even Yü's persuasive prose could not prevail upon the authorities to let Ho sit for the examination. The imbecilic misuse of the taboo regulation had barred him from this forever.

From then on until his untimely death seven years later, a death which was very likely hastened by the dashing of all his hopes for a brilliant official career, Ho was a man ravaged by sickness and disappointment. He seems to have suffered a severe illness – perhaps a nervous breakdown – consequent upon his failure to gain his degree.

> 'I came back home, all skin and bones,
> A fleshless face,
> A murrain lighted on my head,
> My hair fell out'.   (p. 91)

[15]M. T. South, 'Li Ho – a Scholar-Official of the *Yüan-ho* Period (806–21)', *Journal of the Oriental Society of Australia*, 2.2 (June 1964), pp. 64–81.
[16]*Han Ch'ang-li ch'üan-chi, Hui pien*, XX, p. 12a.

From this time on, the melancholy and despair which is the hall-
mark of so much T'ang poetry stamped itself ever more deeply
on his verse.

> Mournfully chanting, I study the sighs of Ch'u,
> My sick bones ache in lonely poverty.
> From gazing at autumns, my hair has turned white,
> Leaves on the trees moan in the wind-blown rain.
>
> (p. 80)

> In Ch'ang-an city lives a lad of twenty
> Whose heart's already so much rotten wood ...
> He knows by now the way is blocked to him,
> No need to wait until his hair turns white.
>
> (p. 145)

> Sparse cassia blossom under snow,
> A crying crow, struck by a bolt came home ...
> The woman he loved asked him no questions,
> But in the mirror he glimpsed her falling tears.
>
> (p. 131)

> Your elder brother is now turned twenty.
> The mirror tells him how his beard is growing.
> Three years ago he left our home – to come to this!
> Begging rice at princes' gates,
> An utter failure.
>
> (p. 97)

> Though I have reached my twentieth year
> I've missed my goal.
> My whole heart sad and withered
> As a dying orchid.
>
> (p. 161)

> The king of Ch'in is nowhere to be seen,
> So dawn and dusk a burning fever racks me ...
> Because I cannot roam round with the moon,
> My hair's grown white before I end my song.
>
> (p. 100)

In one respect, however, Ho was more fortunate than the

countless other young men of his time who were unsuccessful
in the examinations. As the son of an official of the fifth degree he
was entitled to avail himself of the so-called *yin* privilege. This
meant he was allowed to sit for the Selection examination without having first to pass the Doctoral examination. Of course, his
lack of the *chin-shih* degree meant that he could never hope for
promotion or even for a job worthy of his talents. But beggars
cannot be choosers. He was, after all, a man with a widowed
mother and a younger brother to support, as he reminds us in his
verse:

> My whole family welcomes me with joy,
> Counting on me to fill their empty bellies.

(p. 248)

> Born into this world, I have to feed myself,
> So out of my gate I go, with burdened back.

(p. 117)

In the tenth month of 810, he set out from Lo-yang to take the
Selection examination at the capital:

> I'm going to play around with words
> For the Office of Heaven,
> For who would pity a royal scion
> Left unemployed?

(p. 92)

For a man of his abilities and background such an examination
could have presented few problems. In the following years he was
back in Ch'ang-an again, this time as Supervisor of Ceremonies
in the Court of Imperial Sacrifices (奉禮太常). In spite of its
high-sounding title, this was a low-ranking post whose duties
were of the dullest. The two Supervisors were officials of the ninth
degree, third class, a rank well down in the official hierarchy.[17]
Ho was in fact little more than a glorified usher, who had to see

[17]Ho was actually entitled to a higher rank than this, namely the eighth degree,
third class.

that the ceremonial vessels were set out correctly in the imperial
ancestral temple, attend to seating arrangements at court audience
and give the requisite signals which indicated when to bow,
kneel, kowtow or rise during ceremonies.[18] Such a post called for
neither literary talent nor administrative ability. To place a man
of his genius in this position was like using a racehorse to draw a
plough, as he never wearied of reminding his friends.

> This steed is no ordinary horse
> But the very spirit of the Fang star.
> Stand in front, rap on its slender bones,
> They'll ring out like bronze.
>
> (p. 70, No. 4)

> The Office of Rites has forced me from my true nature,
> I look haggard and worn, like a straw dog cast aside.
> In wind and snow I serve at the Altar of Fasting,
> My black belt threaded through a brazen seal.
> The work I do is fit only for slaves and bondmaids
> Who want no more than to wield dustpan and brush.
>
> (p. 146)

> The warm sun leaves me lonely and depressed,
> Blossoms only sadden this Pei-kuo Sao .
>
> (p. 151)

The reference in the last line to Pei-kuo Sao, who, though a man
of genius, supported his widowed mother by weaving nets and
making sandals, sums up succinctly enough what Ho thought
of his own position. We do not know for certain whether he ever
succeeded in rising from this post. Both the T'ang histories state
that he was given the rank of Harmonizer of Pitch-pipes, a post
of the eighth rank and thus one step above his position as Supervisor of Ceremonies.[19] In view of his high reputation as a writer
of songs I am inclined to believe that he was in fact eventually
promoted to this position, though precisely when must remain

---

[18] R. des Rotours, *Le Traité des Examens, Traduit de la Nouvelle Histoire des T'ang* (Paris, 1932), p. 320.
[19] *CTS*, CXXXVII: *HTS*, CCIII.

uncertain. What is certain, however, is that he was highly dissatisfied with whatever post he held in the Court of Imperial Sacrifices and expressed his longing to be away from it all time and time again in his verse, as for example in *After Days of Rain in the Ch'ung-yi District* (p. 143).

> Who can he be, this sad and lonely man,
> Who's come to suffer autumn in Ch'ang-an?
> As a young man I knew a traveller's sorrow,
> Wept in my sleep until my hair turned white.
> I feed my skinny nag on mouldy hay
> As gusts of rain splash in the chilly gutters.
> The Southern Palace is darkened by ancient blinds,
> Its sundials blank beneath a watery sun.
> My mountain home's a thousand leagues away,
> East of here, at the very foot of the clouds.
> Sleeping in sorrow, my sword-case as my pillow,
> In this makeshift room I dream of a marquisate.

The Ch'ung-yi district referred to in the title was a busy quarter of Ch'ang-an close to the Ministry of Civil Office. The cost of living in the capital was very high and Ho's salary regrettably low. Furthermore, he had to support his mother and young brother back in Ch'ang-ku, which must have made considerable inroads on his income. Nevertheless, pleading poverty is a convention of Chinese verse and I find it difficult to believe that he was so destitute he could not afford a servant ('Back from the office, I must shut the gates myself')[20] still less find himself unable to buy wine, as he alleges on at least one occasion. What probably did gall him, as it has vexed many another young bachelor in his position, was to live among all the delights provided by a great city without being able to afford to enjoy them. For Ch'ang-an was a metropolis, populous even by modern standards, with close on a million inhabitants. It was, in fact, the largest city in the world at that time, rivalled in size and splendour only by Haroun

[20] p. 18, *On First Taking up My Post as Supervisor of Ceremonies . . .* line 2.

Al-Rashid's Baghdad, which was then approaching its apogee.[21] In this sophisticated and highly cosmopolitan city a young official on a meagre salary might very well feel that life was passing him by for sheer lack of money, especially if he had a taste for wine and women, as Ho undoubtedly did.

We have already mentioned that a Ch'ing critic alleged that he died of sexual exhaustion, basing his statement partly on the numerous allusions to courtesans which abound throughout his verse.[22] One might perhaps conceivably be persuaded to agree to the assertion that Ho was married: but not even the most casual reader of his poems could reasonably claim that he was monogamous. One of his longest poems, *She Steals My Heart*, is an account of his unhappy affair with a singing-girl who was clearly a good deal too expensive for him to maintain a permanent liaison with her. For the courtesans of Ch'ang-an, many of them exotic blond, blue-eyed foreigners, made heavy demands on both the purse and the constitution, as we know from the short stories (*ch'uan-ch'i*) of the period – demands which Ho was ill-equipped to withstand, both financially and physically. Furthermore, his reputation as the most brilliant song-writer in the empire put him in great demand, exposing him to temptations he might otherwise have avoided. In the preface to his *Outing Among Blossoms* (p. 154), he states that he went off on a picnic with various princes and singing-girls, for whom he wrote a song.

> This morning, drunk outside the city walls,
> Rubbing our mirrors we brush on our rich brows.
> In drizzling mist we fret in clumsy carriages.

[21]See Ishida Mikinosuke, *Chō-an no haru* (Tokyo, 1941) for a brilliant account of life in Ch'ang-an during T'ang.

[22]See *San-chia p'ing-chu Li Ch'ang-chi ko shih*, p. 211, where Yao comments: 'Ho's dying an untimely death must have been due to illness brought on by sexual indulgence.' This theory may, of course, be simply a piece of Neo-Confucian moralizing. But since pulmonary tuberculosis notoriously exacerbates sexuality, my own guess would be that Yao was right.

Red oil-cloth covers up our painted clothes.
These dancing-skirts, though perfumed, are not warm,
Our faces flush but slowly from the wine.

Such outings, where his genius admitted him briefly to the company of rich young playboys and their lovely companions, must have tantalized him with a taste of pleasures just beyond his reach. For Ho, like Keats whom he so much resembles, was a great sensualist, delighting in tastes, sound, and colours.[23] Fine food and wine, music, rich silks and brocades, jewels and beautiful women figure prominently in his verse, so much so that at times we feel we are closer to the languid, erotic world of the later *tz'u* poets than to the lyric verse of mid-T'ang. The pity of it was that – again like Keats – he could not afford the delights he savoured most. So he swings abruptly from contemplation of these joys to sharp condemnation of them; from eulogies of the flesh to grave-yard poetry; from *vers de société* to social satire; from the ballad to something close to the *tz'u*. This dichotomy is vividly illus-trated by his imagery which alternates between vivid colour and stark black and white. All this, I believe, reflects the tensions en-gendered in him by living in Ch'ang-an, that fascinating, deca-dent city whose evanescent pleasures and fugitive splendours mocked him like life itself.

In 814 he gave up his post – whether voluntarily or not we do not know – and returned to his estate in Ch'ang-ku 昌谷, a place to which he was deeply attached. Ch'ang-ku has never found its way into the gazetteers; but all commentators agree that it was located in Fu-ch'ang county, some fifty miles west of Lo-yang. Its proximity to the Eastern capital, still a major centre of intellec-tual life, explains how he managed to acquire his early education. The district was mountainous, thickly wooded and fertile. Ho's family estate, though run-down and dilapidated, could not have been quite as poor as his sense of literary convention would have

[23]See David Ying Chen, *Li Ho and Keats: A Comparative Study of Two Poets* (Unpublished dissertation in Comparative Literature, Indiana University, 1962).

us believe, nor limited to 'a weed-grown patch of stony ground' (p. 224). In his long poem *Ch'ang-ku* (p. 176) he celebrates the tranquil beauty of his countryside and the honest simplicity of its people in some of his most delicately-wrought verse:

> The bamboo's fragrance fills this lonely place,
> Each powdered node is streaked with emerald.
> The long-haired grass lets fall its mournful tresses.
> A bright dew weeps, shedding its secret tears.
> Tall trees form a bright and winding tunnel,
> A scented track where fading reds sway drunkenly . . .
> Cotton-moss winds round the stones in the stream,
> Crimson and purple, mountain fruits hang down . . .
> This precious land is cut in broidered pieces,
> Our villagers prize truth and righteousness.
> No sound of pestles is heard when calamity comes,
> No evil rites are used to drive off plagues . . .
> The county justices have nothing to do,
> No loud-mouthed tax-collectors call on us,
> In bamboo-groves we find our writing paper,
> Our stony streams attract the hook and line . . .
> The fisherman's boy lowers his nets at night,
> Frosty birds soar up on misty wings.
> On the pool's mirror, slippery spittle of dragons,
> And floating pearls spat out from fishes at play . . .
> The mournful moon is curtained with red roses,
> Thorns of the fragrant creeper catch at the clouds . . .
> This man from Ch'eng-chi, now a servant of others,
> Would like to emulate Master Wine-sack's ways.

The last couplet in this long nostalgic poem, which he wrote whilst in Ch'ang-an, means simply that he would like nothing better than to emulate Fan Li, the great statesman who retired into obscurity after saving the state of Yüeh from its enemies. Ho, however, had no hope of ever rising to any office even remotely approaching Fan Li's. Furthermore, however alluring the idea of a life in the country may have seemed from the capital, he soon found that the prospect of retirement for life as an invalid at the age of twenty-three was not to be seriously contemplated,

in spite of the idyllic days he would seem to have spent in his
rural retreat:

> Lying on river sand softly sleeping
> Two ducks in the sun.
> I punt my little skiff slowly past
> The winding shores.
> Magnolias steeped in wine
> Covered with pepper-leaves.
> Friends help the sick man to his feet
> To plant water-chestnut.
>
> (p. 63, No. 9)

Living among the crumbling splendours of this ruined, noble
estate must have been unbearable for him, as was the knowledge
that the household depended largely on his efforts to maintain
them. So after some months of sickness and enforced idleness in
Ch'ang-ku, he was once again in search of an official post. For
some time past he had been seriously contemplating abandoning
a civil career for a military one, as is apparent from several of the
verses in his *Thirteen Poems from My Southern Garden* (pp. 59-65):

> Better to go and buy a sword
> From Jo-yeh river,
> Come back at dawn next day to serve
> The Monkey Duke.
>
> (No. 7)

> Why shouldn't a young man wear a Wu sword?
> He could win back fifty provinces in pass and mountain.
>
> (No. 5)

Over twenty years of incessant study had brought him nothing
except hardship and disappointment. What use was a poet in such
a war-torn age?

> Seeking a style, culling my phrases,
> Grown old carving grubs!
> At dawn the moon hangs in my blinds,
> A bow of jade.
> Can't you see what is going on, year after year,

By the sea of Liao-tung?
Whatever can a writer do
But weep in the autumn wind?

(No. 6)

These lines reveal his dilemma only too clearly. As a disciple
of Han Yü's he shared his master's firm conviction that literature
ought to play an important social role; that the poet was the
guardian of the conscience of society. Yet all his endeavours to
aid his country with his poetic talents had come to nothing. In
fact, his outspoken, satirical poems attacking the abuses of the
time had almost certainly blocked his chances of promotion if not
actually removed him from office.[24] What then was left to him
except to seek service with some military governor or other in
an outlying province? He could then both serve his country and
at the same time further his own ambitions. Once he had established his reputation in such a post, he could return to work for
the central government again, just as Han Yü himself had done
in his youth.[25] Far better to take office under the roughest of
military commands in some distant border region than to starve
in aristocratic poverty and idleness in Ch'ang-ku:

'Not yet thirty but still turned twenty,
Hungry in bright sunshine, living on leaves.
Old man on the bridge! Feel sorry for *me*
And give me a book on the art of war!'

(No. 4)

Fortunately for Ho, his friend Chang Ch'e (d. 821), pupil and
relative of Han Yü, was at that time in the service of Hsi Shih-mei,
a general still loyal to the emperor and commanding an army in

[24]Since the eunuch T'u-t'u Ch'eng-ts'ui, whom Ho had satirized mercilessly,
was recalled to the capital in 814 when that great enemy of the eunuchs, Li
Chiang, fell from favour, it seems reasonable to suppose that Ho would either
have been eased out of his post or thought it politic to resign.
[25]Han Yü had served two military governors, Tung Chin and Chang
Chien-feng, before being appointed to his university post.

c

Lu-chou (Shansi).[26] Since the rebellion of An Lu-shan (A.D. 755) the central government had been gradually losing power to the provincial military governors. The Emperor Hsien-tsung (*regnet* 805–20) had attempted to arrest the decline of the dynasty by bringing these military satraps under the rule of the Ch'ang-an regime. This involved the launching of a number of costly punitive expeditions against those governors who flatly refused to come to heel when called. The most notable of these was Wang Ch'eng-tsung, who could not be compelled to return to allegiance until 818, in spite of the numerous campaigns directed against him. Hsi Shih-mei's army, along with those of five other commanders, was at this time (814) all set to wage a protracted struggle against Wang's forces in Hopeh. Hence Ho must have felt that by putting himself at the service of this general he was directly contributing to the restoration of dynastic greatness.

In the autumn of 814 Ho set out from Ch'ang-ku, heading north-east as he made for Lu-chou. Several of the poems he wrote while on this journey have been preserved, among them the magnificent *Song of an Arrowhead from Ch'ang-p'ing*, (p. 228), a poem which proves that poverty, sickness and misfortune had enhanced, if anything, his poetic powers:

> Flakes of lacquer, dust of bones,
> Red cinnabar,
> The ancient blood once spurted forth
> And bore bronze flowers.
> White feathers and its metal stems
> Have rotted in the rain,
> Only the three spines still remain,
> Broken teeth of a wolf.
> I searched this plain of battle
> With a pair of nags,
> In stony fields east of the post-station,
> On a weed-grown hill.
> An endless wind, the day short,

[26]Chang Ch'e, a *chin-shih* of 809, had married Han Yü's niece. For further details, see p. 87 below. Hsi Shih-mei's biography is in *CTS*, CLVII.

Desolate stars,
Black banners of damp clouds,
Hung in void night.
Souls to the left, spirits to the right,
Gaunt with hunger, wailing,
I poured curds from my tilted flask,
Offered roast mutton.
Insects silent, the wild geese sick,
Reed shoots reddening.
A whirlwind came to see me off,
Blowing the ghost fires . . .

This poem, with its insistent images of death and war, ghosts
and sickness, gives us a disquieting glimpse of Ho's state of mind
as he pushed north through that bitter autumn towards the garri-
son town that was to be his home for the next three years.

We know nothing of his life in Lu-chou, but can only guess
at what it must have been like from the few poems written during
this period that have come down to us. From the length of time
he was there, it is clear that he must have found a post on Hsi
Shih-mei's staff. Hsi's forces were very active in the campaign
against Wang Ch'eng-tsung, so it seems likely that Ho saw something of the actual fighting. Life in a military border-town, in
the thick of a campaign, must have made both the hectic pleasures of Ch'ang-an and the quiet happiness of Ch'ang-ku seem
remote as a fading dream. Two of his poems written at this time
draw a vivid picture of life in a northern frontier post.

Barbarian horns have summoned the north wind,
Thistle Gate is whiter than a stream!
The road to Green Sea vanishes into the sky,
Along the Wall, a thousand moonlit miles.

While dew falls drizzling on our flags,
Cold metal clangs the watches of the night,
Barbarian armour meshes serpent scales,
Horses whinny where Green Grave gleams white . . .

(p. 231)

Even more powerful than these evocative verses is the poem *Down in P'ing-ch'eng* (p. 197).

> Hungry and cold, we stand here in P'ing-ch'eng,
> Night after night, on guard by the shining moon.
> Our keen-edged swords have lost their flowers of jade,
> Our hair is falling out in the Gobi wind.
>
> Where endless desert merges with white sky,
> We see, far-off, sad banners of the Han.
> They sit and play short flutes in their green tents,
> Mist soaks the painted dragons on their flags.
>
> We climb up on the walls as dusk is falling –
> Is something moving out there in the gloom?
> A wind is blowing, stirring the dead weeds,
> Our half-starved horses whinny in their stalls . . .

Verse like this, sober, taut and bare, harking back to the ballad tradition and the concept of poetry as a vehicle for social criticism, is a long way removed from the ornate verse Ho had composed in Ch'ang-an. Yet in what may well be his last poem, written as he lay sick in Ch'ang Che's house in Lu-chou, he evokes once again the strangeness which so distinguished his earlier verse, marries it to the simplicity of his Lu-chou poems and achieves a deeply moving masterpiece which must rank among his finest creations.

> Only when autumn comes to Chao-kuan,
> Will you know how cold it is up here in Chao.
> I tied this letter to a short-feathered summons,
> Cut out a long screed for a recital of woes.
> Through the clear dawn I slumbered in my sickness,
> While the sparse plane-trees cast fresh emeralds down.
> The city crows cried from white battlements,
> Military bugles saddened the mist in the reeds.
> With turban askew, I lifted the silken curtains,
> In dried-up pools the broken lotus lay.
> On the wooden window, traces of silver picture,
> On the stone steps water had left its coins.

The traveller's wine caught at my ailing lungs,
While songs of parting rose from languid strings.
I sealed this poem with a double string of tears,
And culled a single orchid wet with dew.
The sedge is growing old, the cricket weeping,
While broken gargoyles peer from withered pines.
Waking, I sit astride a horse from Yen,
Dreaming, I voyage on a boat through Ch'u.
Pepper and cinnamon poured above long mats!
Perch and bream sliced up on tortoise-shell!
Surely you can't forget the roads leading home,
To spend your youth on river-girdled isles?

(p. 136)

Verse of this quality, written when he was only twenty-five
or so, makes one realize just how great a loss literature sustained
by his untimely death. For at this juncture he was very near the
end. Whatever disease had haunted him for years – probably
pulmonary tuberculosis[27] – was now pressing its attack home for
the last time. He gave up his post in Lu-chou and returned to
Ch'ang-ku, where he died sometime during the year 817, at the
age of 26 or so.[28]

Ho left behind him a corpus of verse which, strangely enough,
has not enjoyed widespread popularity in China since the Sung
dynasty. The standard anthology of T'ang verse *T'ang shih san-
pai shou* (*Three Hundred T'ang Poems*), which was compiled in
Ch'ing times and is familiar to every Chinese schoolboy, does

[27]All the symptoms – the chronic nature of the disease, his greying hair,
fever, weakness and rapid decline to an early grave – indicate pulmonary
tuberculosis. The *Yün-hsien tsa chi* carries the story of a visitor who saw Ho
spit on the floor three times while he was composing three poems. If this is true,
we can be virtually certain Ho was consumptive.

[28]There has been some dispute as to whether Ho died in 816 or 817. The latter
date is now preferred by most scholars, including Suzuki Torao, Arai Ken, Yeh
Ts'ung-ch'i and Chou Lang-feng. The CTS and HTS biographies, along with
the *T'ai-p'ing kuang-chi*, are certainly wrong in saying he died at the age of
twenty-four. Ho's birth and death dates may be taken as 791–817 and not
790–816, the dates erroneously given in several histories of literature.

not include a single poem of his. Even today, he is comparatively little read, though modern critics are paying him increasing attention. The reasons for this neglect are not far to seek. If Chinese culture – to borrow Nietzsche's terminology – is essentially Apollonian, Ho's verse is essentially Dionysian. The only other poet writing in Chinese whose verse seems at all akin to Ho's is, significantly enough, the Manchu poet Singde (1655–85), who had been shaped by a shamanistic culture. There is a wild, exotic air about Ho's poetry which the Chinese mind finds distasteful, an air which has only sporadically made its appearance in Chinese literature since the *Ch'u Tz'u*, those *Songs of the South* from which Ho so clearly drew his inspiration. A Chinese friend of mine, himself a poet and critic of some distinction, once confessed to me that he could never bring himself to read Ho's verse, for it was altogether too mystical and strange. One sees what he means: for there is an air of romantic extravagance about Ho's lines which is quite unmistakable.

> Straddling a tiger, the Prince of Ch'in
> Roams the Eight Poles.
> His glittering sword flashes through the sky,
> Turning heaven sapphire-blue.
> He is Hsi Ho whipping up the sun
> That tinkles like glass . . .
>
> (p. 51)

> Jade from Mount K'un is shattered
> Phoenixes shriek.
> Lotuses are weeping dew,
> Fragrant orchids smile . . .
>
> (p. 10)

> The West's White King was struck with fear
> When it was drawn,
> His demon Mother wailing loudly
> In the autumn wilds.
>
> (p. 26)

Lines like these carry the imprint of Ho's unique style, bearing a strangeness of tone which led an eleventh-century critic to dub him 'the demon-poet'. 'Weird', 'astonishing' and 'demonic' are all adjectives frequently applied to his verse. As Chou Tz'u-chih remarked: 'Li Ch'ang-chi's language is astonishing, verging on the weird.' One does not have to search very far before coming across scores of lines which bear out this remark.

> The Blue Lion kowtows and calls
> To the Palace Spirits.
> With a fearful howl the Dog of Jade
> Opens Heaven's gates . . .
>
> (p. 33)

> On an autumn grave a ghost sits chanting
> That poem of Pao's.
> A thousand years in earth makes emerald jade
> That rancorous blood.
>
> (p. 49)

> Blue racoons are weeping blood
> As shivering foxes die . . .
> Owls that have lived a hundred years,
> Turned forest demons,
> Find emerald fire, laughing wildly,
> Leaps from their nests.
>
> (p. 212)

> A white fox barking at the moon
> Calls out the mountain wind...
>
> (p. 226)

The quality of imagination displayed in the stanzas just quoted is rare in any poetic tradition, let alone in Chinese verse where what one might call the 'shamanistic style' has only sporadically appeared.

> . . . In the west are the Moving Sands stretching
> endlessly on and on,
> And beasts with heads like swine, slanting
> eyes and shaggy hair,
> Long claws and serrated teeth and
> wild, mad laughter . . .

> ... I lashed the Wind God and made him
> ride before me
> Imprisoned the Dark Spirit in the Pit of Night ...

Verses like these last – selected almost at random from David Hawkes's fine translation of the *Ch'u Tz'u*[29] – had their origin in a culture where shamans were employed to call down spirits by means of music, dancing and incantations. This wild, ecstatic quality is echoed in Ho's verse time and time again. Furthermore, several of his poems actually deal with shamans in the act of summoning spirits. I would hazard the guess that Ho was himself by temperament something of a shaman *manqué*, though he expressed his ecstasy in poetry rather than the writhings of trance.

Unusual as Ho's work undoubtedly is, he is nevertheless very much of his time. He does not stand apart from it in the way, say, Blake and Smart stand apart from the eighteenth century. In a sense, his verse simply carries to an extraordinary degree qualities of intensity, floridity and deep-grained pessimism already highly characteristic of T'ang verse. Only in his development of the *Ch'u Tz'u* tradition can he really be called unique. Take for example the prevailingly pessimistic tone of his verse. From the Han dynasty onwards Chinese poetry is on the whole deeply melancholy in tone. T'ang poetry was no exception to this, and even poets like Tu Fu and Li Po (699–762) write verse steeped in sadness. It was not until the Sung dynasty (960–1279) that Chinese poets rid themselves of the burden of sorrow, as the great Japanese critic, Yoshikawa Kōjirō has pointed out.[30] In this respect Ho is

[29] *Ta Chao*, p. 110 and *Yüan Yu*, p. 168 from the *Ch'u Tz'u, the Songs of the South: an Ancient Chinese Anthology* (Oxford, 1959), trans. D. Hawkes This edition will be cited throughout.

[30] Yoshikawa Kōjirō, *Sōshi gaisetsu, Chūgoku shijin senshu*, Series 2, No. 1 (Tokyo, 1962), pp. 34–9. This work has been finely translated by Burton Watson, *An Introduction to Sung Poetry* (Cambridge, Mass., 1967). Yoshikawa remarks (*op. cit.*, p. 41): '[T'ang poems] are full of sorrow, and even a poet like Tu Fu, who tried to free himself from sorrow, could speak of "a whole life of grieving". Indeed, the minor poets of the late T'ang period seem to have regarded it as their duty to sing almost exclusively of sorrow, or rather, of despair.' (trans. Burton Watson, *op. cit.*, p. 29).

typical of his age, for his verse is so imbued with melancholy that the pages seem to darken as one reads.

Any thorough study of Ho's verse would attempt to explain this fully. In doing so, it would have to account for the whole shift in outlook which took place in the poetry of the ninth century, the movement away from the outgoing, assertive verse of Tu Fu to the esoteric, withdrawn poetry of Li Shang-yin. This introduction is no place to attempt such a feat: but I should hazard the guess that the basic factors involved were the decline of the empire after the rebellion of An Lu-shan; the weakening of the central government; the increasing dominance of the eunuchs and the dissociation of literary men from political power. All of these – and especially the last – resulted in what Toynbee would call 'a failure of nerve on the part of the creative minority'. This would account for the pervading sense of melancholy, nostalgia and regret that so characterizes most of the poetry of the *Yüan-ho* period (806–21). Furthermore, this was an age when none of the traditional remedies seemed to make sense any more. Taoism had degenerated into superstition; Buddhism was on the verge of collapse – the persecution of 845 finally struck it a mortal blow – and even the most ardent Confucian reformers found that the time was not yet ripe for revival of the Master's teachings.

What is peculiar, then, about Ho's verse is not his melancholy but the extent of it; not the sentiment itself but the symbols he used to express it. Wada Toshio has analysed Ho's verse statistically and found that expressions directly connected with death occur 74 times; expressions hinting at death 198 times; expressions of sadness 131 times and expressions of anxiety and fear 262 times – a total of 665 in all. On an average there are three expressions concerned with death or unhappiness in every poem.[31] Wada's

[31]Wada Toshio, ' Ri Ga no kishi to sono keisei', *Gumma daigaku kiyō jimbun kagaku hen*, 5.8 (1956), pp. 88–102. Of expressions directly connected with death in Ho's poems, 'death', occurs 24 times; 'ghost', 6 times; 'soul', 8 times; 'bones', 11 times; 'tomb', 'grave' etc., 20 times; and 'corpse-candle' etc., 8 times. 'Old' occurs over twice in every 10 poems; 'night' and 'cold' over 3 times in every 10 poems.

analysis simply lends statistical support to what the reader had
already felt in his senses; namely that Ho's verse is extraordinarily
melancholy even by T'ang standards. Furthermore, the images
he persistently draws on, those of ghosts, demons, spirits, bones,
blood, tombs, corpses, will-o'-the-wisps and so on, are normally
studiously avoided by Chinese poets, as they are avoided by ordinary Chinese, on the grounds that they are unlucky. Admittedly,
during T'ang the weird tale or ghost story (ch'uan-ch'i) enjoyed a great vogue; but these stories are certainly not obsessed
with death and decay as is Ho's verse.

Ho's 'death-wish', as we should style it today, has been noted
by the contemporary writer, Hung Wei-fa, who remarked that
Ho was afraid of death, yet longed for it, for since he was sick of
the world of men, he yearned for heaven.[32] Ho's longing for
death is certainly understandable. For a start, he stemmed from
that most pessimistic of classes, impoverished aristocracy – people
for whom the past recedes ever further in a golden haze. Secondly,
he was unlucky in not being allowed to take an examination
which would almost certainly have led him to fame and fortune –
and for a Chinese to think himself unlucky is to have lost all hope.
Finally, he was a man ravaged by disease, constantly in failing
health and – to cap all this – poor, at least in comparison with his
friends. Small wonder then that he found life a burden which he
would gladly shake off. He would fain have fled the world – but
to what?

Classical Confucianism admits of no life beyond the grave,
beyond the squeaking and gibbering of ghosts. In this it is as
comfortless as the religion of the ancient Greeks. Hung Wei-fa's
assertion that Ho 'longed for heaven' must therefore refer to his
belief in either Buddhism, or Taoism or both. Ostensibly Ho was
no Taoist at least in the conventional sense, for many of his
satirical poems are attacks upon Emperor Hsien-tsung, who

[32]Hung Wei-fa's critique, paraphrased here, is quoted by Chu Tzu-ch'ing,
'Li Ho nien-p'u', Ch'ing-hua hsüeh-pao 10.4 (1935), p. 76, from Ch'ing-nien chieh
5.2 (n.d.).

spent a great deal of time and money which could have been better
employed in the business of government in seeking for elixirs of
eternal life. On the other hand, there can be no denying that Ho
was fascinated with the concept of Heaven, which recurs constantly in his poems as a place of exquisite beauty, where immortals dwell.

> Là, tout n'est qu'ordre et beauté,
> Luxe, calme et volupté.

It seems to me highly probable that at one level of belief Ho
was convinced of the reality of the Taoist heaven. This would
help to explain the stories about his death-bed:

> When Ch'ang-chi was at death's door, suddenly, in broad day-
> light he saw a man in purple raiment driving a red dragon and
> carrying a tablet . . . who said: 'I am here to summon Ch'ang-chi'
> . . . Ch'ang-chi at once got down from his bed and kowtowed
> saying:
> 'Mama is old and ill. I don't want to leave her.'
> The man in purple raiment said with a smile: 'The Emperor
> [of Heaven] has just built the White Jade Tower and summons you
> to come at once and write a description of it. Life up in
> Heaven is delightful: there is no hardship there.' Ch'ang-chi only
> wept the more . . .

Li Shang-yin goes on[33] to state that this story was narrated to
him by Mrs. Wang, Ho's sister, who was present at his death,
adding that her veracity was undoubted.

Now if, in fact, Ho really believed in Heaven, then it is highly
likely that during his final moments he actually saw and described
the events that his sister spoke of. What we have here, indeed, is
a graphic account of Ho's death-bed vision – a consoling dream as
touching and as vividly colourful as many of his poems. But how
can this Taoist belief be reconciled with Ho's avowed Buddhism,
for he states quite plainly in his poem *Presented to Ch'en Shang*
(p. 145) that the *Laṅkāvatāra-sūtra* is his constant companion, along
with the *Ch'u Tz'u*?

[33]Li Shang-yin, *Li Yi-shan wen-chi*, Ssu-pu ts'ung-k'an ed., IV, p. 21a.

I think the explanation lies in the fact that the *Laṅkāvatāra* – a work of notorious difficulty and profundity – was the principal sutra of the Ch'an (Zen) school during T'ang.[34] Ho must therefore have been a devotee of Ch'an Buddhism, a fact which would explain the otherwise puzzling lack of overt Buddhist allusions in his verse, since this school attaches only secondary importance to the scriptures. The Heaven of Ho's visions therefore cannot have been the Western Paradise of Amitābha Buddha, for this is not a belief held by the Ch'an school. He must have envisaged Heaven in Buddhist terms as the abode of the gods, a higher race than men and seemingly immortal by comparison, who were yet doomed to perish as all things in the universe must perish since they too were bound to the Wheel of Life and Death.

When we turn from Ho's thought to a study of the actual texture of the poems themselves we find ourselves on firmer ground. Ho's poems are notoriously difficult and enigmatic. 'Li Ho's poems cannot be read without a commentary', is an old literary saw. His poems, like Li Shang-yin's, present special difficulties for a number of reasons. Firstly, the poems have a logic of their own. His imagination is neither rhetorical nor yet dramatic: it is purely visual. He sees things in flashes, apparently disconnectedly, so that his technique is probably far more familiar to

[34]For a detailed exposition of this work by an eminent authority, see D. T. Suzuki, *Studies in the Laṅkāvatāra Sūtra* (London, 1930) and *The Laṅkāvatāra Sūtra: A Mahayana Text* (London, 1932). Ho probably read the sutra in Sikshānanda's translation of 700–4, which was sponsored by Empress Wu. His attachment to the *Laṅkāvatāra* indicates a real seriousness in his attitude towards Buddhism, for the sutra is one of the most difficult of the whole Buddhist canon. As Su Tung-pei remarked in his preface to the edition of 1085: 'The *Laṅkāvatāra* is deep and unfathomable in meaning, while in style it is so terse and archaic that the reader finds it quite troublesome even to punctuate the sentences correctly, let alone understand their ultimate spirit and purport ...' Suzuki has observed that this scripture 'notes down in a somewhat sketchy style almost all the ideas belonging to different schools of Mahayana Buddhism. It is partly for this reason that the sutra requires a great deal of learning' (*op. cit.*, p. 96). Under the circumstances Ho's involvement with Buddhism must not be underestimated.

modern readers, whose eyes have been trained by years of tele-
vision and cinema, than it was to his traditional audience. This
technique is undoubtedly connected with the method of composition described in his biographies, in which he would jot down
lines and phrases as they occurred to him and then piece them
together like a mosaic on his return home. As a result of this,
some of his long poems, like *Ch'ang-ku* (p. 176) and *She
Steals My Heart* (p. 106) tend to break down into disparate shots in
which the inner unity that should bind them has been lost. In
cinematic terms, Ho's camera-work – whether black-and-white
or colour – is always brilliant. It is his montage that sometimes
fails him.

It is this technique that leads one of his most penetrating modern
commentators, Arai Ken, to complain that Ho jumps about in
time and space, keeps changing his subject and in general lacks
unity. Arai has failed to notice, however, that this disintegration
of the continuity of exterior events is a strikingly modern characteristic, an anticipation of the Bergsonian flux of twentieth-
century Western art. In Ho's verse, landmarks keep moving about
in a most disconcerting fashion. As Ch'ien Chung-shu astutely
observed, his poetry is like the shifting sands of the desert[35] – a
desert, I might add, which has up to now deterred most of those
who would have liked to cross it. As may be imagined, such
poetry presents formidable difficulties for the English translator,
who is forced to be explicit when the original is vague because
of the nature of our language.

Another source of perplexity is found in Ho's imagery. His
metaphors are often difficult to follow until one has grasped their
inner logic.

> He is Hsi Ho whipping up the sun
> That tinkles like glass.

This borders on the synaesthesia of the Symbolists, whom Ho
so much resembles. The sun is like glass because both are white

[35]Ch'ien Chung-shu, *T'an-yi-lu* 談 藝 錄 (Shanghai, 1948), p. 53 ff.

and shining (glass was an exotic substance for T'ang Chinese). Glass tinkles when shattered; the sun is being shattered by time. Therefore it tinkles as Hsi Ho – who drives the sun horse – applies the whip. Ho's verse abounds in images of this nature.

Closely connected with the problem of Ho's imagery is his fondness for kennings. Thus autumn flowers are 'cold reds'; wine is 'liquid amber'; swords are 'jade dragons', jujubes are 'hanging pearls' (or 'hanging reds'). Along with this goes a penchant for coining new words and phrases which is quite uncharacteristic of Chinese poetry. His painstaking craftsmanship, his determination to make his language fresh and novel, seems to indicate the influence of Tu Fu, who once remarked: 'Not even death would stop me from trying to startle my readers.' But Ho went a great deal further than Tu Fu ever dared. As one Chinese critic remarked: Li Ho's poetry is like the art of jade-carving. Not a single word but has been refined a hundred times. This is really the product of work that made him 'vomit out his heart'.[36] Here again he resembles French nineteenth-century poetry, especially the Parnassians, for whom:

> L'œuvre sort plus belle
> D'une forme au travail rebelle,
> Vers, marbre, onyx, émail.

His language has a Keatsian sumptuousness, every rift loaded with ore, a 'devotion to the intensity imbedded within the concrete' giving his lines a 'heavy richness, [a] slow clogged – almost drugged – movement, [a] choked-in fullness . . . which gives him strength with all his luxury and which keeps his sensuousness firm and vital'.[37]

In short then, Ho's work is closer in many respects to modern western poetry than to the classical Chinese tradition. This may explain why T'an Ssu-t'ung (1865–98), one of the martyrs of the

[36]Yeh Yen-lan, *Li Ch'ang-chi chi-pa.*

[37]Walter Jackson Bate, 'Keats's Style: Evolution toward Qualities of Permanent Value', in *The Major English Poets*, ed. Clarence D. Thorpe and others, Carbondale (1957), pp. 66–7.

1898 Reform Movement and Lu Hsün (1881–1936) the greatest writer modern China has produced, both admired Ho's verse.[38] It may also explain why so many of the traditional commentators, especially Confucian rationalists like the Ch'ing commentator Wang Ch'i, have gone so wildly astray at times in interpreting Ho's work, since they understood neither his mystical temperament nor his patriotism.

Ironically enough, modern Chinese communist criticism, which invariably pays lip-service to Lu Hsün, has constantly ignored his praise of Li Ho. Instead the critics have accused Ho of most of the social sins – passivity, aestheticism, lack of patriotism, and a failure to get to grips with reality. Yet even the most cursory reading of his verse will show that Ho was deeply concerned with the problems of his day and used his ballads, which had a wide circulation, to satirize contemporary abuses. His attacks on the eunuch T'u-t'u Ch'eng-ts'ui in particular may have played a part in forcing the emperor to dismiss this singularly incompetent general from his command of the Armies of the Divine Plan in 809.[39]

> A lady-general leads our Chinese soldiers.
> A dainty kerchief tucked into her quiver.
> She's not ashamed of her heavy, gold seal,
> Lurching along with bow-case at her waist.
> Simple old men, just honest villagers,
> Tested the teeth of arrow-barbs last night,
> But she sent her courier to cry victory –
> Must powder and mascara blind us all!
>
> (p. 258, No. 3)

---

[38]T'an remarked: 'His words are clear and strong and need no commentaries. In the long run, there is only Ch'ang-ku.' The Sung patriots Liu Chen-weng (1234–97) and Hsieh Ao (1249–95), as well as the Ming loyalists Chang Tai (1597–1689) and Ch'ien Ch'eng-chih (1612–94) also admired Ho's verse and wrote commentaries to it. Clearly the patriotic element in Ho's verse has attracted attention at the end of every dynasty (except Yüan) since Sung.

[39]*Tzu-chih t'ung-chien* by Ssu-ma Kuang (1019–86), hereinafter abbreviated, to *TCTC*, 4 vols. (Peking, 1956), p. 7668.

Even more dangerous than his attacks on the eunuchs were his scarcely veiled satires on Emperor Hsien-tsung's quest for immortality through Taoist arts – a quest which was eventually to result in his death. Taoists believed that with the aid of the proper drugs, life could be lengthened almost indefinitely. Since most of these drugs were highly toxic preparations of gold, arsenic, lead, mercury and like substances, it is hardly surprising to learn that those who sought immortality the most assiduously were frequently those who departed this life the most precipitately. As early as 810, the Emperor had evinced considerable interest in elixirs of immortality, much to the disapproval of his minister, Li Fan, who had given him a stern lecture on the folly of putting one's faith in Taoist magicians.[40] This seems to have had little effect on Hsien-tsung's ardour, for by 819 we find him 'swallowing drugs daily and so becoming more and more bad-tempered and thirsty',[41] a process which continued until his demise the following year.

Several writers attempted to remonstrate with the emperor on this subject, though to do so was really 'to run up against the dragon's scales', since this was a topic on which he was notoriously short-tempered. Han Yü himself, who had merely alluded indirectly to the subject in his well-known memorial on the Buddha's bone, only narrowly escaped death for his indiscretion. Po Chü-yi, Meng Chiao and other poets preferred to couch their protests in the form of verse gibing at the vain quest for immortality undertaken by previous emperors such as Ch'in Shih Huang-ti, Emperor Wu of Han and Emperor Wen of Wei. Ho himself has a large number of poems on this subject, so many in fact that one wonders how he escaped punishment, for he was undoubtedly running a risk by circulating songs dealing with such a topic.

[40]*CTS*, XIV, Annals of Hsien-tsung, 5th year of *Yüan-ho*, p. 16b.
[41]*TCTC*, p.7775.

Why should we swallow yellow gold,
Or eat white jade?
Who is Jen Kung-tzu
Riding a white donkey through the clouds?
Liu Ch'e lies in the Mao-ling tomb
Just a pile of bones.
Ying Cheng lies in his catalpa coffin –
What a waste of abalone!

(pp. 170-1)

By eating cinnabar you may become
A serpent riding a white mist,
A thousand year-old turtle in a well of jade.
Can't you see yourself transformed to snake or turtle
For twenty centuries,
Dragging your life out, year after year,
On the grain-green dikes of Wu?
Eight trigrams on your back,
Blazoned 'Immortal',
Your cunning scales,
Your stubborn armour
Slimed with a fishy spittle!

(p. 193)

It is difficult at this remove for us to estimate just how many
of the poems are to be understood as satires. Yao Wen-hsieh
ascribes satirical intent to almost every verse Ho wrote, but this,
of course is an exaggeration. However, it is fair to assume that
a great many poems which appear innocuous enough now would
have been read as satires by Ho's contemporaries. Perhaps something like 20 per cent of the verse, at a conservative estimate, can
even now reasonably be labelled satirical, though half the time we
can never be sure just what target he is aiming at. In any case, it is
certain that his involvement with the New Ballad (*hsin yüeh-fu*)
Movement must not be underestimated.[42] Po Chü-yi (772–846)
and Yüan Chen had both come to the conclusion that 'the duty

[42]See M. T. South, 'Li Ho and the New *Yüeh-fu* Movement', *Journal of the
Oriental Society of Australia*, 4.2 (December 1966), pp. 49–61.

D

of literature is to be of service to the writer's generation: that of poetry to influence public affairs'. This conviction was a revival of an ancient belief, dating back to *The Classic of Poetry* and the *Ch'u Tz'u*, that the poet was the social conscience of his time. To ensure the widest possible circulation for their work, Po and Yüan cast their criticisms of existing abuses into ballad form. These ballads, which enjoyed as much vogue as the popular songs of our own time, were songs with a message. As Po puts it in the preface to his own collection of fifty ballads:

> (These songs) are concerned with ideas, not with fine phrases . . . This was the principle behind the three hundred poems (of *The Classic of Poetry*) . . . Their style is smooth and flowing, so they can easily be played and sung. In short, they have been written for the emperor, for his ministers, for the people . . . They have not been written simply for art's sake.

This manifesto of Po's may be considered as the inception of the New Ballad Movement. Po and Yüan were soon joined by a number of other writers – Li Shen, Meng Chiao, Chang Chi and Han Yü among them – who were all concerned in some degree with the use of verse as a vehicle for social criticism. Strictly speaking, the New Ballad had to conform to the criteria Po Chü-yi himself adopted. It had to be simple in expression – Po is said to have tried out all his poems on an old maidservant, deleting anything she could not understand – and conform to the ballad form, while revealing sympathy for the plight of the common people. The poetry, in fact, was in the pity. Ho has comparatively few ballads which meet all these requirements, for he was influenced more by the *Li Sao* tradition (the greatest poem of the *Ch'u Tz'u*) than by *The Classic of Poetry*, and the *Li Sao*, though critical of governmental abuses, was ornate and highly obscure. Nevertheless, Ho would have certainly subscribed to Empson's dictum:

> Politics are what verse should
> Not fly from, or it goes all wrong.

Furthermore, he did write a few ballads which fulfil all the criteria laid down by Po Chü-yi and yet carry his own inimitable stamp, as in the following song describing the miseries of the jade-gatherers, who had taken to this dangerous work to save themselves and their families from starvation:

> On rainy nights, on the ridge of a hill,
> He sups on hazel-nuts.
> Like the blood that wells from a cuckoo's maw,
> Are the old man's tears.
> The waters of Indigo river are gorged
> With human lives.
> After a thousand years the dead
> Still loathe these torrents.
>
> A steep hillside, wind in the cypress,
> Whistle of rain –
> Deep in the springs he hangs from a rope,
> Green curling and swirling,
> Thinking of wife and children back in his poor village,
> In a white-thatched hut.
> Upon stone steps of ancient terraces
> The heartbreak grows.
>
> (pp. 79-80)

Though apparently simple, analysis reveals this to be a far more complex and intricately structured poem than anything Po Chü-yi ever wrote. In modern terms, we can discern within this verse something of that peculiar tension between symbolism and naturalism manifest in the work of so many writers of our own century. But I shall come back to this point later. For the moment we shall simply note that the poem makes its point dramatically and effectively and must certainly be ranked as a ballad of social protest squarely in the tradition.

These two aspects of Ho's verse, his patriotism and his protests, have not received nearly as much critical attention as has his so-called aestheticism, his preoccupation with exotic subjects and fantastic imagery. A great deal of his poetry anticipates the languid, incense-laden atmosphere of the *tz'u*, a kind of song lyric composed to fixed melodic patterns which was to come into being some fifty years or so after his death.[43]

> Clouds tumbling over her jewelled pillow,
> She seeks a spring dream,
> In caskets cold with inlaid sapphires
> The dragon-brain grows chill?
>
> (p. 265)

> She lies resentful in her net of pearls
> Unable to sleep,
> Beneath a robe ornate with golden phoenix
> Her body is chill, ..
>
> (p. 42)

> Drowsy with wine, idle all the white day
> In a moored boat,
> In a plum-breeze by the ferry she waves
> Her singing-fan.
>
> (p. 81)

> Butterflies lighting on China pinks –
> Hinges of silver,
> Frozen water, duck-head green –
> Coins of glass.
> Its six-fold curves enclose a lamp
> Burning orchid-oil.
> She lets down her tresses before the mirror,
> Sheds her gold cicadas,
> Perfume of aloes from a warm fire,
> Smoke of dogwood.
>
> (p. 84)

> A single skein of perfumed silk ,
> Clouds cast on the floor,
> Noiseless, the jade comb tumbles down
> From her lustrous hair,

[43]On the *tz'u* see James J. Y. Liu's invaluable work, *The Art of Chinese Poetry* (Chicago, 1962); Liu Wu-chi, *An Introduction to Chinese Literature* (Bloomington and London, 1966), pp. 101–24.

Delicate fingers push back the coils –
Colour of an old rook's plumes
Blue-black and sleek – the jewelled comb
And hairpin cannot hold.

(pp. 240-1)

Flowers bow down beneath light dew,
Melilote's breath,
Windlass of jade and rope of silk
Draw the dawn water,
Her powdered face, like purple carnelian,
Hot and fragrant.

(p. 140)

Part of this verse – like the last example – is undoubtedly satiric. But in any case, even when Ho's intentions were to mock, he lingered to admire. This world of black-haired, jade-skinned beauties, blushing cheeks, perfumed silks, gauze bed-curtains, flickering tapers, carved screens, golden censers fuming with rare incense, and the mournful drip of rain on the kolanut trees, was to become the sole poetic province of *tz'u* writers like Wen T'ing-yün (812?–70?), Wei Chuang (836–910), Li Yü (937–78), and others. Such a trend was not new in Chinese verse; it had appeared for the first time some three hundred years previously, with the so-called 'palace poetry' of the last years of the Six Dynasties. Ho's natural sensuality could not resist the appeal of this glittering kingdom of pearl and aloes-wood, jasper and cassia, though he invested it with a significance lacking in later writers. Not only does Ho anticipate the great poets of the *tz'u*: he also looks forward to the two outstanding romantics of the ninth century, Tu Mu and Li Shang-yin. Like them he delights in wine and spring flowers, beautiful women and the moon on the water. Ho takes love as seriously as the Confucian poet took friendship. Li Shang-yin, one of the greatest poets of love writing in Chinese, was a devoted admirer of Ho's and must have found support for his passionate affairs of the heart in Ho's verse:

What sort of love am I seeking?
That of Hsün Feng-ch'ien.
O sun above the city wall,
Forever stay above the city wall!
Let a single day be as a thousand years,
And never sink to rest.

(p. 160)

Some critics give the impression that Ho's love of beauty was somehow incompatible with the Confucian gravity and sense of purpose associated with the New Ballad Movement: that aestheticism and naturalism could not go together. This is a misleading dichotomy. T'ang poetry, even the best of it, is inclined to be florid: but one should never mistake this for a lack of high seriousness. One has only to look at Han Yü's own verse to see that it abounds in quaint conceits and odd expressions, breaks many of the time-hallowed rules of composition and deals with subjects which no earlier poet would have thought fit to mention in verse.[44] I hazard the opinion that both the intricate nature of Ho's own poetry and his choice of subjects were in fact partly the result of a deliberate attempt to please his patrons. There is certainly nothing in Ho's verse which Yü or his fellows would have thought frivolous. Critics have failed to see that there is a difference between Ho's verse and the effete, palace poetry against which Yü fulminated. Palace poetry was mere empty rhetoric; once penetrate its glossy surface and there was nothing underneath. But Ho's verse, even when concerned with the very subjects that formed the sole staple of the palace poets, never wavered from the Li Sao tradition. Beneath the intricately patterned surface lay solid layers of meaning. Ultimately, Yü waged war on the poetry of Ch'i and Liang not because of its 'decadent' subject-matter but because it was void of social content: he praised Ho's verse because it came to grips with reality, whether it dealt with soldiers starving in a frontier-post or a princess getting drunk at

[44]See the selection of Yü's poems in A.C. Graham, Poems of the Late T'ang (London, 1965).

a banquet. Ho was astute enough to realize, as so many later critics have not, that if verse was to mirror the complex, sophisticated and disintegrating fabric of T'ang society it could not confine itself to simple ballads. It is only because he possessed this poetic range that he could so successfully hold up the mirror to his age: and it was precisely for this quality that Yü admired him. His verse in its own way reflects the realities of T'ang life just as faithfully as the poems of Tu Fu and Po Chü-yi. The parallel with our own times when naturalism and symbolism, aesthete and realist flourish together, is quite striking. One is reminded of Mallarmé congratulating Zola on the publication of *L'Assommoir*, both having, as Durkheim pointed out, a common need to destroy the real or escape from it.

The contention that the main difference between Ho's poetry and the verse of Ch'i and Liang, which it sometimes superficially resembles, lies in their content brings us directly to the problems of meaning in Chinese verse. Ho was brought up in a poetic tradition which laid great stress on metaphor (*pi*) and allegory (*hsing*): 'The parables employed in the *hsing* appear subtle, but they are so apparent!' wrote the critic Liu Hsieh (c.465–522) in the chapter on metaphor and allegory of his *Wen-hsin tiao-lung* (*The Literary Mind and the Carving of Dragons*).[45] Subtle they certainly are; but they are not always as apparent as they might be. Thus the first song of *The Classic of Songs* begins with the line:

Kuan-kuan cry the fish-hawks.

The commentators point out here that fish-hawks are a symbol of virtue, because male and female do not mix promiscuously; hence the poem is a eulogy to the virtue of Queen Wen, wife of Wen of the Chou. So Liu Hsieh adds sagely: 'Do not let these birds of prey distract your mind, because the important thing is the virtue of sexual separation. Such parables are like the first rays of light before the break of dawn, still enveloped in ambiguity.

[45]Liu Hsieh, *The Literary Mind and the Carving of Dragons*, trans. by Vincent Y. C. Shih (New York, 1959), p. 194.

This is the reason why commentators are required to make the meaning clear.'[46]

Liu then goes on to deal with the difference of metaphor, whose most important function, he implies, is to act as a further means of remonstration. 'Thus gold and pewter are used to stand for illustrious virtue, a jade tally signifies an outstanding man, a caterpillar means education, cicadas and grasshoppers denote howling and shouting, washing clothes symbolises sadness of the heart and the rolling up of a mat denotes firmness of will.'[47]

Now Ho's style is admittedly based not on the *Songs*, from which all the above examples are drawn, but on the *Ch'u Tz'u*. Yet ultimately this makes no difference to our argument, for as Liu points out, the *Sao* was created in the spirit of the *Songs* and has 'adopted its formal remonstrations'. We may protest, of course, that the *Ch'u Tz'u* is not really like that; for its dragons do not always betoken men of virtue any more than its clouds and rainbows invariably stand for flatterers and sycophants. But this is after all rather to miss the point. What matters in this context is that Ho's views on the nature of the *Ch'u Tz'u* must have been essentially those of Liu Hsieh.

Western sinologists have very much inclined to ignore the part played by *pi* and *hsing* in Chinese verse, largely because the tradition of a work possessing several levels of meaning died out in Europe during the seventeenth century and has only recently been revived. I. A. Richards's 'multiple definition', Kenneth Burke's 'multiple causation', William Troy's attempt to revive the medieval 'four levels of meaning' are all of them relevant to any attempt to read Chinese literature in depth. Unfortunately, very little, if anything, has as yet been done towards applying modern critical methods to the study of Chinese poetry. A. C. Graham's recent excursions into this field in his *Poems of the Late T'ang* have the distinction of being the first serious attempt of its kind. In general, due credit has not been given to traditional Chinese

[46]*Ibid.*, p. 195.
[47]*Ibid.*, p. 195.

explanations of the meanings hidden in verse. Hence in my own
annotations to Ho's poems, I have attempted to bring out this
aspect of the verse wherever possible, while attempting to avoid
falling into the pitfall that Yao Wen-hsieh tumbled into in his
anxiety to suppose every bush a bear.

A point closely connected with this is the question of plurisignation[48] (a better term than 'ambiguity') in Ho's verse. Lack of
literary professionalism among sinologists has all too often led to
a concern with outmoded, pre-Empsonian ideas about the meaning of a poem. The notion has persisted that the denotative aspect
of language is more important than the connotative: that a line –
or a whole poem – must mean one thing and one thing only. In
fact, Chinese poetry has consciously employed plurisignation
since the Six Dynasties period; by late T'ang times, when Ho
was writing, multiple meanings had become quite as involved as
those of Shakespearian verse.[49] This poses special difficulties for
the translator, who is in any case forced by the very nature of the
English language to be precise where Chinese is vague and
suggestive. At times, he may be lucky enough to hit upon a
rendering which will convey something of the ambiguity of the
original; but most of the time he can only laboriously spell out
the other possible meanings of the line in a footnote.[50]

A reluctance to annotate poems copiously has been one of the
main reasons, I think, why Ho has not received the attention that

[48]A term first suggested by Philip Wheelwright in his article 'On the
Semantics of Poetry', *Kenyon Review*, II, 3 (Summer, 1940), pp. 263-83. Austin
Warren's 'concurrent multivalence' approximates this.

[49]As A. C. Graham has pointed out (*Poems of the Late T'ang*, p. 20), a Japanese
critic, Kurokawa Yoichi, has asserted that Chinese verse does not become
ambiguous until the second half of the eighth century, with the late verse of
Tu Fu. But this is manifestly untrue. Paronomasia has been a feature of Chinese
poetry since very early times and during the Six Dynasties period became a
common literary device. Syntactical ambiguity, of course, is another matter.

[50]The problem is complicated by the fact that the text of Ho's poems contains a fair number of variants, most of them poetically suggestive. The ideal
translation would clearly have to include all these variants and discuss what
overtones they added to the poem.

is his due from Western translators. From the end of the eighth century onwards, Chinese poetry becomes steadily more complex and allusive. The Chinese poet has always relied heavily for his effect on allusions. Pound's characterization of a poem as a form that should be able to do as much in a line as a whole page of prose is strikingly true of Chinese verse, which can sum up a situation, draw an analogy or reveal a contrast in the minimum of words through the use of the shorthand of allusion. As the corpus of literature increased there was a tendency on the part of poets to refer not only to the Confucian and Taoist classics but to the whole ever-growing body of earlier writings. This means that the later T'ang poets tend to be rather more difficult to read than their predecessors, if only because they have incorporated so much into their verse. This is not to say that there is a great deal of purely literary allusion in Ho's verse; on the contrary, there is far less of this than in, say, the fifth-century poet Hsieh Ling-yün. But there is enough general use of allusion to ensure that there are very few poems in Ho's collected works that can be understood without at least some notes and a good many poems that require a great deal of annotation indeed.

Here the Western reader is at a considerable disadvantage compared with even the Chinese reader who has received no formal classical education; for the latter has acquired, by cultural osmosis as it were, a great deal of information which the unfortunate Westerner has painstakingly to imbibe. All this goes to swell the already excessive volume of footnotes, until the translator half begins to wonder, with Pound, whether he is not obscuring the text with philology. Nevertheless, I myself am convinced for one that this is the only way in which Chinese verse can be made intelligible to the European reader, without fobbing him off with mere *chinoiserie*.

It may be objected that a great deal of the essential poetry of the original is lost through such a method of translation. I doubt this. Such a belief can be traced back to the French Symbolist view that poetry, 'which is made with words, not ideas', as

Mallarmé expressed it, must evaporate like spilt perfume when poured into the alien flask of another language. This contention has come up against some very sharp and perceptive criticism of recent years, the most telling onslaught on this cherished doctrine coming from the Chicago critics. They reject the doctrine that literature is only a question of particular arrangements of words on the page, as Leavis puts it, in favour of the view that we are moved not by the words but by the things the words stand for. One can test this for oneself. Flecker's line:

> A ship, an isle, a sickle moon –
> With few, but with how splendid stars.

loses nothing when rendered into any language. The quality of the imagery here is such that it passes unscathed through the refining fires of translation. It is precisely this characteristic of Ho's verse, the giving of sharp perceptions in images of extraordinary colour and clarity, that makes him a peculiarly translatable poet. Whatever else may be lost, this at least is not.

But Ho has other advantages for the translator besides the vividness of his imagery. Chinese poets, on the whole, are impersonal, self-effacing and inclined to generalize in a way which sometimes muffles the impact of their verse on the Western reader, who is accustomed to as forceful a display of individualism in his poetry as in his culture. The Western poet, at least since the Romantics, has almost invariably been endowed with a personality which makes itself strongly felt through his verse. In this respect, Ho is an aberration from the Chinese standard; for though he very seldom consciously intrudes himself into his verse, the stress of his personality is there all the same. One is continually aware of a sort of controlled violence in his poems, informing even the most casual-sounding lines. He is a poet of exaggerated gestures and moods, swinging between despair and exultation in a way that leads one to guess that he must have been something of a manic-depressive. It is, I suspect, this violence of gesture that makes him so irritate his Chinese readers, who are vaguely conscious all the time that the proprieties are being offended. An image like the following illustrates what I mean:

> Like the blood that wells from a cuckoo's maw
> Are the old man's tears.

Occurring as it does in a poem of social protest, which we are accustomed to think of in terms of the gentle, conversational ironies of Po Chü-yi, this image brings one up with a start. It is altogether too vehement. What is more, it has a peculiar telling-ness about it which is hard to explain. The Chinese reader would at once link this with the story of the Emperor of Shu who abdicated his throne, fled into the wilds and was changed into a cuckoo. But what has this allusion to the weeping emperor to do with an old peasant? The most likely explanation is that the blood the old man weeps (another exaggeration) makes him kin to the cuckoo and hence an animal; at the same time, the cuckoo is an emperor, so the old man's grief is imperial. Linking cuckoo, peasant and emperor in this way through the highly unpleasant image of blood flowing from the eyes and mouth works on the reader powerfully and upsettingly. For a Chinese, the implied social confusion of man with animal, peasant with Son of Heaven, would have been not the least disturbing thing about this com-parison.

Another factor which is not lost in translation but can be brought over unscathed is Ho's evocative use of colour to sym-bolize emotion.[51] White, gold, silver, black, red, green, yellow, blue-green, emerald, vermilion, scarlet, purple, turquoise and cinnabar run riot through his work. Furthermore, his palette is a highly idiosyncratic one in which certain colours, notably white, red and blue-green are dominant, with white standing far above the rest. The table below, compiled from my own analysis, shows the frequency with which the principal colours are dis-tributed through Ho's poems. They fall neatly into six groups:

[51]Ishikawa Kazunari, 'Ri Chō-kichi no shikisai kankaku', *Chūgoku bunka kenkyūkai kaihō* (1955), pp. 18–22: Arai Ken, 'Ri Chō-kichi no shi: toku ni sono shikisai ni tsuite', *Chūgoku bungaku hō*, 3 (1955), pp. 61–90.

COLOUR	NUMBER OF OCCURRENCES IN POEMS
White (*pai*)+ecru (*su*)	113
Jade or jade-white (*yü*)	79
Gold or metal (*chin*)	73
Red (*hung*)	67
Blue-green (*ch'ing*)	63
True green or emerald (*lü*)	44
Yellow (*huang*)	39
Luminescent blue-green *or* sapphire (*pi*)	25
Silver (*yin*)	21
Purple (*tzu*)	20
Turquoise *or* kingfisher-blue (*ts'ui*)	20
Black (*hei*)	13
Vermilion (*chu*)	9
Azure (*ts'ang*)	9
Russet or dark red (*ch'ih*)	3
Cinnabar (*tan*)	3
Deep red (*chiang*)	3
Reddish-brown (*che*)	2
Greenish-white (*p'iao*)	2
Indigo (*lan*)	2
Powder-blue (*p'iao-fen*)	1
Rosy-red (*ch'eng*)	1
Blood-red (*hsüeh se*)	1

Ho's liking for white, a colour associated in China not with purity and virginity but with mourning and misfortune, is highly significant.[52] To the Chinese, white is an unlucky colour, suggesting death and old age. In the Han system of correspondences it was linked with autumn, the west (and hence the setting sun), and the element metal, which interestingly enough ranks second in

[52]Even in Ho's death-bed delirium, we note that he refers to a White Jade Tower.

Ho's list. Moreover, since 'jade' as an adjective always means 'jade-white' in Chinese and never 'jade-green', the combination of white, metal, and jade – 265 instances in all out of 613 – represents a quite extraordinary preference for white. Even in the West, psychologists tend to associate a strong liking for white with psychic abnormality: in China, where white has all the emotional overtones that in Europe would be carried by black, such a predilection would be considered morbid and ill-omened.

Ho's landscapes, drenched in this white radiance, shine with an unearthly pallor.

> In the ninth month, the great wilderness is white.

> The entire mountain bathed in a white dawn.

> Horses' hooves trampling in white.

> Autumn whitens the infinite heavens.

> White grasses, dead beneath invading mist.

> A white sky, water like raw silk.

> Where endless desert merges with white sky.

> Vast autumn gleamed white.

> Jade mist over green damp
> Like pennants of white.

> To an islet where white duckweed grows . . .

> The cloud-towers are half-revealed,
> Walls slant and white.

> Above cold gardens, deserted courtyards,
> A limpid, white void.

> The white glare returns to the Western Hills.

There seems little doubt that Ho's obsession with white was in some way connected with the premature and sinister whitening of his own hair, a physiological quirk which he refers to several times in his poems. He was haunted by the mystery of whiteness as another great poet, Lorca, was haunted by the spell of green.

Against this pallid background the other colours burn with a brilliant flame:

> Under massing clouds red nets darken,
> Over broken stones slant purple coins.

> Beyond the frontiers like rouge from Yen,
> Night's purple congeals.

> Who is this girl shedding vermilion tears?

> Cold candles, kingfisher-green . . .

> Smoky yellow mantles the willows.

> A thousand hills of darkest emerald.

> A flame-red mirror opens in the east.

> His glittering sword flashes through the sky,
> Turning heaven sapphire-blue.

> On the scarlet walls hang girdle-gems of jade.

> Under the white sun, a thousand hills
> Look darkest green.

> Black waters of the Pine Stream
> Bear new dragon-eggs.

> Emerald smoke swirling . . .

> Cold reds weeping dew . . .

> What hungry beetles would not eat
> Piles up in broken yellows.

> Twilight purple freezes in the dappled sky.

> Only black waters' waves sobbing at dawn.

> Pattern of golden snakes on her dancing-rug.

Along with this striking use of colour goes a wholly personal imagery which, again, is unique in Chinese if not in world literature. The following images all occur in Ho's verse, some of them

several times: shrieking phoenixes; lonely simurghs; ageing simurghs; shivering hares; old fishes; gaunt dragons; crying mole-
crickets; weeping raccoons; dying foxes; white foxes barking;
snarling dogs; wailing crickets; drooling lions; slavering griffons;
whinnying and half-starved horses; crying crows; serpents riding
a white mist; old turtles in jade wells; poisonous, horned dragons;
demon-owls and weeping bronze camels. The last figure leads
us to the next class of imagery, that of normally inanimate objects
which in Ho's verse become endowed with a mysterious life of
their own. This is the world of T'ang ghost stories: swords that
roar, swords that fly, painted dragons ridden by rain-elves,
haggard straw-dogs, weeping statues and gargoyles peering out
of stunted trees. It is but a step away from the realm of gods and
spirits proper, ranging from cave-dwelling demons, mountain
trolls, witches and Weird Crones to Nü Kua, the Purple King and
the Mother who is Queen in the West. Against the flickering background of a hallucinatory universe, where mountains crumble
away in the wind and land lurches out of the sea only to disappear
again. Ho's phantasmagoria dances wildly past. The only constant
here is the inexorable passing of time: the dripping water-clock,
the booming drum mark men's progress towards the graves
where the fireflies dance like corpse-fires and lonely candles burn.
Nor are men alone in their predicament. In the Buddhist vision
of things even the gods must perish; and Ho's heaven is a place of
funerals where the blessed themselves are borne in never-ending
procession to the tomb.

Ultimately, Ho was at heart a mystic, as we might have guessed
from his preoccupation with the *Laṅkāvatāra*, the central theme
of which is the doctrine of self-realization (*svasiddhānta*) and inner
enlightenment (*pratyātmagati*). Many of his poems are clearly
records, not of hallucinations, but of genuine, if elementary
visions, in which he transcends the world of egoic experience, the
illusions of Maya, entering a realm in which he contemplates a
higher state of being than our own. Today, we have so completely
lost touch with inner reality that very few of us can believe in its

existence, a fact that makes it difficult for us to respond adequately to Ho's greatest poems where the vision shines the most resplendently. Nevertheless, we must realize that the world of his visions was not a mere fantasy into which he retreated from the miseries of 'reality'. Rather, his Buddhist training enabled him to journey to places far removed from 'the weariness, the fever and the fret' of his existence without losing his orientation, while his poetic genius enabled him to describe vividly what he had seen.

Ho's feeling for religion, whether for Zen or for Shamanism, his sense of the ultimate identity (*samatā*) of the world-of-birth-and-death (*saṁsāra*) and Nirvana, is central not peripheral to his poetic art. He wrote verse ultimately not for aesthetic pleasure but to express what the *Laṅkāvatāra* calls *pratyātmāryajnāna-gocara* – the state of intuitive awareness of inner truth.[53] It is perhaps this which makes the perceptive Western reader want to link him with that great occult tradition which includes Baudelaire and Blake, Rimbaud and Yeats. Though his visions are admittedly never more than two-fold (to use Blake's term) they are intensely felt and realized, even if they do lapse at times when the spirit fails him into mere fantasy. His moments of epiphany occur when he realizes – to quote his favourite sutra – that 'this world of error is eternity itself, truth itself' ('*Bhrāntiḥ śāśvatā, bhrāntis tattvam*'); when he glimpses as Yeats puts it, 'the uncontrollable mystery on the bestial floor'.

To say this is not to overlook the fact that Ho's poetry lacks the

[53]The *Laṅkāvatāra* devotes a long passage to attacking the erroneous belief that words can express the highest reality: 'Mahāmati, words are not the highest reality, nor is what is expressed in words the highest reality. Why? Because the highest reality is an exalted state of bliss, and as it cannot be entered into by mere statements regarding it, words are not the highest reality. Mahāmati, the highest reality is to be attained by the inner realization of noble wisdom: it is not a state of word-discrimination: therefore, discrimination does not express the highest reality.' (D. T. Suzuki, *The Laṅkāvatāra Sūtra*, p. 77). In the light of this and other passages, it would seem clear that Ho must have realized the limitations of the world of words to which he had devoted himself, knowing that 'the truth (*tattva*) is beyond words'. He can thus hardly be accused of poetic aestheticism.

E

serene assurance of the mystic who has achieved realization and enlightenment. Since for much of his life he was a sick man, a great deal of his verse betrays all the feverish and heightened sensibility of the consumptive. In this he is very much of his age. As Yoshikawa Kōjirō remarks: 'T'ang poetry burns with intensity. The moment in which the poem is born is one of the most vital instants in a man's life in his headlong plunge towards death. He must fix his eyes upon the instant and pour his feelings into it. The emotion must cohere, it must jet forth, it must explode'.[54]

Never was this truer than of the poetry of Li Ho. In his sensuality and the despairing intensity with which he strives to hold the passing moment burning eternally in his art, like a frozen flame, he is akin to Keats: and like Keats – or Beddoes, whom he also resembles[55] – he is half in love at times with easeful death. He wrote in the shadow of the grave: and no philosophy, no religion, no consoling belief could quite keep out its ineluctable cold. Only at the white radiance of his own poetic visions could he warm himself for a while before making his final journey to those cypress-shadowed tombs where he had wandered so often during his brief lifetime like some pallid and melancholy ghost. Yet it would have been some consolation to him, I feel, to learn that now 'after a thousand years in earth', his 'rancorous blood' shines forth in the light of day as emerald-jade.

[54]*Sōshi gaisetsu*, pp. 43–4. The translation is from Burton Watson, *An Introduction to Sung Poetry*, p. 32. Elsewhere, Yoshikawa remarks, finely, that 'the tension of T'ang poetry is produced by the strain of trying to discover some cause for hope in a life that seems entirely given over to despair' (*Sōshi gaisetsu*, p. 35; translated, Watson, *op. cit.*, p. 25).

[55]The resemblance to T. L. Beddoes was first noted by Ch'ien Chung-shu, *T'an-yi-lu*, p. 59.

ABBREVIATIONS

The following abbreviations occur very frequently in the text: Full details can be found by consulting the list of sources.

Wang	=	Wang Ch'i (Source No. 4)
Yao	=	Yao Wen-hsieh (Source No. 4)
Yeh	=	Yeh Ts'ung-ch'i (Source No. 5)
Arai	=	Arai Ken (Source No. 6)
Suzuki	=	Suzuki Torao (Source No. 7)
Saitō	=	Saitō Shō (Source No. 8)

Tu Mu's *Preface* to the Songs and Poems of Li Ch'ang-chi

In the tenth month of the fifth year of the *T'ai-ho* period (A.D. 831) there came a sudden shout outside my house at midnight from some-one bearing me a letter. 'This must be something out of the ordinary', I exclaimed, as I hurriedly took a torch and went outside. When I opened it, it turned out to be a letter from the Scholar of the Hall of Assembled Sages, Shen Tzu-ming, which read:

> During the *Yüan-ho* period my dead friend Li Ho and I were very loyal and affectionate to each other. Day and night we rose and rested, ate and drank together. When Ho was dying, he gave me all the songs and poems he had written during his lifetime. These were divided into four sections, numbering 233 pieces altogether. For several years now I have been wandering all over the place, till I had begun to think these poems were already lost. Tonight as the wine wore off me, I found I could not get to sleep again, so I decided to go through my trunks and set things in order. Suddenly I came across the poems which Ho had given me and my thoughts turned to days gone by. I re-collected all my conversations and pleasant outings with him. Every place, every season, every day, every night, every goblet, every meal came back to me with such clarity, no detail forgotten, that I found myself shedding tears.
>
> Since Ho no longer has a family or children that I can support or sympathize with, I regret that all I have done up to now has been to think of him and enjoy his words as I recited them. You have always been very good to me. Would you now somewhat solace my thoughts by writing a preface to Ho's works for me, explaining their worth?

I was unable that night to send him a letter saying I could not do this, but went to see him next day to excuse myself from this task, remarking that people considered that Ho's genius surpassed those of his predecessors.

For several days after this refusal I pondered this matter, reflecting that Shen had a profoundly subtle and extraordinarily comprehensive knowledge of poetry as well as a thorough understanding of both Ho's poetic abilities and his shortcomings. Hence if I did not definitely decline to write this preface I would certainly leave him dissatisfied. What could I do then but go and make my excuses to him once more, explaining to him in detail why I did not dare write a preface to Ho's works? However, he insisted that I must write it or he would feel humiliated, so that I did not dare refuse again. I have tried my best to write this preface but am still very much ashamed of it.

Ho was a descendant of the T'ang imperial house. His style was Ch'ang-chi. During the *Yüan-ho* period, Han Yü, the President of the Ministry of Civil Office, praised his songs and poems. Clouds and mist gently intermingling cannot describe his manner; illimitable waters cannot describe his feelings; the verdure of spring cannot describe his warmth; the clarity of autumn cannot describe his style; a mast in the wind, a horse in the battle-line cannot describe his courage; earthenware coffins and tripods with seal-characters cannot describe his antiquity; seasonal blossoms and lovely girls cannot describe his ardour; fallen kingdoms and ruined palaces, thorny thickets and gravemounds cannot describe his resentment and sorrow; whales yawning, turtles spurting, ox-ghosts and serpent-spirits cannot describe his wildness and extravagance.

He is in the tradition of the *Li Sao*. Even though he does not come up to it in high seriousness he sometimes surpasses it in expression. The *Li Sao* is full of resentment and criticism of the rule and misrule of princes and ministers. Often it goads men into thought; though this quality is sometimes lacking in Ho's work. Ho has the ability to delve into the past. Heaving deep sighs, he would grieve over things which nobody had ever recounted either now or in days gone by. We may instance his *Song of the Brazen Immortal Bidding Farewell to Han*, or the songs in which he supplemented the Palace Poetry of Yü Ch'ien-wu of Liang. In hunting out facts and collecting material he broke with tradition and went far into the distance along paths of the brush and ink. We cannot really claim to understand him.

Ho died when he was twenty-seven. We, his contemporaries, all believe that if he had added a little more high seriousness to his work and had not died when he did, he could have treated the *Li Sao* itself as his servant.

I, Tu Mu of Ching-chao, write this preface some fifteen years after Ho's death.

Finding-list of Li Ho's Poems Mentioned
in the Text

3

Song: Li P'ing at the Vertical Harp[1]

7-character: 5 rhymes

SILK from Wu, paulownia from Shu,
Open high autumn.[2]
In the white sky the frozen clouds
Falling, not floating.[3]
Ladies of the River weeping among bamboos,
The White Girl mournful;[4]
Such is Li P'ing playing his harp
In the Middle Kingdom.

Jade from Mount K'un is shattered,
Phoenixes shriek.[5]
Lotuses are weeping dew,
Fragrant orchids smile.

[1]Li P'ing was one of the emperor's musicians, from the famous Pear-garden School. The *k'ung-hou* was a vertical, angular harp with from sixteen to twenty-three strings, according to size.

[2]Shu (Szechwan) was famous for its *t'ung* trees (*paulownia imperialis*), from which these harps were made. Similarly, the best silk came from Wu, in south-east China. 'High autumn' is a term used for the ninth lunar month.

[3] Reading 空白 in preference to the 空山 ('deserted mountain') of some editions. The music is so exquisite the clouds come down to hear it.

[4]The Ladies of the River Hsiang are the two daughters of the legendary Emperor Yao, consorts of the Emperor Shun. Their teardrops, falling on the bamboos growing by the latter's grave, left speckled marks on them. The White Girl played a zither with fifty strings (a *se*) for the Yellow Emperor. The tune she played was so sad that he was forced to break her *se*, leaving her with only a twenty-five-stringed instrument.

[5]Mount K'un-lun was a mythical mountain in the west, said to produce the finest jade. Here the Peaches of Immortality were to be found.

Before the twelve gates of the city
The cold light melts.[6]
The twenty-three strings have power to move
The Purple King.[7]

The goddess Nü Kua smelts her stones
To weld the sky.[8]
Stones split asunder, the sky startles,
Autumn rains gush forth.
He goes in dreams to the Magic Mountain
To teach the Weird Crone.[9]
Old fishes leap above the waves,
Gaunt dragons dance.[10]

Even Wu Kang, unsleeping still,
Leans on his cassia tree,[11]
While wing-foot dew drifts wetly
Over the shivering hare.[12]

[6]Both Ch'ang-an and Lo-yang had twelve gates. The light melts because music had power over the elements.

[7]One of the three foremost rulers of Heaven.

[8]Nü Kua (or Wa) was a goddess with a snake's body, consort of Fu Hsi. When the demon Kung Kung butted his head against the north-west pillar of heaven, tilting the earth downwards to the south-east and making a hole in the sky, Nü Kua repaired the hole by fusing minerals of five colours. (This may possibly be an early reference to glass-making.) See *Huai-nan-tzu*, 'Lan Ming'.

[9]The Weird Crone is perhaps the Ch'eng Fu-jen of the *Sou-shen chi*, who is said to have been an expert performer on the vertical harp.

[10]*Lieh-tzu* mentions a certain Hu Pa, who was such a performer on the classical zither (*ch'in*) that fishes danced and dragons leapt whenever he played. See A. C. Graham, *The Book of Lieh-tzu* (London, 1960), p. 107.

[11] Read 剛 for 貫. Wu Kang was banished to the moon, where he must forever unavailingly try to cut down the cassia tree growing there. The music makes him pause from his endless toil.

[12]The moon was believed to contain a hare, a toad and a cassia tree; 'shivering hare' is a kenning for 'cold moon'.

Song: Gossamer[1]

7-character: 3 rhymes

IN the aging leaves of weeping-willows,
Orioles feed their young,
The gossamer is vanishing,
Yellow bees go home.

Black-haired young men, and girls
With golden hairpins,[2]
From goblets, powder-blue, are quaffing,
A liquid amber.

Twilight over flower-decked terraces,
Spring says goodbye,
Fallen blossoms rise and dance
To eddying airs.
Elm-tree seeds are now so thick,
They can't be counted,
Shen's green money strewn along
Our city roads![3]

---

[1]'*Ts'an-ssu*' ('remnants of silk') means 'lingering heat-haze', (*kagerō*) according to Suzuki. Saitō prefers 'gossamer'.

[2]Singing-girls.

[3]Elm seeds look like strings of copper cash. During the Chin dynasty Shen Ch'ung coined his own cash, which became known as 'Shen's money'. The fallen seeds mark the end of spring.

Song: Returning from Kuei-chi[1]
5-character: 1 rhyme

When Yü Chien-wu was living, during the Liang dynasty (A.D. 502–57), he used to write songs in the palace poetry style to harmonize with those of the Crown Prince. When the state was subverted, Chien-wu fled to hide from the danger in Kuei-chi. Later, he was able to return home. I thought that he would have left some poems on this subject but none of them has been found. So I myself wrote this song about his return from Kuei-chi to express his sadness for him.

> WILDERNESS crumbles the yellow walls of pepper,[2]
> Wet fireflies fill the palaces of Liang.[3]
> Once poet to a prince in the T'ai-ch'eng palace,[4]
> I dream of bronze carriages under an autumn quilt.
> Home again, Wu frost whitens my hair,[5]
> My body grown old, like the rushes in the pools.
> Sleeplessly staring, the Golden Fish now lost,[6]
> This wandering courtier must live in poverty.

[1]This poem is really an exercise in verse, an imitation of the style of the Liang dynasty poet, Yü Chien-wu (487–551), father of the more famous Yü Hsin (513–81). Yü Chien-wu was a favourite of Emperor Wu of Liang, who made him Prime Minister of State. He was a practitioner of the art of 'palace poetry', a new type of rather exotic, languid verse very much in fashion at the Liang court. The rebellion of Hou Ching (548), a revolt which took three years to subdue, forced Yü to take shelter in Kuei-chi (Chekiang). He returned to find the capital in ruins, while he himself was too old for high office.

[2]The apartments of the Empress were traditionally said to have walls painted with a substance containing pepper and fagara to give them fragrance and warmth.

[3]Fireflies were supposed to be born spontaneously from damp.

[4]He is referring to the Crown Prince, Hsiao T'ung (501–31), compiler of the famous anthology, *Wen-hsüan*. The T'ai-ch'eng palace of the Crown Prince stood in Shang-yüan county, now a suburb of Nanking.

[5]Wu (Kiangsu) was the site of the capital.

[6] Read 眽眽 for 脉脉. cf. *Ch'u Tz'u, Chiu Ssu, Feng Yu*, p. 172: 'And I lie all the morning in staring wakefulness.' 'Golden Fish' – a type of purse worn at the belt by officials of the third degree and upwards during T'ang. Our line is an anachronism, since during Liang Golden Tortoises, not Fish, were worn.

Sent to Ch'üan Ch'ü and Yang Ching-chih When I Left the City[1]

7-character: 1 rhyme

WARM grasses, darkening clouds, compose
Ten thousand leagues of spring.
The palace flowers bid me farewell,
Caress my face.
I tell myself that a sword of Han
Should fly away.
Why does this homeward carriage bear
Only an ailing man?[2]

[1]This poem was perhaps written in 814 when Ho left Ch'ang-an after resigning from his post in the Court of Imperial Sacrifices. It could also have been written after he had been refused his *chin-shih* degree in 810. Ch'üan and Yang were two friends of his, both of them *chin-shih*.

[2]Old swords were supposed to have magical properties, among them the power to rise in the air. When a fire broke out in the palace in 284, the sword with which Liu Pang had slain the son of the White King of the West (a huge snake) flew away and was never seen again. Ho is saying that if he had really been an exceptional person he would not be leaving the capital in this way.

To Be Shown to My Younger Brother[1]

5-character: 1 rhyme

THREE years ago, I left my younger brother,
Already I've been home ten days or so.[2]
Tonight we have the good wine of Lu-ling,[3]
And our yellow-covered books of long-ago.
I've managed to keep my ailing bones alive.
But in this world our troubles come in packs.[4]
Why bother to ask who's ox and who is horse?[5]
You throw your dice, then take your 'owls' or 'blacks'.[6]

[1] Written when Ho returned to Ch'ang-ku from Ch'ang-an, in 814.
[2] Yeh reads ✝ for — with Sung edition.
[3] A famous wine made from the water of Lake Ling, in Heng-yang, Honan.
[4] An old saying.
[5] 'Ox' and 'horse' were the names of two of the symbolical animals in the Chinese system of 'branches'. These branches were used in divination. Note that 'ox' and 'horse' were also terms used in the *Shu-p'u* game described below. The couplet is rich in meanings. Success and failure in life depend mainly on chance. (a) Why then be concerned about one's fate? (b) Why bother consulting fortune-tellers? (c) Why care about who holds what official rank?
[6] In the game known as *Shu-p'u wu-mu*, played with 5 wooden black and white counters, 5 blacks was the best throw. The owl – an unlucky bird – was the name given to the worst throw, namely 2 whites and 3 blacks.

Bamboo

5-character: 1 rhyme

ITS patterns of light ripple over water,
Thrusting into air, it greenly shadows spring.
Flowers of dew beget the young bamboo,
Its frosty roots caressed by coloured moss.
Woven into mats, it's damp with fragrant sweat,[1]
Cut into rods, it catches ornate scales.
Once it was used to make three-layered caps,
One section I present to you, my prince.[2]

[1]Beautiful women will sleep on these mats.
[2]In ancient times, princes had worn caps lined with three layers of bamboo. Ho is offering his services to some prince or other. Perhaps this poem accompanied a present of bamboo.

Harmonizing with a Poem Written by Shen,
the Imperial Son-in-law, Entitled:
'The Waters of the Royal Canal'[1]

5-character: 1 rhyme

FLOWING through the park, white water broad and deep;[2]
Palace ladies put on their yellow patches.[3]
Winding round hills, its dragon-bones are cold,[4]
Brushing the banks, its duck-head green is fragrant.[5]
It startles concubines from fading dreams,
Cups stop circling, little goblets float.[6]
I was lucky enough to wander for a while
Beside this wavy stream with Master Ho.[7]

[1]Shen Tzu-ming (the friend who wrote the letter mentioned in Tu Mu's *Preface*) had married the Princess An-lo, a daughter of Emperor Hsien-tsung.

[2]Wang understands this line as meaning: 'When I enter the royal park, I see white waters broad and deep.' I have followed Suzuki.

[3]'Yellow-star beauty-spots' were all the rage at this time. The ladies are using the clear water as their mirror.

[4]A reference to the stone slabs lining the sides of the canal.

[5]'Duck-head' was the name of a green dye.

[6]It was an old custom for guests to float wine-cups on a stream during parties.

[7]Ho Yen, style P'ing-shu (190–249), was a man of exceptional good looks and talent who, like Shen, had married a princess.

On First Taking up My Post as Supervisor of Ceremonies My Thoughts Turn to My House in the Mountains of Ch'ang-ku[1]

5-character: 1 rhyme

HORSES' hoof-prints have been brushed away,
Back from the office, I must shut the gates myself.[2]
In the long saucepan, River rice is cooking,[3]
On little trees the jujubes flower in spring.[4]
Up on the wall I hang my lotus-sceptre,[5]
Inspect my pointed turban by the screen.[6]
I sent my dog to carry a letter to Lo,[7]
The crane fell sick, regretting its wanderings in Ch'in.[8]
The tea is sealed away in earthen jars,
My mountain wine locked up with the bamboo stumps.
Nothing so fine as moonlight on a boat . . .
But who is punting on that cloud-filled stream?

[1]This poem was written in 811, when Li Ho first assumed office. Ch'ang-ku was in south-east Fu-ch'ang county, some fifty *li* south-west of Lo-yang. Ho was working far away in Ch'ang-an.

[2]He has few visitors and no servants, because he is so poor.

[3] Rice from south of the Yangtze is cooking in a *ch'eng* 鎗, a type of pot. Suzuki thinks *ch'eng* is the name of a type of rice.

[4]'Jujubes': the fruit of *zizyphus vulgaris*, Lam.

[5]*Ju-yi* ('as-you-like-it') was a double-curved sceptre, often used as a back-scratcher, in the form of lotus-flower and stalk. It was normally made of jade or other valuable material and was presented as a token of esteem.

[6]A kind of turban with peaked corners worn at home.

[7]The poet Lu Chi (261–303) was supposed to have owned a dog named Yellow Ears, said to have carried a letter all the way from Lo-yang to Lu's family in far-off Wu and then to have come back with an answer, performing in a fortnight a journey that would have taken a man several weeks. Yellow Ears' grave is still pointed out near the site of the Lu family ancestral temple at Hua-t'ing. See *Chin-shu*, LIV.

[8]With his body as wasted as that of a sick crane, he regrets he ever came to the capital. Wang and Yeh, however, understand this line as: 'The crane fell sick, regretting my wandering off to Ch'in' and presumably believe Ho is referring to a mistress of his who was pining away for him. In defence of this they cite an old ballad entitled 'A pair of white geese' one version of which (in *Yüeh-fu shih-chi*, XXXIX, p. 56) reads 'crane' for goose.

Seventh Night[1]

5-character: 1 rhyme

THE Shores of Parting are dark this morning,[2]
The silken bed-hangings mournful at midnight.[3]
Magpies leave the moon of threaded silk,
Flowers fill the towers where clothes are aired.[4]
Up in the sky, half of a golden mirror,[5]
Down among men, we gaze at a jade hook.[6]
In Ch'ien-t'ang city, Su Hsiao-hsiao
Endures the autumn of yet one more year.[7]

[1]On the seventh night of the seventh lunar month the festival of the Herd-boy and the Weaving Lady was celebrated. These two lovers, exiled to heaven as stars and parted by the river of the Milky Way, were allowed to meet on this night. They crossed the river on a bridge formed by magpies (see line 3), but had to part at dawn.

[2]'Shores of Parting' – the Milky Way.

[3]Probably a reference to the Weaving Lady, now left desolate again. It might, however, refer to Ho himself.

[4]It was the custom on this night for women to leave seven needles threaded with silk in the moonlight and pray for greater skill in sewing. It was also the custom to air books and clothes in the sun during the day. Yeh reads 'fireflies' 螢 for 'flowers'.

[5]The crescent moon. 'Half a mirror' hints at a story of parted lovers who each kept half a mirror as a love-token.

[6]Yeh understands 鈎 as 'return'. 'Down in the world of men, we hope that these jade stars will meet again.'

[7]See the poem Su Hsiao-hsiao's Tomb, p. 30 below.

Passing by the Hua-ch'ing Palace[1]

5-character: 1 rhyme

SPRING moon, crows crying at night,
Palace screens shutting out royal flowers.
Under massing clouds, red nets darken,[2]
Over broken stones slant purple coins.[3]
Jade bowls now filled with fallen dew,
Silver lamps have blackened antique silk.[4]
No news of late about the Prince of Shu,[5]
Around the springs young parsley grows.[6]

Song: Seeing off Shen Ya-chih
(Together with an Introduction)

7-character: 4 rhymes

In the seventh year of the *Yüan-ho* period (812) the scholar,
Shen Ya-chih, failed his Doctoral Examination in Calligraphy
and went back to Wu-chiang. I was sad at his going, but had not

[1]This winter palace, built in A.D. 644 at the foot of Mount Li in Shensi,
famous for its hot springs, had been one of the resorts of Emperor Hsüan-tsung
(*regnet* 712–56) and his ill-starred favourite, the beautiful Yang Kuei-fei
(d. 756). Passing by it half a century later, Ho was stuck by the poignancy of
its fading glories.

[2]Suzuki and Saitō believe the term 'red threads' 朱 絡 refers to the jewelled,
red nets stretched across the windows to keep out bird-droppings, insects and
dust. Yeh understands this as 'red-lacquered window-frames'.

[3]Mosses.

[4]The palace contained many shrines to various deities. Saitō suggests this
was the shrine of Lao-tzu. Since the bowls are full of dew (rain) the roof must
be leaking. They should have held sacrificial wine. 'Silk' refers to silk screens.

[5]During the rebellion of An Lu-shan (755–63), Hsüan-tsung fled to Shu, in
south-west China. Hence he was known derisively as the 'Prince of Shu'.

[6]The famous hot-springs are so deserted that no one comes there even to
pluck parsley. *Ch'in* 芹 is 'Chinese celery' (*venanthe stolonifera*, DC), which in
appearance rather resembles parsley. We know it as 'curled cress'.

the money to buy wine to console him. Furthermore, I was moved by his pleas. So I sang these stanzas as I escorted him on his way.[1]

> THIS talented man from Wu-hsing[2]
> Resents the winds of spring.
> Peach blossom burgeons over the roads –
> A thousand leagues of red!
> With purple reins and a snapped bamboo[3]
> On a small piebald nag,
> He's riding home to Ch'ien-t'ang –
> East, then east again.
>
> From criss-cross shoots of white rattan,
> His book-basket was woven.
> Short bamboo-slips, all of a length,
> Like Buddhist texts.
> His flashing strength, his precious ore,
> Offered to Spring Officials.[4]
> He skimmed the waves beneath the mist,
> Riding a single leaf.[5]

[1]Shen Ya-chih, style Hsia-hsien, was noted for his literary talents. He was not only a fine poet but had also gained fame as a writer of tales of the supernatural (*ch'üan-ch'i*). He finally succeeded in gaining his doctorate three years later, in 815. The song deals with Shen's leaving Ch'ang-an, where he had sat for his examinations, to return home.

[2]Hu-chou, in Chekiang, was Shen's home.

[3]The bamboo was for use as a whip. Yeh thinks 'purple silk' also refers to the whip.

[4]Officials attached to the Department of Rites, who conducted the *chü* examinations. Read 才 for 材.

[5]A small boat. This section describes Shen's coming to Ch'ang-an for the examinations.

The Spring Officials garner talent
Wherever the white sun shines,
But threw away this yellow gold,
Let slip this dragon-horse.
So satchel in hand, he returned to the River,[6]
Back through his gates,
Weary and worn – yet who was there
To give him sympathy?

I hear a brave man always treasures
His heart and his bones.
Three times that ancient ran away,
Yet never lost his head.[7]
I beg you now to wait till dawn
Before you ply your whip.
Your carriage will come back one day
To the tune of autumn pipes.[8]

[6]To the Wu-chiang, i.e. to Wu-hsing. Yeh reads 家 for 江 with Sung ed.

[7]Kuan Chung (d. 645 B.C.), prime minister to Duke Huan of Ch'i, once confessed he had run away from battle three times, for the sake of his old mother. See *Shih-chi*, LXII. Read 猝 for 捽.

[8]Each month of the year was allotted a certain note on the pitch-pipes. Since the examinations were held in autumn, Shen would return then.

Expressing My Feelings[1]

5-character: 1 rhyme

No. 1

CH'ANG-CH'ING was deep in thought at Mao-ling,
Where emerald grasses drooped by a stone well.
As he played his zither, he watched Wen-chün,
The spring breeze stirring her shadow-dappling hair.
The Prince of Liang and Emperor Wu
Had cast him aside like a snapped-off flower.[2]
All that he left was a single memorial,
Buried in liquid gold on top of Mount T'ai.[3]

[1]Ssu-ma Hsiang-ju (179–117 B.C.), styled Ch'ang-ch'ing, is mentioned several times in Ho's poems, always with admiration. Hsiang-ju was the finest writer of *fu* of his time – probably the finest in Chinese literary history. He resigned his first appointment under Emperor Ching (r.157–141 B.C.) to take office under Prince Hsiao of Liang, who had brought together a brilliant group of poets at his court. On the death of Prince Hsiao, he returned to his native Sze-chwan, where he eloped with Wen-chün, daughter of a local millionaire named Cho Wang-sun. Later he took service under Emperor Wu (r.141–87 B.C.). He retired to Mao-ling (Hsing-p'ing county, Shensi) and died there of diabetes after many years of illness. In this poem Ho is comparing the dying poet's plight with his own.

[2]This is quite untrue. Both rulers had shown Hsiang-ju great favours. Ho is simply projecting his own situation on to Hsiang-ju.

[3]'Liquid gold' was a mixture of gold and mercury. The document in question, which dealt with the imperial sacrifices, was handed over to the Emperor after Hsiang-ju's death.

No. 2

5-character: 1 rhyme

AT DUSK, when I have done with writing,[1]
Surprised by frost, my white silk starts to fall.[2]
I laugh at myself in the mirror for a while,
How can I live as long as the Southern Hill?
I wear no turban wrapped around my head,[3]
The bitter-cork has already dyed my clothes.[4]
Cannot you see the fish in the clear stream
That drink its water and do just as they please?

Written after the Style of a Poem by Liu Yün[5]

5-character: 2 rhymes

TO AN islet where white duckweed grows,
Liu Yün comes home, riding upon his horse.
The head of the river is fragrant with quince,[6]
Over its shores butterflies flutter about.

[1]One edition reads 看 for 著.

[2]His hair has turned prematurely white.

[3]He cannot wear the turban, that symbol of the life of ease (see p. 18, note 6. above), because he is so hard at work.

[4]Bitter-cork (*phellodendron amurense*: the Siberian cork-tree) is a mountain tree, the bitter yellow bark of which is used as a drug and a dye. In early folk-songs, it is a symbol of suffering (e.g. *Tzu-yeh*, No. 11). Hence the line means not only that Ho is out of office and dressed like a commoner – for during T'ang all the common people had to wear yellow clothes – but also that he has suffered a great deal.

[5]Liu Yün, style Wen-ch'ang, was governor of Wu-hsing during the Liang dynasty (502–57), He wrote a famous *yüeh-fu* ballad, which begins:

'On an islet I gather white duckweed,
Sunset, spring south of the River.'

[6]Literally: '*cha* trees' (*cydonia japonica*: the Japanese quince tree). This is a thorny tree with yellow, red or white flowers, that grows on hillsides.

Wine in the cups like dew from bamboo-leaves,[1]
Her jade-pegged lute of hollow paulownia from Shu.[2]
A waterway runs past the scarlet tower,[3]
Where the sand is warm, you'll find a pair of fish.[4]

Song of the Sword of the Collator in the Spring Office[5]

7-character: 1 rhyme

ELDER, within your casket glints
Three feet of water,[6]
That once plunged into a lake in Wu
To behead a dragon.[7]
A slash of brightly slanting moonlight,
Polished, cold dew.
A sash of white satin, smooth and level,
Unruffled by wind.
Its hilt of ancient shark-womb skin,
Bristles with caltrops,[8]
Damasked blade, tempered with sea-bird's grease,
A white pheasant's tail.

[1]A pun. The villages of Upper Bamboo (Shang-jo) and Lower Bamboo (Hsia-jo) in Wu-ch'eng county, Hu-chou, not far from Wu-hsing, were famous for their wine made with the water of the Bamboo River. Hence the line also means: 'Wine in the cups from Jo-hsia'.

[2]For paulownia from Shu, see p. 10, note 2, above.

[3]Where the singing-girl lived.

[4]The two lovers. Note that this poem, modelled on Liu Yün, is quite different in style from Ho's other works.

[5]Ho's twelfth elder cousin held the post of Collator in the Spring Office (Secretariat) of the household of the Crown Prince, as we know from the poem *Autumn Cold*, (p. 185 below.). This was a post of the ninth rank, upper class.

[6]'Elder' (*hsien-pei*) was a term used by second-degree graduates when addressing those who had taken their doctorates.

[7]A reference to Chou Ch'u (Chin dynasty), who dived into a lake to kill a dragon that was plaguing his district. See *Chin-shu*, LVIII, p. 1a.

[8]The finest swords had hilts of shark skin.

It is, in short, a sliver
Of Ching K'o's heart.[1]
May it never shine on the characters
In the Spring Office![2]
Twisted sashes, whorls of gold.
Hang from its hilt,
Its magic beams can cut clean through
A Blue-field jade.[3]
The West's White King was struck with fear
When it was drawn,
His demon mother wailing loudly
In the autumn wilds.[4]

Song: A Nobleman at the End of the Night

SMOKE of aloeswood curls and swirls,[5]
Crows cry the tattered end of night.
Lotus and ripples in a winding pool –
White jades around the waist strike cold.[6]

[1]Ching K'o was the epitome of the knight-errant, a hero who tried to assassinate the detested First Emperor of Ch'in. Ho's cousin is his spiritual descendant. Even though he works in a civil service office he has all the valour of a true knight.

[2]The commentators cannot explain this line satisfactorily. I follow Saitō.

[3]Lan-t'ien (Indigo-field) in Shensi, was famous for its 'jade' which was actually a green-and-white marble quarried in the Chung-nan hills.

[4]Liu Pang, founder of the Han dynasty, once killed a huge snake which lay across his path. That night an old woman appeared to him in a dream, lamenting loudly, and told him that the snake was the son of the White King of the West.

[5]Ch'en-shui hsiang ('The perfumed wood that sinks in water') was the most popular aromatic of T'ang. Derived from a tree of the genus aquilaria, it is variously known in English as aloeswood, eaglewood, agalloch or garoo. Schafer, The Golden Peaches of Samarkand (Berkeley & Los Angeles, 1963), pp. 163–5 (henceforward referred to as Golden Peaches), has an excellent discussion of this very popular incense, which includes a translation of the above poem.

[6]A girl sits alone in her room waiting for her lord to return? Or possibly, a nobleman, not yet in bed after a night's hard drinking, waits for the dawn which must summon him to court.

Ballad of the Grand Warden of Goose Gate[1]

7-character: 2 rhymes

BLACK clouds whelm on the city,
Till it seems the city must yield.
Our chain-mail glitters under the moon,[2]
Metal scales agape.

Clangour of horns fills the sky
With colours of fall.[3]
Beyond the frontiers, like rouge from Yen,
Night's purple congeals.[4]
Our scarlet banners, half unfurled,
Withdraw to the river Yi,[5]
So cold the drums, in the heavy frost,
Their sound is dulled.
We requite the king for his favours to us
At Yellow Gold Tower,[6]
Clutching our Dragons of Jade
We die for our lord.[7]

[1]The title is that of an old *yüeh-fu* ballad. Grand Warden (*t'ai-shou*) was a rank roughly equivalent to Governor. Yen-men ('Goose Gate') commandery was in Shansi. Yao believes that this poem deals with a rising which took place in the north (actually in Shensi) in the winter of 814. But another source, the *Yu-hsien ku-ch'ui* of the T'ang writer, Chang Ku, claims that it was this poem which attracted Han Yü's attention to Ho, round about the year 809. Ostensibly the poem deals with the defeat of a Chinese army during the Later Han.

[2]Some editions read 'sun' for 'moon'.

[3]These horns, which were of non-Chinese origin, were being sounded at dawn.

[4]A dark-red cosmetic made in Yen from the safflower (*carthamus tinctorius*) Read 上 for 土.

[5]The army is in retreat. Three rivers which rise in Hopeh province are all called 'Yi'.

[6]During the Warring States period King Chao of Yen, anxious to attract to his court all the finest men of his time, offered a thousand pieces of gold to those who came to have audience with him in this tower and were subsequently accepted into his service. The ruins of this tower stood 18 *li* south-east of the river Yi.

[7]'Jade Dragon' was a favourite name for a sword during T'ang times.

Song: Great Dike[1]

Irregular: 3 rhymes

In Heng-t'ang is my home,
Red, sendal curtains filled with fragrant cassia.
Black clouds have taught me
To pile up my hair,[1]
Bright moons have made me
Pearls for my ears.[3]

A lotus wind stirs
On the spring river-bank.
Down in Great Dike
They detain northerners.
You, sir, eat tails of carp,
While I eat gibbons' lips.[4]

Oh, do not point to
The road to Hsiang-yang!
Down the river's green reaches
Few sails return.
Today a flowering sweet-flag,
Tomorrow a withered maple-tree.

[1]A girl from Heng-t'ang, near Nanking, is begging her love not to linger in the gay quarters of Ta-t'i ('Great Dike'), but to come home quickly. Ta-t'i, near Hsiang-yang, in south Hupeh, was famous for its wine and its brothels. Heng-t'ang was also noted for its singing-girls, one of whom is here begging her lover to stay away from her rivals. The poem is closely modelled on a *yüeh-fu* ballad by Liu Tan (433–59).

[2]Saitō interprets: 'I have piled up my hair in dark-blue clouds.'

[3]'Bright moons' – pearls.

[4]Great delicacies for the gourmet. The term *hsing-hsing* referred to three types of gibbon, namely the black gibbon, the white-handed gibbon and the hoolock gibbon.

Music for Strings from Shu[1]

5-character: 2 rhymes

UNDER the maples, tranquil flowers at twilight,[2]
In Brilliant River, the southern hills' reflection,[3]
Fearsome rocks are falling, apes are wailing,[4]
Bamboos and clouds have saddened half the peaks.

A cold moon rises over the autumn shores,
Jade sand glistens through translucent waves.
Who is this girl shedding vermilion tears?
She cannot bear his journey through Ch'ü-t'ang Gorge.[5]

[1]Name of a type of *yüeh-fu* ballad.
[2]Lotuses on calm water.
[3]The Cho-chin river in Szechwan (Shu).
[4]Wang and Saitō interpret this line as meaning: 'Among the fearsome rocks the apes, looking as though they are falling from the trees, are wailing.' I have followed Suzuki.
[5]She weeps tears of blood at the thought of the dangers her lover must endure while journeying down-river through the terrifying Ch'ü-t'ang Gorge, in K'uei-chou, Szechwan.

G

Su Hsiao-hsiao's Tomb[1]

Irregular: 3 rhymes

DEW upon lonely orchids
Like tear-brimmed eyes.
No twining of love-knots,
Mist-wreathed flowers I cannot bear to cut.

Grass for her cushions,
Pines for her awning,
Wind as her skirts,
Water as girdle-jades.
In her oil-silk carriage[2]
She is waiting at dusk.
Cold candles, kingfisher-green,
Weary with shining.[3]

Under the Western Grave-mound,
Wind-blown rain.[4]

[1]Su Hsiao-hsiao was a renowned singing-girl from Ch'ien-t'ang (Hangchow) who lived during the Southern Ch'i dynasty (479–502). Two tombs, said to be hers, are in existence, one in Chia-hsing county, north Chekiang, the other on Mount Ku, near Hangchow. The T'ang writer, Li Shen, recounts the story that sounds of music and singing could be heard coming from the tomb on stormy nights. Ho was clearly inspired by an old ballad, ascribed to Su Hsiao-hsiao herself, which runs:

> 'I ride in an oil-silk carriage
> My love rides a piebald horse.
> Where shall we twine our love-knots?
> Under the pine and cypress of
> the Western Grave-mound.'

> (*Yü-t'ai hsin-yung*, X)

[2]Singing-girls rode in carriages with oil-cloth sides. Su's carriage must have been buried with her.

[3]The will-o'-the-wisps are like candles lit for the lovers who will never come. After burning for over 300 years, they seem faint and feeble.

[4]In spite of the legend that her lovers visited her on stormy nights, she is waiting in vain. The Western Grave-mound (Hsi-ling) was near Hangchow.

A Dream of Heaven[1]

7-character: 2 rhymes

THE ancient hare, the shivering toad,[2]
Weep sky-blue tears,
The cloud-towers are half-revealed,
Walls slant and white.[3]
Jade wheel creaks upon the dew,
Wet globes of light,
Simurgh-bells and girdle-gems meeting
On cassia-scented roads.[4]

Now yellow dust, now clear water,
Below the Three Hills.[5]
Sudden the changes of a thousand years
As a galloping horse.
From far above, the Middle Kingdom
Is just nine wisps of cloud.[6]
All the clear waters of the sea
A spilt cup.

---

[1]The first four lines describe the moon; the next two the Islands of the Immortals; the last two describe the earth, all as seen from heaven.

[2]Animals in the moon.

[3]Or: 'cloud-towers' – the Jade Towers of the moon.

[4]Fairy-maidens in the moon ride in carriages jingling with simurgh-bells, their girdle-gems tinkling. The roads are cassia-scented because of the cassia tree there.

[5]The Three Islands of the Immortals endure throughout geological epochs of time, while the seas cover what was once land and then recede again.

[6]An allusion to the nine provinces of the empire. The last lines suggest a famous passage in *Chuang-tzu*, XVII. Tsou Yen (4th century A.D.), however, believed the world consisted of 9 continents in an environing ocean. See J. Needham, *Science & Civilization in China*, II (Cambridge, 1956), p. 236.

Song for the Boy T'ang[1]
Son of Tu, Duke of Pin

7-character: 1 rhyme

SKULL like jade, hard as stone,
Blue-black eyelashes.
Master Tu has certainly begotten
A very fine boy.
Serious of face, pure of spirit,
A temple-vessel,[2]
With a pair of eyes that can see through men
Like autumn water.
His bamboo horse shakes its green tail
In the wind,[3]
On his short sleeves, simurghs of silver
Prance glittering.
His eastern neighbour's pretty daughter,
In search of a husband,
With a dazzling smile is writing on air
The character 'T'ang'.[4]
His eyes are big, his heart is brave,
So he knows why.
May he never forget the man called Li
Who wrote this song!

[1]This boy, T'ang-erh, was a young son of Tu Huang-t'ang, Duke of Pin. His mother was a princess of the reigning house; hence the name 'T'ang'.

[2]A vessel used in the Imperial Temple.

[3]The horse's tail is formed from bamboo leaves.

[4]"Eastern neighbour's daughter" is a stock expression for a pretty girl, stemming from the *Teng T'u-tzu hao se fu* of Sung Yü. Chinese often write characters with the forefinger, either in the air or on the palm of the hand.

Sealing up Green Prayers
A Sacrifice Performed at Night by the Taoist Master, Wu[1]

7-character: 4 rhymes

THE Blue Lion kowtows and calls
To the Palace Spirits.[2]
With a fearful howl the Dog of Jade
Opens Heaven's gates.[3]
Pomegranate-blossom in full bloom
Covers the ford.
Maidens bathe blossoms in the stream,
Dyeing white clouds.[4]

Sealing up the green prayers
We pray to the Primal Father.[5]
On the six highways horses' hooves
Run wild and masterless.[6]
From an empty sky the wind's breath comes,
Hot and impure.
Short robes and little hats
Huddle in dust.[7]

[1]The Sealing up of the Green Prayers was a Taoist rite in which prayers written in red characters on greenish paper were sealed in a box and offered to Shang-ch'ing 上清, one of the Three Pure Ones 三清. The rite had originally been called Pure Prayers, the character 'blue-green' 青 later being substituted for 'pure' 清. See Lü Yüan-su, *Tao-men ting-chih* VI, p. 8b, *Tao-tsang*, 974. The sacrifice described in this poem was presumably to drive away the demons of plague and drought.

[2]Understanding 青霓 as a mythical beast. Wang and Suzuki prefer to keep to the original text, thus: 'Clad in blue rainbow, he kowtows . . .'. 'Palace' refers to the palace of Shang-ch'ing.

[3]The Jade Dog was one of the guardians of Heaven. Most commentators understand 鸿龍 as 'goose and dragon' or 'goose-dragon', taking it as some fabulous beast or beasts guarding the gates of Heaven. Suzuki, however, points out that the expression should be written 鸿龍 and is simply onomatopoeic.

In perfumed lanes of the Chin family,
Noise of a thousand wheels,
But no one mentions the autumn rooms
Of poor Yang Hsiung.[8]

I want to call up his bookish ghost
With a halberd of Han.[9]
May his rancorous bones not be interred
In a weed-grown grave!

[4]The girls were handmaidens of the spirits. Pomegranate blossom still has magical significance among the Hokkiens today, who float it in water for divination.

[5]The Father of the Primal Unity, or Emperor of Heaven.

[6]Ch'ang-an had six main highways. Suzuki translates: 'Empty-headed people are running aimlessly all over Ch'ang-an.'

[7]Yeh believes that drought and plague were wreaking havoc among the common people. Presumably these lines mean 'While rich and foolish people are running aimlessly around on horseback, bent on pleasure, the poor are dying like flies.'

[8]Chin Mi-ti (134–86 B.C.) was a foreigner whose family acquired great wealth and power during the Former Han. Yang Hsiung (53–18 B.C.) was a literary man of the same period, who was so poor he once served as a common soldier. Ho is contrasting the affluence of the *nouveau-riche* foreigners (Uighurs and Tibetans) in the capital with his own plight. Yeh believes these lines mean: 'Even if the rich die in this plague, they will have enjoyed life. Yet poor scholars like me will die filled with resentment.'

[9]When calling up a ghost it was customary to use some article which the dead man had handled frequently and would recognize. Hence to summon Yang Hsiung the medium would employ an antique halberd, a weapon Yang had once carried.

*Twelve Lyrics for Music on the Theme of the Twelve
Months of the Year (Together with an Intercalary
Month) Composed While Taking the Examinations in
Honan–Fu*[1]

First Moon

7-character: 3 rhymes

WE climb a tower to greet the spring,
As spring returns newly.[2]
Smoky yellow mantles the willows,
The palace-clock drips slowly.[3]
A scant veil of lightest cloud
Stirs on the face of the wilds.
Through chill greens the desolate wind
Raises silk stubble.

Asleep in her rich bed at daybreak
Skin cool as jade,
Her dewy face, not yet in bloom,
Turned to dawn's pallor.

You cannot yet cut willow-sashes
On the public roads,[4]
When will the leaves of the sweet-flag
Be long enough to tie?[5]

---

[1]These poems were written in 809 when Ho was a candidate for the district
examination of Honan-fu. They were almost certainly intended to demonstrate
his poetic gifts to the examiners before the actual examination.

[2]One version reads: 'In the first month we climb a tower to welcome spring's
return.'

[3]The clepsydra.

[4]Perhaps a reference to the cutting of willow-branches at the Cold Food Festival, held in early April.

[5]When the leaves can be tied spring will really have arrived.

Second Moon

7-character: 2 rhymes

DRINKING wine in the second month[1]
By Gather-mulberries ford.[2]
Day-lilies bloom there,
Smiling orchids too.
Like crossed swords the rushes,
Wind like incense,
Northern swallows, hard at work,
Chide the heightened spring.[3]
Lingering mist in curtains of roses
Conjures green dust,[4]
Golden hairpins, high-piled tresses,
Shame the evening clouds,[5]
With billowing dresses, they dance
In skirts of pearl.

They bid us farewell at the ferry
Singing 'Water flows'.[6]
Wind chills the drunkards' spines,
South Mountain dies.[7]

---

[1]The two characters 二 月 are missing from some editions.

[2]A ford in south-west Ch'ü county, north of P'ing-yang, Honan.

[3]The northern swallow is noted for its loud cry.

[4]Nobody seems quite sure what this line means. Arai translates: 'In the rose-bush curtains the mist is caught and green dust is produced.' Presumably the picnic-spot is screened by roses, very much as the Japanese still curtain their cherry-viewing picnics (*hanami*).

[5]Arai reads 金 翅, explaining Golden Wings as the name of a mythical, dragon-eating bird. Saitō and Suzuki read 翅.

[6]Probably a line from a 4th or 5th century song, the *Ch'ien chi ko*, which was sung on such occasions.

[7]At sunset the party ends.

Third Moon

7-character: 3 rhymes

A WIND comes blowing from the east,
Filling our eyes with spring.
Willows darken in this city of blossoms,
Breaking our hearts.

Through deep halls of the storied palace
Stirs a bamboo breeze,
We dance in new collars of emerald-green,
Translucent as water.
A sunny wind bends the melilotus
Over a hundred leagues,[1]
A genial mist urges on the clouds,
Caressing heaven and earth.

Adorned like warriors, palace-girls
Closely brush on their brows.[2]
Embroidered banners wave their state
Along the warm, walled road,[3]
The wind-borne fragrance wafts away
Across the Serpentine.[4]
Pear-blossom scattered everywhere
Brings autumn to the park.[5]

[1] *Kuang feng* is a wind that blows when the sun comes out after rain.
[2] Suzuki interprets *ch'ien* as 'close to the eyes'. So: 'They brush on their eye-brows close to their eyes.'
[3] A walled road ran from the women's apartments in the palace down to the Serpentine.
[4] The Serpentine was a winding lake in the grounds of the palace.
[5] For the palace-maidens who have been left behind, spring seems as melancholy as autumn, while the fallen pear-blossoms look like withered leaves.

Fourth Moon

7-character: 3 rhymes

COOL at dawn and cool at dusk,
Trees like a canopy.
A thousand hills of darkest emerald
Beyond the clouds.

Vaguely a scented rain is falling
Through a haze of green.[1]
Glossy leaves and curls of blossom
Shining through side-gates.[2]

Water in its golden pools,
Jade-green ripples trembling.
Vistas heavy with ageing spring,
No startled petals fly.
Faded pinks and fallen calyx
Dappled in the shade.

Fifth Moon

5-character: 2 rhymes

CARVED jade heavy on screen-lintels,
Light gauze veils the open gates.
From leaden wells we draw the flowering water,[3]
Our fans ornate with mandarin ducks and drakes.[4]

[1]The rain is scented because of the blossoms. The green haze refers to the leaves.

[2]'*Ch'ü-men*' could mean 'gates opening onto a curving path' or 'gates in the corner of a garden or a city-wall'.

[3]The finest wells were lined with lead. Wang says that water drawn at break of day was known as 'flowering water'. Suzuki believes the term referred to water used for putting on cosmetics.

[4]Symbols of love.

Whirling snow dances through the Hall of Coolness,[1]
Sweet dew washes the emerald air.[2]
Silken sleeves are wheeling and hovering,
The fragrant sweat that soaks them, jewels of grain.[3]

Sixth Moon

Irregular: 2 rhymes

WE snip raw silk,
Hew speckled bamboo,
Sleeveless robes dusted with light frost,
Mats of autumn jade.[4]

A flame-red mirror opens in the east,
A haloed cartwheel journeying on high,
With a roar of flames comes the Scarlet Emperor
Riding his dragons.[5]

[1]The sleeves or skirts of the palace dancers look like whirling snow.

[2]The 'sweet dew' of the K'un-lun mountains was said to make plants dazzle as though covered with snow.

[3]'Sweet dew' and 'fragrant sweat' probably both refer to the perspiration of the dancers in the summer heat. The last line would seem to mean that the dancers' bodies are beaded with sweat which looks like seeds of grain.

[4]The raw silk used for their robes looks as though it has been dusted with frost. The speckled bamboo makes mats as cool as jade feels in autumn.

[5]The Scarlet Emperor is Chu Jung, guardian-spirit of the South. He has a man's face on the body of a beast, rides on two dragons and is an attendant of the Fiery Spirit. The term *chiu-chiu* is glossed by Arai as 'roaring flames'.

Seventh Moon

5-character: 1 rhyme

COLD glint of starlight round the Cloudy Island,[1]
Upon the plate the beaded dew-drops fall.[2]
Fine flowers are born out of the tips of twigs,[3]
Deserted gardens grieve for dying orchids.
The night-sky turns to terraces of jade,[4]
Leaves in the lotus-pool are big, green coins.
Vexed at the thinness of her dancing-gown
She feels a chill creep through her flowery mat.
A wind wakes sighing just at break of day,
The Northern Dipper glitters down the heavens.

Eighth Moon

5-character: 1 rhyme

THE widowed wife must dread these weary nights,
The lonely traveller dreams he's back at home.[5]
Beside the eaves insects twist their silk,[6]
Along the wall a lamp lets fall its flowers.[7]
Outside the screens, the moon exhales its light,
Inside the screens, slant shadows of the trees.
The dew flies all around in loveliness,[8]
Adorning even the lotus in its pool.

[1] The Milky Way.
[2] The plate was put out to catch the dew.
[3] Hibiscus, according to the commentators.
[4] A cloud formation which looks like terraces of white jade.
[5] This couplet has the style of an old *yüeh-fu* ballad.
[6] This could refer either to the cricket, whose cry sounds like the reeling of silk, or to the spider. One version reads 'spin' for 'twist'.
[7] 'Lamp-flowers': a peculiar twisting of the snuff of the wick, thought to be lucky.
[8] Or perhaps: 'Leisurely flies the dew in loveliness.'

Ninth Moon

7-character: 4 rhymes

IN THE summer palace scattered fireflies –
A sky like water.
Bamboos turn yellow, pools grow chill,
The lotus dies.

Moonlight glints on golden door-rings,
Purposeful beams.[1]
Above cold gardens, deserted courtyards,
A limpid, white void.

Flowers of dew are flying, flying
On an unhurried wind.[2]
Kingfisher brocades in gorgeous hues
Strewn along galleries.[3]

The Cock-herald chants no longer –
Refulgence of dawn![4]
Ravens cry by the brazen well
As kola-leaves flutter down.[5]

---

[1]'*P'u-shou*': brass animal-heads into which the rings of the knockers were set.
[2]'Flowers of dew': dewdrops about to freeze.
[3]'Kingfisher brocades': autumn leaves.
[4]A term used for the palace watchmen who announced the dawn each day.
[5]Leaves of the kolanut tree (*sterculia platanifolia*), a symbol of autumn, are falling very slowly, one or two at a time.

Tenth Moon

7-character: 3 rhymes

THE jade vase with its silver arrows
Can scarcely pour,[1]
Lamp-flowers smile upon the night
Where light and dark congeal.[2]

Slivers of frost dance slantingly
Across gauze curtains,
Two rows of candle-dragons[3] shine
In her winged pavilion.[4]

She lies resentful in her net of pearls,
Unable to sleep,
Beneath a robe ornate with golden phoenix
Her body is chill,
She stares at the moon, her long brows
Vie with its curved jade.[5]

[1]The water in the palace clepsydra is close to freezing.

[2]The snuff of the wick forms a flower as the lamp burns: since this is a lucky omen, the lamp is said to smile. Yet it is so cold that the light the lamp gives, burning there unmoving, seems to be frozen too, as are its motionless shadows.

[3]Candles in dragon-shaped holders. Read 龍 for 籠 with Sung edition.

[4]The corridors linking the women's apartments with the main palace were built high off the ground: hence 'winged'.

[5]She is melancholy as the crescent moon of winter. Clearly, the poem is concerned with one of the emperor's neglected favourites.

Eleventh Moon

7-character: 3 rhymes

THE palace walls lie coiled and shivering[1]
In the cold, stark light.
The white sky, shattered in pieces,
Drops diamantine fragrance.[2]

Strike the bells! Drink your fill
Of this thousand-day wine![3]
Fight to conquer the freezing cold!
Quaff the lord's health!

The royal canal is locked in ice,
Like a circle of silk.
Where is the Well of Fire?
Where are the Warm Springs?[4]

Twelfth Moon

7-character: 1 rhyme

FROM the sun's feet a wan light
Is shining redly.[5]
The thin frost does not melt at all
Beneath the cassia branches.
Rarely a warmer air will try to banish
The bitter winter.
For now we run to longer days –
Farewell to the long nights.

[1]Or: 'Go coiling into the distance, shivering', if we read *chiung* for *hui*.
[2]Snow.
[3]Wine from Chung-shan that would make you drunk for a thousand days, as it was reported to have done to Liu Hsüan-shih.
[4]Both these places were in Lin-ch'iung county, Szechwan.
[5]The feet of the sun-crow.

Intercalary Month[1]

Irregular: 2 rhymes

OUR emperors add to their glory,
The year adds to its days.
Seventy-two periods wheel about
Urging each other on.[2]
The astronomer with tubes of jade,
Has sent the ashes flying.[3]
Why must this year be so long,
The next so late?

The Western Mother plucks her peaches,
To give to the Emperor.[4]
Hsi Ho drives his dragon-car
The long way round.[5]

[1]This was an extra month added from time to time to make the lunar year agree with the solar year. The intercalary month for A.D. 809 was inserted after the third month.

[2]A lunar year was composed of 72 periods of 5 days each.

[3]To determine which month it was, the court astronomer would set twelve pitch-pipes on a tube and fill them with bullrush-ash. The ashes were supposed to fly away when the appropriate month arrived. There was no tube for the intercalary month.

[4]'Western Mother' - Hsi Wang Mu (the Mother who is Queen in the West) was ranked among the chief Taoist deities. The peaches of the Mother ripen only once every six thousand years. They confer immortal life on all who eat them.

[5]Hsi Ho: the charioteer of the sun.

A Ballad of Heaven[1]

7-character: 4 rhymes

THE River of Heaven wheels round at night
Drifting the circling stars.
The Silver Stream floats through the clouds,
Mimics the murmur of water.[2]
By the Palace of Jade the cassia blossoms
Have not yet fallen,
Fairy maidens gather their fragrance
For their dangling girdle-sachets.[3]

The Princess from Ch'in rolls up her blinds,
Dawn at the north casement.[4]
In front of the window, a straight-backed kolanut
Dwarfs the blue phoenix.
The King's son plays his pipes'
Long goose-quills,[5]
Summoning dragons to plough the mist
And plant Jade Grass.[6]

With ribbons of powdery dawn-cloud pink,
Skirt of lotus-root silk,
She walks on Green Island,[7] gathering
Orchids in spring.

[1]Yao interprets this poem as another satire directed against Hsien-tsung, who had commanded all the Taoist adepts of the empire to appear at his court with recipes for immortal life. These are the real Immortals, he would have Ho say. How can we hope to imitate them?

[2]The 'Silver Stream' is part of the ' River of Heaven' (the Milky Way).

[3]The Palace of Jade, the Cassia Tree and the fairy maidens are all found in the moon.

[4]Lung-yü, daughter of Duke Mu of Ch'in, married the Immortal Wang Tzu Ch'iao (the 'King's son' of line seven).

[5]The jade pipes of his *sheng* (mouth-organ) were shaped like goose-quills.

[6]'Jade Grass': a mythical plant.

[7]A legendary island in the Eastern Seas, abode of the Immortal Maidens, generally called Ch'ing-ch'iu.

H

She points to Hsi Ho in the eastern sky,
Deftly urging his steeds,
While sea and land rise again and again
Below mountains of stone.[1]

I Shout My Song[2]

7-character: 6 rhymes

THE south wind blows upon the mountains,
Levelling them flat.[3]
God sends T'ien Wu to sweep away
The waters of the sea.[4]
As the Queen Mother's peach-blossoms redden again
The thousandth time,
How often have Grandfather P'eng and Wizard Hsien
Come to their deaths?[5]

---

[1]Gods and Immortals can afford to be careless of the passing of time. To them whole epochs during which land rises out of the sea and sinks back beneath it again are as nothing.

[2]The title hints at the *Ch'u Tz'u*, *The Nine Songs* (*Chiu Ho*), *The Lesser Master of Fate* (*Shao Ssŭ Ming*), p. 41: 'Wildly I shout my song into the wind'.

[3]In the immense stretches of time that have elapsed since the world came into being (a Buddhist insight) the wind has levelled the mountains to the plain.

[4]T'ien Wu, god of the waters, turns sea into dry land over geological epochs of time.

[5]The peaches of the Mother who is Queen in the West ripen only once every six thousand years. During the passing of these millennia Grandfather P'eng (the Chinese Methusaleh) and Wizard Hsien (a doctor during the reign of Yao who became a spirit and so knew the date of every man's death) will themselves have died countless times. For Ho, the so-called Immortals have a life-span as ephemeral as a gnat's in comparison with the eons of time that the universe has endured.

The blue-black hair of my piebald horse
Dappled with coins,
Willows of the graceful spring
Wreathed in light mist.

A girl with a zither coaxing me
To a golden goblet,
Before blood and spirit had yet congealed,
Who then was I?

No point in drinking ocean-deep,
Governor Ting![6]
The finest men in this age of ours
Will own no master.
Let us buy silk to embroider the image
Of the Lord of P'ing-yüan.[7]
And then pour out a libation of wine
On the soil of Chao.[8]

Hurrying drops of the water-clock
Choke the jade toad,[9]
The Wei girl's tresses grow so thin
She cannot bear the comb.[10]

[6]Sung Wu-ti sent Ting Wu 丁旿 to recover the body of his son-in-law who
had fallen in battle. Later, during the reign of Sung Hsiao Wu-ti (r. 453–64) a
mournful yüeh-fu ballad appeared based on this event in which the words
'Governor Ting!' figured in a chorus. Ho is remembering this song.

[7]The Lord of P'ing-yüan (3rd century B.C.) was famous for his munificence
in supporting large numbers of retainers. Ho regrets that there is now no one
who would employ him as the Lord of P'ing-yüan would have done.

[8]Ho is mistaken here. The Lord of P'ing-yüan ruled in Chao but was not
buried there, so the libation could not have been poured on his grave.

[9]The jade toad in the water-clock, which caught the drops in its mouth.

[10]Perhaps the girl with the zither who was coaxing him to drink?

Autumn eyebrows in an instant
Replace our fresh green!¹
Why must lads of twenty
Fawn and scramble for office?²

Coming of Autumn

7-character: 2 rhymes

WIND in the plane-trees startles my heart
To a man's bitter grief.
In the guttering lamplight, spinners cry
Their icy silk.³
Who will ever read these slips
Of green bamboo,⁴
Or forbid the ornate worm
To pierce its powdery holes?⁵

---

¹A difficult line: Arai suggests it means: 'The autumn scene changes before one's eyes to a fresh green.' Suzuki translates: 'In an instant green eyebrows change to autumnal white.' This line could also mean: (a) Age must give way to youth; for the old with their grizzled brows are replaced by the young with their brows painted green. (b) Age must give way to youth just as grizzled eyebrows (like mine, which are prematurely white) must give way to black ones ('ch'ing' means both green and black). (c) Last year's leaves ('eyebrows' often stands for 'leaves') must be replaced by those of the new spring.

²Read 刺 with *Yüeh-fu shih-chi*, LXVIII, not 刺. Why must young men waste their precious youth in a dreary scramble to become the servants of others?

³The cricket is called 'the spinner', since its cry sounds like the reeling of silk. For the plane tree (*sterculia platanifolia*) see p. 41, note 5, above.

⁴Before the invention of paper early in the second century A.D., books were written on slips of green bamboo which had been burnt to remove the oily outer layer. Here Ho is referring to his own verse, which no one will ever read.

⁵Most commentators think that 花 虫 means 'bookworm'. Suzuki disagrees.

Such thoughts tonight must disentwine
My knotted heart.
In the cold rain comes a fragrant spirit
To console this poet.[6]
On an autumn grave a ghost sits chanting
That poem of Pao's.[7]
A thousand years in earth makes emerald jade
That rancorous blood.[8]

[6]Arai takes this to mean 'a dead girl's spirit'.

[7]The 'Graveyard Lament' (*Tai Hao-li Hsing*) of the fifth-century poet, Pao Chao, begins: Rich and poor, all meet the same end,

'Differing wishes granted or unfulfilled
Galloping waves urge on eternal night,
Falling dew hastens the brief dawn.'

Ho is comparing himself to Pao Chao.

[8]*Chuang-tzu*, XXVI, 'Ch'ang-hung died in Shu (*circa* 500 B.C.). Ch'ang-hung had been unjustly put to death. Three years after his burial his blood had turned to emerald jade.' I think this means that the resentment Ho felt, embodied in the poems he has written (metaphorically) with his very blood, will turn into precious jade with the passage of time.

Song of the Emperor's Daughters[1]

7-character: 2 rhymes

BRIGHT moonlight over Tung-t'ing lake
A thousand leagues around.[2]
In the chill wind wild geese are crying,
Water reflects the sky.
Nine-jointed calamus lies dead
Upon the stones.[3]
The goddess of Hsiang, playing her lute,
Welcomes the Emperor's daughters.

[1]Wu Cheng-tzu believes these were the daughters of Emperor Yao, the spirits of the river Hsiang. Wang thinks they were rain-goddesses who lived round Tung-t'ing lake. Yao interprets this poem as a comment on the death of Hsien-tsung's mother in the autumn of 816. This event was accompanied by destructive floods, which were taken as a sign of heaven's displeasure with the Emperor. Yao contends that Ho is once again satirizing Hsien-tsung's futile quest for the elixir of life – futile, since in spite of all his own efforts he could not save his mother. The poem is largely a tissue of allusions to *The Nine Songs* of the *Ch'u Tz'u*.

[2]Wang prefers the reading: 'The Emperor's daughters rule the territory around Tung-t'ing lake for a thousand leagues.' Cf. *The Nine Songs, The Lady of the Hsiang, (Hsiang Fu Yen)*, which begins:
     'The Child of God, descending the northern bank . . .'

[3]An allusion to the inefficacy of the drugs which should have cured the empress. *Acorus calamus*, or stone-calamus, is a water-plant with spiky, yellow flowers. It grows among stones. The best type contained nine joints within the space of an inch from the root. The plant was thought to confer immortality.

On the mountain-top stands an ancient cassia
Of age-old scent.
A woman-dragon chants her sorrow,
Water glints cold.
By the sandy shores where fishes swim,
Goes the Lord of White Stone.[1]
Idly he casts a precious pearl
To the dragon-hall.[2]

The Prince of Ch'in Drinks Wine[3]

7-character: 5 rhymes

STRADDLING a tiger, the Prince of Ch'in
Roams the Eight Poles.[4]
His glittering sword flashes through the sky,
Turning heaven sapphire-blue.[5]

He is Hsi Ho whipping up the sun,
That tinkles like glass.[6]
The ashes of kalpas all fly away,
The world is at peace.[7]

---

[1]A minor water-spirit.

[2]*Ch'u Tz'u, The Nine Songs, The Lady of the Hsiang;*, p. 39:
> I'll throw my thumb-ring into the river,
> Leave my thimble in the bay of the Li.'

Ibid. The God of the Yellow River (Ho Po), p. 42:
> Of fish-scales in my palace, with a dragon-scale hall;'

[3]According to one interpretation, the poem is a hymn of praise to Emperor Te-tsung (*regnet* 779–805), who had died when Ho was only a boy of fourteen. (It is certainly not a satire directed against Te-tsung's tyranny and licentiousness, as Yao contends.) Ho styles the emperor 'Prince of Ch'in', as he had distinguished himself when he was enfeoffed in Yung-chao, which was in former Ch'in territory. The poem is not to be read as a eulogy of the First Emperor of Ch'in.

[4]The eight points of the compass (*pa chi*).

From a dragon's head spouts wine enough
To call down the wine-stars[8].
Golden lutes are singing softly
Throughout the night.[9]
The feet of rain on Tung-t'ing lake
Come blown on the pipes.[10]
Flushed with wine, he commands the moon
To run back in her course.
Beneath dense drifts of silver clouds
The jaspar hall glows.

At the palace portals the Gatekeeper cries
The first watch of the night.
In the ornate tower, a jade phoenix sings,
Faltering and sweet.[11]
From ocean-pongee, patterned in crimson,
A faint, cool scent.[12]
The yellow beauties reel in their dance.
A thousand years with each cup![13]

[5]The military prowess of the Emperor was manifest everywhere.

[6]Hsi Ho is the charioteer of the sun.

[7]A kalpa was an Indian (later Buddhist) unit of measure for a cosmic cycle. Fourteen *mahāyuga* of 4,320,000 years each constituted one kalpa. At the end of each kalpa came a great dissolution (*Mahāpralaya*), when the universe was reduced to ashes. Such ashes were believed to have been found in 120 B.C., during the digging of the artificial lake of K'un-ming, in Shansi. (See E. Zurcher, *The Buddhist Conquest of China* [Leiden, 1959], p. 20). The reign of Te-tsung, Ho is saying, was a time of unexampled prosperity, a new era rising out of the ashes of the old.

[8]A large wine-vessel shaped like a dragon spouted wine from its mouth for the guests.

[9]Literally: 'Short lutes with golden sound-boxes . . .'

As fairy candlesticks waft on high[14]
A light, waxy smoke,
Eyes rapt with wine, those Emerald Lutes[15]
Shed seas of tears.

[10]A line that has led to a good deal of speculation on the part of the commentators. Literally it reads: 'Tung-t'ing rain feet come blow mouth-organ'. The
line is a complex one, fusing many images together: but the basic allusion is to
the music played for the Yellow Emperor on Tung-t'ing lake in northern
Hunan (see *Chuang-tzu*, XIV), which sounds like raindrops on water. The
mouth-organ (*sheng*) is formed from thirteen or so bamboo pipes of different
length opening into a wind-chest of lacquer by an aperture covered with a
copper reed.

[11]The phoenix is not a musical instrument, but a singer.

[12]The dancers were clad in ocean-pongee (*hai-shao*), a rare and costly fabric
said to be woven by the mermen or sharkpeople who lived under the sea off the
coast of Champa. See Schafer, *Golden Peaches*, p. 109.

[13]Wang suggests that Yellow Goose 黃 鵝 is perhaps the name of a dance.
Suzuki and Arai both read 黃 娥 'Beautiful girls with yellow make-up'. This is
very plausible since the expression occurs again on p. 109, line 7.

[14]Literally: 'Immortal candle-trees'. This could denote either candles decorated with paintings of Immortals or candlesticks in the shape of Immortals.

[15]The text reads 'pure lute'. I have followed Wang, who reads 青 'emerald'
instead of 清 'pure', understanding this as the name of a fairy maiden. Here, of
course, it refers to the palace beauties.

Pearl – A Lo-yang Beauty

7-character: 5 rhymes

MY Lady Pearl came down to earth
From the blue void.[1]
To a Lo-yang park on a scented wind
She flew slowly down.

Hairpins aslant in her cool tresses,
Sheen of jade swallows,[2]
Singing to the moon in her tall tower,
Beating time on a pendant.

Orchid breezes and cassia dew
Sprinkle dark, blue leaves.
Red-string music writhes to the clouds,
As she sobs out her grief.[3]
Flowered jacket and white horse –
He has not come back.
Dark moth-eyebrows, double willows,
Lips fragrant with wine.[4]

Gold geese screen her from the wind,
She dreams of Shu mountain,[5]
Simurgh skirt and phoenix sash
Heavy with mist.[6]
As sunlight dazzles at all eight windows,
Her eyelids stir.[7]

[1]Like a fairy.
[2]Hair-ornaments.
[3]Music from her *cheng*, which had reddish brass strings.
[4]'Moths' and 'willows' were synonyms for the arched, painted eyebrows of
a Chinese lady. The girl is drunk, trying to forget her loneliness.
[5]A reference to Mount Wu, in Shu, where a Prince Hsiang made love to a
goddess. 'A Shu-mountain dream' is a dream about love-making.

Rays of the setting sun are pouring
Through gauzy curtains.
'In the gay quarters, south of the city,
The fall is not cold.[8]
Waists of Ch'u, hair-styles of Wei,
Fragrant all year.
Crystal voices from throats of jade
Brush the lights of heaven.
Pulling at clouds, tugging at snow,
They detain Master Lu.'[9]

[6]The goddess of Mount Wu controlled the clouds and the rain. Hence mist (clouds and rain) here mean 'an amorous dream'.

[7] Reading 臆 for 聰 with Suzuki.

[8]The last four lines are spoken by the girl herself who is contrasting her own loneliness (bird in a gilded cage!) with the lively life she once enjoyed as a singing-girl.

[9]'Clouds' and 'snow' stand for a man's robes. Lu Yü, who was notorious for his dissipations, was a favourite of Ch'en Shu-pao (553–604), the last emperor of the Ch'en dynasty, who was also famous for his love of wine and women. Lu Yü is mentioned again in Ho's *Song: Sitting through the Night*, p. 194 below.

The Lady Li[1]

7-character: 3 rhymes

WHERE the Purple Emperor's halls and towers
Rear their storeyed heights,[2]
Among those towers of chalcedony
The Lady has flown away.

When will the emerald incense fade
From her broidered hangings?
Blue, so blue and lustreless the clouds
Over sobbing palace waters.
Cassia flowers come fluttering down
From the autumn moon.
The lonely simurgh gives a startled cry,
As a *shang* note sounds from the strings.[3]

On the scarlet walls hang girdle-gems of jade,
Abandoned now.
Singing in the tower, the dancing-girls
Gaze into the distance.[4]
From out of the Jade Toad water drips,
The Cock-herald chants.[5]
Dewy flowers and orchid leaves
In dazzling disarray.[6]

[1]Lady Li was a favourite of Emperor Wu of Han (*regnet* 141–87 B.C.) whose premature death plunged the Emperor into despair. Ho's poem would appear to be an elegy for some favourite or other of the reigning Emperor. Yao contends that Ho is lamenting a concubine of Emperor Te-tsung (*regnet* 779–805) who had died many years previously, in 786. This seems rather far-fetched.

[2]The Purple Emperor is one of the three highest divinities dwelling in the Nine Palaces of the Great Purity.

[3]Here the lonely simurgh stands for the Emperor. *Shang* was the note of the pentatonic scale associated with autumn and sadness.

[4]See p. 120, note 1, below.

[5]The Jade Toad was a clepsydra made in the shape of that animal. For the Cock-herald, see p. 41, note 4, above.

[6]I suspect this line is a hint to the Emperor that though his favourite is dead, there are still many other beautiful women at his command.

Song of the Horseman[1]

5-character: 1 rhyme

I LEFT my native village with a sword
Whose edge of jade could cut a cloud in two.
Among the youthful horsemen of Hsiang-yang,[2]
My spirits were as fresh as spring itself.
At dawn I grieved the sword's fair blade was clean,
At dusk I grieved the sword's bright gleam was cold.[3]
Gripping it firm, I go to kill my man;
A sword is not conducive to reflection.

[1]The *Ku-chin chu* states that a certain Shu-li Mu-kung once slew a man to avenge his father and then flew to the hills. Here he was awakened one night by the whinnying of a supernatural horse, which warned him he was in danger. He is supposed to have composed the original *yüeh-fu* of this title in honour of his visitant. The commentators have failed to see the connection between this story and Ho's poem. To understand these verses, we must realize that this is a poem about revenge and that Shu-li Mu-kung himself is speaking. We may note, incidentally, that this is yet another example of Ho's fascination with swords.

[2]During the Six Dynasties period, Hsiang-yang, in Hupeh, was famous for its warriors. One edition reads 'Ch'ang-an' for 'Hsiang-yang'.

[3]The blade was clean and cold because he had not yet slain his enemy.

The Ladies of the Hsiang[1]

7-character: 2 rhymes

BAMBOO that has lasted a thousand years,
Growing old, yet not dying.
Antique companion of these spirit ladies
It surrounds Hsiang's waters.[2]

Songs of native girls of the south
Fill the cold sky.[3]
On the Nine Mountains, tranquil and green,
Grow red tear-flowers.[4]
Departure of simurgh, farewell of phoenix,
In mist-hung Ts'ang-wu,[5]
Clouds of Wu and rain of Shu,
Love reaching afar.[6]
Drearily, sadly, the spirit of autumn
Mounts the green maples.[7]
In the icy night among those waves,
The ancient dragon roars.[8]

[1]Legend had it that when Emperor Shun died his two wives, the daughters of Yao, buried him on Mount Ts'ang-wu in Hunan. They wept so bitterly that their tears of blood left stains on all the bamboos of this region. Then they threw themselves into the river Hsiang, were changed into spirits, and became wives of the River God.

[2] Reading 神 for 秦 with Yeh and Suzuki.

[3]The sound of the wind through the bamboos.

[4]Nine Doubts Mountain is another name for Mount Ts'ang-wu. 'Tear-flowers': the red-speckled bamboos of this region.

[5]This alludes to the deaths of Shun and his wives. The line also suggests the meaning: ' . . . among mist-hung kolanut trees'.

[6]Clouds and rain on Mount Wu in Shu are generally a symbol of love. In this context, however, as Yeh points out, the expression refers simply to the comings and goings of the spirits.

[7]For which this region was famous.

[8]It is not clear whether the dragon is found in the Hsiang river or in Tung-t'ing Lake. The style of this poem has been heavily influenced by the *Ch'u Tz'u.*

Thirteen Poems from My Southern Garden[1]

7-character: 1 rhyme

No. 1

BUDDING branches, stems of flowers,
Blossom while I watch.
Touched with white and streaked with crimson –
Cheeks of a girl from Yüeh.[2]
Sad to say, once dusk has come,
Their wanton fragrance falls.
They have eloped with the spring wind,
Without a go-between.[3]

No. 2

NORTH of the palace over the furrows
Full flush of dawn,[4]
Yellow mulberries, drinking dew,
Rustle on palace blinds.
Tall girls, sturdy girls stealthily
Breaking branches,
Feeding the eight-fold silkworms,
Of the King of Wu.[5]

---

[1]Poems written in Ho's home in Ch'ang-ku, while he was making up his mind to take office in Lu-chou in 814.
[2]Hsi-shih, most renowned of all Chinese beauties, came from Yüeh.
[3]No respectable Chinese girl would ever get married without a go-between or match-maker.
[4]The ruined Fu-ch'ang palace in Ch'ang-ku.
[5]Suzuki believes this refers to a type of silkworm that produced as much as eight ordinary silkworms.

No. 3

The spinner in the bamboos
Turns his spinning wheel.[1]
A green cicada sings alone
In the setting sun.
Amber fragrant, peach-tree sap
Welcomes the summer,
I order my native gardener
To plant out melons.[2]

No. 4

'NOT yet thirty but still turned twenty,
Hungry in bright sunshine, living on leaves.
Old man on the bridge! Feel sorry for *me*
And give me a book on the art of war!'[3]

[1]No commentator has explained this line satisfactorily.
[2]The gardener came from Yüeh, in south-east China.
[3]*Shih-chi*, LV, biography of Chang Liang (d. 189 B.C.) recounts how Chang met a poorly dressed old man on a bridge in Hsia-p'i. The old man tested him by dropping his shoe under the bridge and then ordering Chang to pick it up. Later, after testing his patience still further, the old man presented him with a book on the art of war which brought him to success.

No. 5

WHY shouldn't a young man wear a Wu sword?[1]
He could win back fifty provinces in pass and mountain.[2]
I wish you would visit the Ling-yen pavilion,[3]
How can a student ever become a rich marquis?[4]

No. 6

SEEKING a style, culling my phrases,
Grown old carving grubs!
At dawn the moon hangs in my blinds,
A bow of jade.
Can't you see what is going on, year after year,
By the sea of Liao-tung?
Whatever can a writer do
But weep in the autumn wind?[5]

[1]Wu-kou (Hook of Wu) was the name of a famous type of sword used by the southern aborigines.

[2]Over 50 Chinese districts in Honan and Hopeh were in the hands of tribal peoples at this time. See *TCTC*, p. 7689, for A.D. 812.

[3]The portraits found in the Ling-yen pavilion were of military men who had aided T'ang T'ai-tsung in his struggle for power.

[4]Literally: ' . . . a marquis of ten thousand households'.

[5]Ho has been studying all night, perfecting his literary style. ('Carving grubs' was a contemptuous expression for writing verse). There is no point to all this, since a country incessantly at war has little use for poets. The quickest way to gain renown is to fight on some distant frontier, like the Liao-tung peninsula.

I

No. 7

CH'ANG-HSIANG was lonely and wretched
In his empty house.[1]
Man-ch'ien was always joking –
Too anxious to please.[2]
Better to go and buy a sword
From Jo-yeh river,[3]
Come back at dawn next day to serve
The Monkey Duke.[4]

No. 8

FIRST flush of spring waters,
Swallows with fledglings flying.
Small-tailed yellow bees come home
From flying round the flowers.
The window brings a distant scene
To my study curtains.
Fish throng round my scented hook
By river-washed stones.

[1]When the poet Ssu-ma Hsiang-ju returned home after eloping with Wen-chün, he found his house in ruins. See *Shih-chi*, CXVII.

[2]The Han statesman and philosopher Tung-fang Shuo (154–93 B.C.), style Man-ch'ien, was noted for his sense of humour – a trait which enabled him to criticize the Emperor yet remain in office. See *Han-shu*, LXV.

[3]A river in Shao-hsing, Chekiang, famous for its copper. Ou-yeh Tzu cast swords there.

[4]See the story in *Wu Yüeh Ch'un-ch'iu*, V, about an old man who changed into a white monkey to elude his girl-opponent. This is another poem about the futility of a literary career.

No. 9

LYING on river sand softly sleeping
Two ducks in the sun.
I punt my little skiff slowly past
The winding shores.
Magnolias steeped in wine,
Covered with pepper-leaves.[1]
Friends help the sick man to his feet
To plant water-chestnut.

No. 10

PIEN Jang this morning was thinking
Of Ts'ai Yung,[2]
Lying down in the spring breeze
No heart to chant songs.
South of my house there grow bamboos[3]
For writing-slips.
When old, I'll go up-river and live
As an ancient fisherman.

[1]Magnolias and pepper gave fragrance to the wine. Read 蘭 for 闌.
[2]Pien Jang (*floruit* late 2nd-early 3rd centuries A.D.) was a brilliant young man who was given high office when still a youth thanks to the sponsorship of Ts'ai Yung (133–192), an outstanding poet and writer of the Later Han. Here Ho is referring to his relationship with Han Yü – a shade ironically perhaps since he himself had not achieved office.
[3]He will use the bamboos for fishing-rods, rather than write poems on them.

No. 11

HsI's house stands near a little peak,
By a valley-mouth.[1]
Under the white sun, a thousand hills
Look darkest green.
Roaming around in cane sandals,
Gathering honey from stones,
I pull away strands of moss
From long water-plants.

No. 12

BLACK waters of the Pine Stream
Spawn new dragon-eggs.[2]
The Cassia Cave bears sulphate –
Old horses' teeth.[3]
Who has tailored Taoist robes
For this Yü Ch'ing,
Out of a length of light chiffon
Dyed with pink mists of dawn?[4]

[1] A reference to the poet Hsi K'ang (223–62), who here stands for Ho himself.
[2] Pine Stream and Cassia Cave were places in Ch'ang-ku. Dragons always lived in deep, black water. Wang says the eggs were lizard eggs.
[3] Ma-ya hsiao (horse-tooth sulphate) was a name for purified sodium sulphate (Glauber's salt).
[4] Yü Ch'ing (Warring States period) wrote the Yü-shih Ch'un-ch'iu when in great misery. Wang argues that there was probably a hermit named Yü, who was a friend of Li Ho's, living near Ch'ang-ku.

No. 13

5-character: 1 rhyme

UNDER small trees a path opens at dawn –
Long, thick grasses soaked by the night mist.
Willow catkins startle the snowy banks,
Wheat-rains flood the fields down by the stream![1]
Occasional boom of a bell from the old monastery,
Distant storm-clouds hang from a shattered moon.
I light a fire on the sandy shores, striking stones together –
Burning bamboo flares on the fisherman's boat.

Song of the Brazen Immortal Bidding Farewell to Han[2]

7-character: 3 rhymes

In the eighth month of the first year of the *Ch'ing-lung* period (233)
of Emperor Ming of Wei (*regnet* 226–39), it was decreed that
the palace officials should harness their chariots and go westwards
to obtain the statue of the Immortal holding a dew-plate which

---

[1]The 'Wheat-rain season' begins on 20 April.

[2]Yao interprets this poem as a protest against Hsien-tsung's extravagance in
building two new palaces and constructing an ornamental lake, the Dragon-
head Pool. All these activities, Ho is saying, are as futile as the quest for immortality. Han Wu-ti also sought for eternal life, surrounding himself with every
luxury. Yet where is he now? Nothing remains of all his glory. Even his Brazen
Immortal fell into the hands of others. The latter was a statue which Wu-ti had
set up on top of his Shen-ming tower. Pan Ku, in his *Fu of the Western Capital*,
describes this statue as 'placed high on a metal column, holding a bowl to catch
the dew; reaching beyond the vile, clogging dust of the world to obtain the
limpid elixir of the pure, translucent ether'. Wu-ti was accustomed to collect
the dew from this vessel and drink it, mixed with powdered jade, in the hope
that this would make him immortal. Over three hundred years later, Emperor
Ming tried to have the statue brought to his capital. But it proved too heavy to
transport over such a distance; so it was eventually left forlornly standing on the
banks of the river Pa, in Shensi, with its dew-plate broken from its hands.

had belonged to Emperor Hsiao Wu of Han (*regnet* 141–87 B.C.).
The Emperor wanted to have this set up in his front hall. When
the palace officials had broken off the dew-plate and were trying
to load the Immortal on a cart, it shed tears. I, Li Ch'ang-chi,
descendant of the royal house of T'ang, have therefore written
this *Song of the Brazen Immortal Bidding Farewell to Han.*

> In the Mao-ling tomb lies the lad named Liu,
> Guest of the autumn wind.[1]
> At night we hear his whinnying horse –
> At dawn not a hoof-print there.
> From painted balustrades, the cassia trees
> Cast down autumnal fragrance.[2]
> Over six-and-thirty palaces grow
> Emerald earth-flowers.[3]
>
> The courtiers of Wei harnessed their chariots
> To travel a thousand leagues.
> The vinegar wind from the eastern passes
> Arrowed their eyes.
> Vainly bearing the moon of Han
> I went out of the palace gates.[4]
> Remembering the emperor, my pure tears
> Dropped down like molten lead.

[1]Han Wu-ti (whose surname was Liu) was buried in the Mao-ling tomb in
Hsing-p'ing county, 80 *li* north-west of Ch'ang-an. 'Guest of the autumn wind'
is a reference to Wu-ti's having written a song called *Autumn Wind*, about the
brevity of life. It also suggests that his life was as brief as summer; that he is
now one with the dead leaves of autumn; that instead of wine and singing-girls,
he now has only the cold wind of autumn to entertain him as it whistles through
his bones.

[2]Cassia trees are growing among the ruins of balustrades.

[3]The thirty-six palaces of Ch'ang-an. 'Earth-flowers': moss.

[4]Yao understands the expression 'moon of Han' as a kenning for the dew-
plate. Wang, however, takes it as meaning: 'Hopelessly, under the moon of
Han, the statue went out of the palace gates.' The statue still looks on the moon
as belonging to Han, though everything else has been usurped by Wei.

Withering orchids bade them farewell
On the Hsien-yang road.[1]
If God could suffer as we do
God too would grow old.[2]
Bearing my dew-plate, I journeyed alone
By the light of the cold, wild moon,
Already Wei-ch'eng lay far behind
And its waters faintly calling.[3]

Ballad:[4] Time Goes on for Ever

5-character: 1 rhyme

THE white glare returns to the Western Hills,
The jasper blossom soars into the distance.[5]
When will past and present ever end?
Thousands of years have whirled away on the wind.
Sands of the sea turn into stone,
Fish blow bubbles at the bridge of Ch'in.[6]
The heavenly lights float far, far off,
Pillars of bronze melt with the years.[7]

[1]Hsien-yang was the ancient capital of Ch'in.
[2]A famous line, much admired by Ssu-ma Kuang.
[3]Wei-ch'eng was the name given by Han to the district around Hsien-yang.
The change of names suggests the passing of the dynasties.
[4]'Hsing' – not a verb here. It means 'ballad'.
[5]'Jasper blossom' – the moon? Or perhaps 'dark blue clouds at night'?
[6]Ch'in Shih Huang-ti tried to build a bridge across the sea, to reach the
islands of immortality, only to have it pulled down by spirits.
[7]'Pillars of bronze': both the pillar on which the Brazen Immortal of Han
Wu-ti stood and those pillars, 3,000 li in circumference, which held up the
sky over Mount K'un-lun.

The Man with a Yellow Hat[1]

Irregular: 3 rhymes

MAN with a yellow hat,
You've taken your boat and gone away,
Not yet come home.
Lotus shadow by south shore,[2]
Sad, red petals wilting alone.

Murmer of water,
Girdle-jades of the Lady of Hsiang.[3]
Bamboos sobbing, moon over dew-drenched hills.
On a jade zither she plays 'Green Gates',[4]
Hill-clouds drenching yellow arrowroot.[5]

Deer-parsley flowers on sand,
Already blooming in the autumn wind.[6]
Holding a spray, she sweeps fine, silken mats,
Perfume wafting from warm mandarin-ducks.[7]

[1]A boatman.

[2]'South shore' suggests parting, as in the *Ch'u Tz'u, The Nine Songs, The Lady of the Hsiang*.

[3]See p. 50, note 1, above.

[4]'Zither' – actually a *se* 瑟, a zither with 25 strings.

[5]Saitō believes 'yellow arrowroot' is also the name of a ballad.

[6]Lotus blooms in early summer, deer-parsley (*gracilaria confervoides*, Grey) in autumn. She has waited in vain for her husband's return all these months.

[7]Incense-burners in the form of ducks, symbols of conjugal love.

Twenty-three Poems about Horses[1]

All 5-character: 1 rhyme

No. 1

DRAGON-SPINE marked with strings of cash,
Silver hooves whitely trampling the mist.
No one can weave brocade caparisons.
Who will make a golden whip for him?

No. 2

IN the twelfth month, grass roots are sweet,
In the capital's streets, snow looks like salt.
Has he a hard-mouth or a tender?
Let's try him out with a caltrops bit![2]

No. 3

SUDDENLY I remember that Emperor of Chou,[3]
Urging his chariot on, up Jade Hill at a gallop.
Rattle of horse and chariot out of Phoenix Park –
Red Bayard was his favourite horse of all.

[1]These poems, though ostensibly concerned with horses, are in fact about the neglect and misuse of men of genius. Ho's patron, Han Yü, frequently employed this very metaphor, insisting that though there were 'thousand league horses' in plenty, nobody had the wit to recognize them.

[2]Suffering bitter hardship, the poor scholar finds still more misery in store.

[3]The Emperor of Chou, at least, knew a thoroughbred when he saw one.

No. 4

THIS steed is no ordinary horse
But the very spirit of the Fang star,
Stand in front, rap on its slender bones,
They'll ring out like bronze.[1]

No. 5

ON the mighty desert, sand seems snow,[2]
Over Mount Yen, a moon like a hook.[3]
If only their heads could ever be bridled with gold!
Swiftly they run, pure autumn under their hooves.

No. 6

HE lies there starving, a huddle of bones,
Rough coat branded with broken flowers.
From his burnt mane the red hair falls,
His jagged forelock hacked by the long rope.[4]

[1]The constellation Fang was said to be composed of four horses.
[2]A reference to the sand-dunes.
[3]Mount Yen-jan, now known as Mount Hang-ai, in Mongolia.
[4]Another vivid picture of Ho at the end of his tether.

No. 7

THE Western Mother's party is almost over,
The Eastern King is finishing his meal.[1]
Should Your Majesty want to attend the banquet
What would you harness to your carriage-shafts?[2]

No. 8

No other man could straddle Russet Hare,
It had to be Lü Pu who rode him.[3]
But I have heard that fruit-tree ponies[4]
Can be haltered and whipped even by native boys.[5]

[1]Mu Kung, or the Eastern King, is the male principle of the air, while the Mother who is Queen in the West is the female. From these two principles heaven and earth are formed.

[2]High-king Mu of Chou was said to have feasted with the Mother who is Queen in the West and the Eastern King at the Peach Blossom Banquet, which takes place at the side of the Jade Lake and is attended by all classes of Immortals. He was driven to their palace in the K'un-lun mountain by his eight famous horses. Ho's prince would be unable to do this since his horses are worthless. This poem is a thrust at rulers who (a) spend their time seeking immortality; (b) employ only third-rate men.

[3] Russet Hare was a renowned horse ridden by the hero Lü Pu during the period of the Three Kingdoms.

[4]'Fruit-tree ponies' were dwarf ponies from Korea, used to pull carts for the palace ladies, add colour to processions and so on. The name (pronounced kua-ha in T'ang Chinese) 'must originally have been a word from some north-eastern language whose meaning was then forgotten and rationalized by the Chinese' (Schafer, Golden Peaches, p. 68). It was written with two characters meaning 'under a fruit-tree', the explanation given being that these ponies were so small that a man could ride them beneath the low-hanging branches of a fruit-tree. For an excellent discussion of these little animals, see Schafer, loc. cit.

[5]Literally: ' . . . by boys of the Man tribes'. The Man were southern aborigines. Yao believes that this poem is a protest against Hsien-Tsung's appointment of the eunuch T'u-t'u Ch'eng-ts'ui as Commander-in-Chief of the forces attacking Wang Ch'eng-tsung (10th month of 809).

No. 9

SHU of Liao died suddenly,
So no one knows how to care for dragons.
At nightfall, frost thick on the stable,
The west wind splits the thoroughbred's hooves.[1]

No. 10

WITH rapid pole he crossed the River Wu,
Divine Dapple wept, breasting the wind.
'My lord has taken his sword and slain himself.
Where will I find another hero now?'[2]

No. 11

A ROYAL horse given to a palace lady,
Silver trappings embroidered with unicorns,
At midday, on that hill of salt,
A foundering steed is struggling through wind and dust.[3]

[1]Legend has it that a descendant of Shu An of Liao, called Tung-fu, could tame dragons, which he then presented to the emperor Shun (*Tso-chuan*, 29th year of Ch'ao; Legge, *The Chinese Classics*, V, p. 731a). In this poem 'dragons' stands for 'fire horses.'

[2]*Shih-chi*, VII, relates that Hsiang Yü, defeated by the founder of the Han dynasty in the struggle for the empire, gave away his steed, Dapple, to the man who had ferried him across the river Wu. Shortly afterwards, he killed himself.

[3]Not a satire against rulers who were over-fond of women, as Yeh would have it, but rather another protest against their wanton neglect of genius. *Chan-kuo ts'e*, XVII, 2, tells how Po-lo, a famous judge of horseflesh, came across a magnificent horse dragging a load of salt up a steep hill. 'Its hooves were swollen, its knees were gashed ... When Po-lo saw it he sprang down from his carriage and wept ... This bayard then hung down its head and snorted, raised its head and neighed ... because Po-lo had recognized its true worth.'

No. 12

EARS like bamboo-slivers, close together,
No peach-blossom showing on its coat,
In a few years' time, it will smash a battle-line,
So take this horse and lend him to a general.[1]

No. 13

WHAT house owns this beringed young gallant?
I've heard a dead knight's bones are fragrant,
But he bought a bayard's bones for a heap of gold
Just to present them to King Hsiang of Ch'u.[2]

No. 14

PERFUMED saddle-cover of fresh, scarlet sendal.
Coiled dragons' scales around his stirrups,
As he gazes all around the southern road,
How can you say he has not met with spring?[3]

[1]A description of a new-born colt. Peach-blossom markings were the sign of a fine horse.

[2]A difficult poem, which has the commentators puzzled, for King Hsiang of Ch'u was notorious for his love of women, not horses. Yeh explains that since there are no connoisseurs of horseflesh left, the young man in question can only present the bones of a fine horse to King Hsiang's spirit; for since King Hsiang has the power to dream of horses, perhaps he at least will know a fine horse when he sees one. Line 3 refers to the story, found in *Chan-kuo ts'e*, of the man who bought a dead thoroughbred's bones for five hundred pieces of gold, in order to induce people to offer him a live one.

[3]A satire on some rich, successful and worthless young man?

No. 15

IF it hadn't gone hunting with Duke Huan,
It could never have frightened tigers![1]
One morning it will leave its fields and dikes –
Just watch it soar to brush against the clouds![2]

No. 16

WHEN T'ang swords beheaded the Dukes of Sui,
Ch'üan-mao was the horse T'ai-tsung loved best.
No one gave a thought to its heavy armour,
For it was fleet enough to catch a whirlwind.[3]

No. 17

WHITE steel cuts down green grain,
Between mortar-stones drop tiny leaves,[4]
Nowadays people want dainty-necked ponies,
Wealthy owners fear long-toothed steeds.[5]

[1]Duke Huan of Ch'i (685–643 B.C.) had a piebald horse which frightened off tigers.

[2]When a genius meets the right patron, he will rise from obscurity and become famous overnight.

[3]A genius labours under heavy disabilities. But when it comes to the test, he will outstrip all others.

[4]Pampered horses are fed on cereals, not grass.

[5]Long teeth were the sign of a horse that could run 1000 *li* in one day. The poem means that those in power are afraid of men of genius.

No. 18

ONCE Po-lo looked at this horse,
Saw its hair grow in whorls on its belly.[1]
So far they've fed it on white grass[2] –
When will it leap across the emerald hills?

No. 19

THIS horse, whose native land is India,
Brought back scriptures to Hsiao temple.[3]
We know this is a noble animal
That does not want to run round Chang-t'ai street.[4]

No. 20

YOUR double baldric, like a swallow-tail,
Your jewelled sword like Fish-gut itself.[5]
You want a horse can run a thousand leagues?
First try looking for the gleam in its eye.[6]

[1]Po-lo – Sun Yang of Ch'in, a famous judge of horseflesh. A horse with whorls of hair on its belly was said to be capable of covering 1,000 *li* a day.

[2]*Vitis serjaniaefolia*, Bge., a plant found in North China – poor feed for thoroughbreds.

[3]Legend has it that the first Buddhist scriptures were brought to China on the back of a white horse. Hsiao was the surname of Emperor Wu of Liang (*regnet* 502–49), a pious Buddhist who built many temples.

[4]Chang-t'ai street, in Ch'ang-an, was in the quarter where the singing-girls lived. Ho would seem to be writing about himself; for he was, after all, a Buddhist.

[5]'Fish-gut': name of a famous sword.

[6]A young prince wearing a belt and sword needs a fine horse. So a ruler needs a talented man around him if he is to establish a reputation.

No. 21

TYING up Prancing Yellow for a while,
The Fairy climbs his coloured tower.
The groom who waits with jade bridle and whip –
Why must he be banished to Kao-chou?[1]

No. 22

BLOOD-SWEATING steeds came to the royal house,[2]
Following the bells, shaking jade bridle-gems.[3]
Shao-chün rode one by the sea,
Yet in men's eyes it was only a black mule.[4]

[1]Why does the emperor dismiss his patient officials simply because the empire is temporarily at peace? Yeh believes this poem refers to the resignation of the Prime Minister, Li Chiang, early in 814. Kao-chou was a malarial region in Kwangtung to which many officials were banished.

[2]The blood-sweating horses of Ferghana, on the Jaxartes, were famous throughout antiquity. The bloody sweat may have been caused by a parasite, *parafiliaria multipapillosa.* 'Royal house' – the house of Han.

[3] Read 轡 for 鑾. Bells adorned the bits of the horses.

[4]Li Shao-chün was an Immortal who was seen riding a black mule in P'u-pan, over three months after his supposed death. When his coffin was opened, it was found to be empty. Ho is saying that Li was not riding a mule but a blood-sweating steed: but the times are so out of joint that men cannot tell one from the other. Hence it is not surprising that men of great talents – like Ho himself – are allowed to go unrecognized.

No. 23

EMPEROR Wu longed for Gods and Immortals,
Trying to make gold, he got nothing but purple mist.[1]
All he had in his stables were horses of flesh,
They did not know how to mount the blue heavens.[2]

Song: Bearded Shen Playing His Tartar Horn[3]
5-character: 1 rhyme

Preface:

Bearded Shen was the servant of a northern friend of mine. This northerner, who belonged to an old and honourable branch of the Li family, was entitled to offer sacrifice in the temple of the Prince of Chiang-hsia.[4] He had once committed some small offence or other, lost rank and been posted to a commandery in the north.[5] He claims to be highly proficient in 5-word and 7-word verse: yet fame has for long eluded him. In the fourth month of this year, when I was a neighbour of his in the Ch'ung-yi quarter of Ch'ang-an, after pawning his clothes to buy wine, he invited me to join him in a drinking-party. When our spirits were high and all of us well in our cups, he said to me: 'Li Ch'ang-chi! You can only write 7-word poems. You can't handle 5-word poems. You may force the tip of your brush to write something, but you'll never come within miles of the verse of T'ao Yüan-ming and Hsieh Ling-yün.'[6]

[1]Emperor Wu of Han dabbled in alchemy, trying to make gold by smelting cinnabar. The purple mist was given off when making chemical compounds.
[2]Emperor Wu invaded Ferghana to seize its blood-sweating horses; but even they were not truly divine.
[3]The pi-li was a type of flageolet.
[4]The Li family of Lung-hsi constituted the imperial house of T'ang. Li Tao-tsung was Prince of Chiang-hsia.
[5] Reading 郡 for 部.
[6]T'ao Yüan-ming (365–427) and Hsieh Ling-yün (385–433) were perhaps the greatest poets of the pre-T'ang period.

After I had replied to this I asked if I could write a 'Song for Bearded Shen Playing His Tartar Horn'. When I'd finished my song, all the guests started shouting for us to sing it together. My northern friend was quite delighted. He stood up raised his goblet to toast me, and then called for his concubine, Hua-niang, to come out from behind the curtain and walk up and down paying her respects to the guests. I asked her which type of music she was best at. She replied that 'Peaceful and Slow'[1] was the mode she preferred. Then we sang my verses together, while Shen accompanied us, wishing me long life with his music.

Faces glowing from your wine, sir,
We savour the sound of the reeds,
Hua-niang, her hair in careful disarray,
Wakes from her sleep behind the screen.
Who cut the flute of Perfect Peace,[2]
Bored these holes like stars in the sky?
Piercing and sudden, a wind opening blossoms,
It sends the clouds scudding through the heavens.
Tonight the flowers of our years are falling,[3]
Breaking my heart for days beyond recall.
My passions surge as wild as waves,
I sit here startled time and time again.
The northerner rides on a white horse,
Grasping his sword with orchid-tasselled haft.[4]
He is strong and quick as a wild monkey,
Yet catches fireflies in tumbleweed.[5]

[1]*P'ing-nung* 平弄 emphasized the *kung* mode.

[2]The *t'ai p'ing kuan* was a reed instrument with nine holes and a mouthpiece like the Tartar horn.

[3]*Sui-hua* 歲華 here means 'age'; 'time'.

[4] Read 杷 for 弝.

[5]Chü Yin, of the Chin dynasty, was so poor that in the summer he studied by the light of fireflies which he caught himself. See *Chin-shu*, LXXXIII. Hence our line means that Ho's host, though poor, was an assiduous student.

Song of the Old Jade-hunter[1]

7-character: 3 rhymes

HUNTING for jade! Hunting for jade!
Only water-emeralds will do[2]
For cutting into Shake-as-she-walks
Only the finest colours![3]
For an old man hungry, shivering with cold,
Even dragons must grieve,
Where the vaporous waters of Indigo river
Run turbid, not white.[4]

On rainy nights, on the ridge of a hill,
He sups on hazel-nuts,
Like the blood that wells from a cuckoo's maw
Are the old man's tears.[5]
The waters of Indigo river are gorged
With human lives;
After a thousand years the dead
Still loathe these torrents.[6]

[1]A ballad of social protest, very much in the style made popular by Po Chü-yi, Yüan Chen and others.
[2]Water-emerald (*shui-pi*) was one of the most sought-after types of jade during T'ang.
[3]'Shake-as-she-walks' (*pu-yao*) was a woman's hair-ornament, with its top made of jade. It shook as the wearer walked.
[4]Indigo Field (Lan-t'ien) among the mountains of Shensi south of Ch'ang-an provided the finest 'jade', actually a type of green-and-white marble.
[5]During summer the cuckoo – believed to be the soul of a banished emperor – cried day and night, so the story went, until its mouth ran with blood. See *Erh-ya yi*, XIV, 2.
[6]An indirect way of saying that their ghosts hate the officials whose depredations drove them to their death while hunting for jade.

A steep hillside, wind in the cypress,
Whistle of rain –
Deep in the springs he hangs from a rope,
Green curling and swirling,
Thinking of wife and children back in his poor village,
In a white-thatched hut.
Upon stone steps of ancient terraces
The heartbreak grows.[1]

Ballad of an Aching Heart[2]

5-character: 1 rhyme

MOURNFULLY chanting, I study the sighs of Ch'u,[3]
My sick bones ache in lonely poverty.
From gazing at autumns, my hair has turned white.
Leaves on the trees moan in the wind-blown rain.
The lamp burns blue, its orchid-oil run dry,[4]
Round its falling sparks the flying moths are dancing.[5]
On ancient walls the dust grows thicker still,
The vagrant spirit mutters through its dreams.[6]

[1]A type of creeper also called 'think-of-your children' (ssu-tzu-man). 'Ancient terraces' means 'mountains' here. His search is so hazardous that this mountain-plant forever reminds him of the children who depend on him and may be fatherless at any moment.

[2]This poem was written when Ho was living in either Lo-yang or in Ch'ang-an.

[3]Ho's fondness for the Ch'u Tz'u is mentioned again on p. 145 below.

[4]Cf. Ch'u Tz'u, The Summons of the Soul (Chao Hun), p. 108: 'Bright candles of orchid perfumed fat . . .'

[5] Reading 蛾 for 娥.

[6]Wang glosses chi-hun as 'the traveller's spirit' (chi-k'o chih hun). This misses the force of Ho's idea of the spirit journeying through endless reincarnations, lodging for a while in the body. Yeh understands chi as chi-hsieh: 'The haltered spirit mutters through its dreams.' This is also very powerful.

Song: On the Lake

7-character: 3 rhymes

GIRL with long eyebrows crosses the sands,
Gathering orchids and iris.[1]
Cassia leaves and smartweed spread
An ambient fragrance.[2]
Drowsy with wine, idle all the white day
In a moored boat,
In a plum-breeze by the ferry she waves
Her singing-fan.[3]

Jade forks of her swallow-hairpins gleam
In the clear canal,[4]
The king of Yüeh's handsome son
Sends her a delicate letter.[5]

Paper from Shu, wrapped in a kerchief,
Tells this cloud-haired girl,[6]
They will meet tonight when the water-clock
Has stilled its drops.

[1] Wang believes she tries to gather these plants but finds only cassia and smart-weed.

[2] Read 香 for 春, since the fourth line refers to summer, not spring.

[3] The plum-breeze is the wind that blows down the plums in the fifth lunar month. A singing-fan was used to screen the face when singing.

[4] Reading 清 for 青.

[5] Crown Prince Shih of Yüeh was sent as a hostage to the King of An-yang. The king's daughter, Mei-chu, fell in love with him and yielded herself to him.

[6] Shu produced a very fine writing-paper. The expression I have rendered as 'a delicate letter' reads literally 'a letter in small characters'. The fineness of the calligraphy was a mark of the good-breeding of her lover. Wang wrongly construes this line as 'A letter written on a kerchief and sealed in Shu paper'.

The Caves of the Yellow Clan[1]

7-character: 2 rhymes

TREADING like sparrows, they kick up the sand
With sibilant feet,
Horn-trimmed bows a yard in length,
Arrowheads of green stone,
Jet-black banners with triple marks,
Bronze drums calling,[2]
High-pitched voices shrilling like apes,
They shake their quivers.

[1]The region of south Kwangsi and west Kwangtung was inhabited by aborigines called the Yellow Cave Natives (taking their name from their leader, Huang Hsiao-ch'ing) who were for long a nuisance to the imperial government. In the winter of 816 they staged a large-scale rising, plundered many towns and harassed the government armies. See *TCTC*, p. 7725.

[2]Bronze drums were the finest artifacts of aboriginal culture.

[3]Their war-paint was evidently reddish-purple, like the flowers of the arrowroot.

[4]*Pen-ts'ao*, XLIII, notes that the alligator 'makes a noise like a drum and sounds the watches of the night'.

[5]The bamboo-viper (*trimeresurus gramineus*) was a particularly venomous variety, also known as the *ch'ing-k'uei* 青蛙. 'Flying crawlers' (*fei-tu*) is explained by Suzuki as 'flying hairy caterpillars'. (Yeh suggests that 'snakes' and 'caterpillars' are symbols for the poisoned arrows used by the natives.) Both these creatures are as deadly as the *yü*, a fabulous beast said to spit sand onto the shadows of people that fall on the stream in which it lies hidden. The person affected sickens and dies.

[6]'Bamboo-horse' can only have been the name of some type of vehicle. Horses could not survive in the jungles of the south.

At the heads of rivers their war-bands muster
Gorgeous as arrowroot,[3]
In mist-wreathed mountain tarns at dusk
White alligators boom,[4]
Bamboo snakes, flying crawlers,
Spurters of golden sand.[5]
Quietly trundling their bamboo-horses,[6]
They slowly go home,
Leaving the government armies to kill
The natives of Jung-chou.[7]

[7]Literally: '. . . the *ch'a* of Jung-chou'. '*Ch'a*' 槎 normally means 'raft'. Hence some commentators interpret as 'destroyed the rafts to stop the aborigines from advancing'. Wang mistakenly understands '*ch'a*' as meaning 'to cut off branches; to prune'. It seems best to follow Saitō's suggestion that '*ch'a*' is an aboriginal word for 'people'. While the aborigines quietly go home with their plunder, the government armies wreak vengeance on the harmless inhabitants of Jung-chou (Jung county, Kwangsi), in order to lay claim to a resounding victory. The satirical force of this last line is quite clear. The imperial armies of this period were notoriously unwilling to engage the enemy. Han Yü himself wrote a scathing memorial on this subject.

Song: The Screen[1]

7-character: 1 rhyme

BUTTERFLIES lighting on China pinks –
Hinges of silver,
Frozen water, duck-head green –
Coins of glass,[2]
Its six-fold curves enclose a lamp
Burning orchid-oil.[3]
She lets down her tresses before the mirror,
Sheds her gold cicadas,[4]
Perfume of aloes from a warm fire,
Smoke of dogwood.[5]
Goblets of wine joined with a sash,
A new bride in raptures,[6]
Wind by moonlight blowing the dew,
Cold outside the screen,
As crows cry from the city walls,
The girl from Ch'u sleeps on.[7]

[1]A poem about a newly married couple whose bed is surrounded by an elaborate screen. The atmosphere of this poem is very close to that of a *tz'u*.

[2]The hinges of the screen look like glass coins. 'Liu-li' was coloured, ornamental glass widely used during T'ang for decorations.

[3]There were 12 screens arranged in pairs across the bed.

[4]Gold cicada-shaped hairpins. I read *chieh* 解 for *chiang* 將, with Suzuki.

[5]Literally: 'smoke' of *shu-yü* 茱萸, a name used for three completely different plants. The smoke from the aloeswood rises straight up, like the smoke from *shu-yü*. Alternatively the line might refer to the purplish colour of the smoke.

[6]The tying of wine-goblets with a sash was part of the wedding ceremonies.

[7]Ch'u girls were famous for their slim waists.

Ballad of the South Mountain Fields

Irregular: 2 rhymes

THE autumn wilds bright,
The autumn wind white.[1]
Pool-water deep and clear,
Insects whining.
Moss on the cloud-roots,
Stones on the mountains.[2]
Cold reds weeping dew,
Gracefully crying colours.[3]

Fields in the wild, in the ninth month
Forks of rice.
Torpid fireflies flying low,
Start across dike-paths.
Water flows from veins of rocks,
Springs drip on sand.
Ghost-fires' lacquer lamps,
Shining on pine-flowers.[4]

[1]White was the colour assigned to autumn, being the colour of mourning.
[2]'Cloud-roots': a poetic term for 'crags'.
[3]Dew drips from the dying flowers.
[4]The will-o'-the-wisps burn as feebly and as sinisterly as the black lacquer lamps placed in tombs. Pine-flowers are yellow.

Joys of a Princess Travelling in Battle-array[1]

7-character: 4 rhymes

BONDMAIDS on horseback in linked chain-armour
Of yellow bronze,
Silken banners on perfumed staves
With gold-painted leaves.[2]

In Ho-yang city, drunk with wine,
The leader lingers,[3]
Her graceful Purple Swallow whinnies,
Pawing the flowers.[4]

The pink-jade general of cavalry riding
Through her vernal camp,
Shaking a whip, mounts the green void
On her galloping steed.

A pale moon over the battlements
As the horns crow out,
Though the pennoned tent is not yet open,
They share the brocades.[5]

[1]Wang sees this poem as a satire directed against a princess of the time going out to a banquet in Ho-yang accompanied by her retinue, many of whom are her own handmaids accoutred for war to act as her bodyguard. It must be remembered that women during the T'ang period enjoyed far more freedom than they did in the later eras, when the spectacle of a princess behaving in this way would have been quite unthinkable. It is highly likely, however, that the poem is a satire on the eunuch-general T'u-t'u Ch'eng-ts'ui, here ridiculed as a 'princess'.

[2]The poles are made of costly, aromatic wood.

[3]In Honan, 80 *li* north-east of Lo-yang. This was a strategic centre.

[4]'Purple Swallow' – name of a famous thoroughbred of the early Han. Ho-yang was renowned for its flowers.

[5]A serrated pennon stood before the tent of the commanding officer. Though the general herself has not yet risen, brocade clothes are bestowed on the ladies of her retinue.

'After a Drinking-party'
Chang Ch'e, My Elder, Once Presented Me with a Poem on
This Theme. At That Time Chang Was Serving
as Adviser in Lu-chou.[1]

7-character: 3 rhymes

LONG-BEARDED Master Chang
Is thirty-one,[2]
A poet sent down from Heaven
With flowers for bones.
Who of our company could replace
This dragon-headed man,[3]
That a princess sent to hold
The fish-barb tablet?[4]

The green grass of T'ai-hang
Has climbed your robe.[5]
Essays, memorials in your casket
Rolled tight as silk-worms:
Golden Portals, Stone Pavilion,
I know you will have,[6]
Horn of unicorn, fragrant cloves,
Dawn and dusk you'll employ.[7]

[1]Chang Ch'e (d. 821), the pupil and nephew-in-law of Han Yü, was one of Ho's closest friends. He took his doctorate in 809, eventually rising to the rank of Censor in the Court of Palace Affairs. He met his death at the hands of rebellious soldiery, 'his mouth still uttering grave admonitions'. Lu-chou is in Shansi.

[2] Reading 'thirty-one' with Arai: other editions read 'thirty-eight'.

[3]'Dragon-head' was a sobriquet applied to the foremost of a group of friends. See *San-kuo chih, Wei-chih*, XIII, p. 10a, commentary.

[4]Chang was a descendant of Chang Chi-shang, Princess of Ning-ch'in. As a kinsman of the royal house, Chang could have obtained office by privilege, even if he had not held the doctoral degree. Bamboo tablets decorated with fish-barbs were part of the insignia of the highest officials.

But Ch'ang-chi of Lung-hsi
Is a wreck of a fellow,[8]
Waking from drunken sleep
With unquiet heart.
Coarse, linen clothes all tattered
Though it's autumn in Chao-ch'eng,[9]
Chanting poems the whole night long,
Till the east grows white.

[5]Arai, Yeh and Suzuki all read 太行: other editions read 水行. Lu-chou was on the highest part of the T'ai-hang range, which cuts across Shansi. Officials of the sixth and seventh ranks wore green robes. Hence the line means: 'As you crossed the T'ai-hang range to take up your first post, your white (commoner's) robes turned green.'

[6]The Golden Horse Portals and the Stone Culvert Pavilion both stood in the capital during Han times. Here they denote high office. The gateway led to the offices of the officials. The pavilion, built by the Han general Hsiao Ho, was used for storing records. See *Chiao-cheng san-fu huang-t'u, Ku-tien wen hsüeh ch'u-pan she*, III, p. 22: IV, p, 48.

[7]The *chih* (loosely rendered 'unicorn') was a fabulous, one-horned beast which gored only the wicked. It was used as a symbol on the caps worn by the President and Vice-President of the Tribunal of Censors when they were preferring charges. Great officers of state had to put cloves in their mouths to sweeten their breath when they addressed reports to the emperor, a practice that dated back to Han.

[8]It will be remembered that Ho, whose style was Ch'ang-chi, came from Lung-hsi commandery in Kansu, the native-place of the T'ang royal house.

[9]Chao-ch'eng county, Shansi.

Verses on Being Presented with a Length of Summer Cloth by the Mountaineer of Lo-fu[1]

7-character: 2 rhymes

IT was surely woven when the rain-drenched sky
Clings to the river,
In the Orchid Terrace breeze that blows
In rainy July.[2]
When the ancient Immortal of Lo-po[3]
Brings the cloth from his cave,
From thousand-year-old beds of stone,
Demon weavers wail.[4]

Venom of serpents, thick and congealed,
Soaks the caverned halls,
Fish in the river will not eat,
Mouths sunk in the sand.[5]
I want to cut a foot of sky
Out of the river Hsiang,[6]
Let the maidens of Wu never dare to say
Their blades are blunt.[7]

[1]Summer-cloth is woven from the *ke* plant (*pueraria thunbergiana*). The Mountaineer was a Taoist Immortal living on Mount Lo-fu, a mountain in Kwangtung famed in both Buddhist and Taoist lore. *Li Ch'ang-chi wen-chi* title reads 羅 敷 交 與 葛 篇.

[2]On the Orchid Terrace of King Hsiang of Ch'u, mentioned by Sung Yü in his *Fu of the Wind*, every breeze was delightful.

[3]Another name for Lo-fu.

[4]The demons cry out because the precious cloth they have woven has been given away.

[5]In July the heat is so great that snakes lose their venom and fish burrow into the sand of the river-bed.

[6]The cloth is brilliant as the sky.

[7]Wu was renowned for its steel.

A Few Remarks Addressed to Huang-fu Shih from the Jen-ho Quarter[1]

7-character: 5 rhymes

FROM my father's brother I've borrowed a horse,
With a lean and hungry look,
A kinsman has lent me a house of his,
With ruinous walls.
Round its courtyard's bare and trampled earth
The rat-tracks run,
Over the fence grows a big date-tree,
Its pendant reds all spoilt.[2]

A gentleman from An-ting
Cut off his yellow ribbon,
Removed his cap-strings, shed his robe,
Drank wine day and night.[3]
He went back to his family
No white brush on his head,[4]
No wonder my reputation fell
Far behind others![5]

[1]This poem was written in the winter of 810, when Ho was setting off to
Ch'ang-an to take his Selection examination, after having failed to qualify for
the doctorate. He was entitled to do this since his father had been an official
of the fifth-degree, first class. Huang-fu Shih had taken his doctorate in 806
and been appointed to the post of Chief of Staff at Lü-hun, Honan. Two
years later he found himself involved in an examination scandal along with Li
Tsung-min and Niu Seng-ju. The papers of these candidates were so critical
of one powerful faction in the government that the Emperor dismissed and
demoted the examiners. Huang-fu Shih himself was a protégé of Han Yü's
and a patron of Ho's. The Jen-ho quarter of Lo-yang was a pleasant, sparsely
settled district near the Ch'ang-hsia gate.

[2]Reading 朱 for 珠.

In vain you deigned to call me friend
I offended your eyes,
Just when you were going to haul me up,
Your strong rope snapped.
With the Lo-yang wind to escort my horse
I rode the long pass,
But before the palace gates swung wide,
The mad dogs found me.[6]

Who would believe that Chien or Tu
Were careless judges?[7]
Lonely on my traveller's pillow
I watched spring grow old.
I came back home, all skin and bones.
A fleshless face,
A murrain lighted on my head.
My hair fell out.[8]

[3]A reference to Huang-fu's debacle in the special examination of 808, which obviously led him to lose his official position. Suzuki reads 暝 for 瞑: 'grew giddy with wine every morning'. During T'ang, Chiefs of Staff, who were officials of the ninth rank, wore no red ribbons; Ho is referring to a Han dynasty practice.

[4]Officials of the seventh grade and upwards wore white writing-brushes in their hair. Huang-fu Shih had clearly missed being promoted to the seventh grade.

[5]Ho was also affected by the disgrace of his patron.

[6]Reading 獌 for 獥.

[7]Tao Chien and Ting Chün-tu were renowned as judges of horses. Here Ho is referring to his patrons Han Yü and Huang-fu Shih.

[8]This suggests a nervous breakdown consequent on the shock of his rejection.

I'm going to play around with words
For the Office of Heaven,[9]
For who would pity a royal scion
Left unemployed?
Tomorrow, midway through the tenth month,
I'm heading west once more.[10]
In the K'ung-t'ung hills I'll be far from you,
Far as the sky.

[9]*Chuang-tzu*, XXVI: 'He dressed up little phrases in order to get a job as a district magistrate.' The Office of Heaven was a name for the Ministry of Civil Office. Clearly, Ho was going to sit for another examination.

[10]Candidates for the Selection examination were supposed to be in Ch'ang-an by the twentieth day of the tenth month. Ho had thus left himself only five days to cover close on three hundred miles of rugged country.

Song of a Palace Beauty[1]

7-character: 4 rhymes

LIGHT of tapers, hung on high,
Shines through the gauzy air.[2]
In the flowery chambers at night they are pounding
Red palace-wardens.[3]

The elephant's mouth puffs incense forth,[4]
My Persian rug feels warm.
When Seven Stars hang over the city-wall,[5]
I hear the clepsydra's gong.

The cold creeps in past the eaves-net[6]
As palace shadows darken.
The brilliant simurghs on lintels of blinds
Bear scars from the frost.
Crying mole-crickets mourn for the moon,
Beneath curved balustrades.
Crook-knee hinges and door-plates of bronze
Lock in this poor Chen.[7]

---

[1]The summer of 813 was marked by severe floods, alleged to be due to a predominance of the Yin (female) element. The Emperor therefore sent three hundred of his harem back to their homes. Yao interprets this poem as being written by one who was not sent back, although fallen from favour. In view of the persistent water-imagery of the last lines, he may well be right.

[2]The candle-light is seen through the gauze of her bed-curtains.

[3]'Palace-wardens' was a name given to geckos, which were fed on cinnabar until they turned red. They were then pounded up in mortars, the resulting paste being used to mark the bodies of the Emperor's concubines. It was believed that such spots would not disappear until the woman had sexual intercourse. Thus a check could be kept on the behaviour of the women of the harem – hence the name 'palace-wardens'. The girl lies awake listening to the noise of the mortars, reflecting bitterly that she will never have need of the palace-wardens again.

[4]Incense-braziers were often made in the form of animals, generally ducks or elephants.

L

In dreams I go through the gates of my home,
Up past sandy isles.
Where the River of Heaven curves down through the air
Lies the Long Island road.[8]
I wish that my lord, who is dazzling bright
As the Great Light itself,
Would set me free to ride off on a fish,
Attacking the waves.[9]

[5]The seven stars of the Dipper.

[6]A net stretched across the edge of the eaves. See p. 20, note 2, above.

[7]Lady Chen was a discarded favourite of Emperor Wen of Wei (*regnet* 220–6). She was eventually forced to commit suicide.

[8]Long Island (Ch'ang-chou) was the old name of a county in Kiangsu, in the ancient territory of Wu. Like the Lady Chen, the girl came from Suchow, a place famous for its beautiful girls. The Long River (the Milky Way) seems to curve down the sky in the direction of Ch'ang-chou, forming a watery pathway which will lead her home.

[9]Wang finds her straddling a fish rather odd, but finally decides, owlishly enough, that she chose this way to travel because it would be faster than any boat! I suspect she is promising to drive back the floods in exchange for her freedom.

Splendour on Splendour[1]

Irregular: 1 rhyme

SPLENDOUR on splendour, splendour on splendour again!
The red is gone, the plum-tree ashes still fragrant.[2]
For tens of years wood-worm have bred
In painted beams,
What hungry beetles would not eat
Piles up in broken yellows.
Orchid petals wither,
Peach-leaves grow long.
Hanging blinds of the Palaces
Exclude imperial light.
In Hua-ch'ing springs, arsenic stone
Boils in the water,[3]
Where once white phoenixes wandered,
Following their prince.[4]

---

[1]A song of this title was first written by the last emperor of the Ch'en dynasty. Ho is once again visiting the ruins of the Hua-ch'ing palace (see p. 20 above). Suzuki says the first line is meaningless. I disagree. It clearly refers to the palace. Yeh takes it literally: 'Hall after hall'.

[2]Suzuki points out that this refers to the story that when a temple in Shao-hsing dedicated to the legendary emperor Yü was being repaired, during the Liang dynasty (A.D. 502–57), a beam of plum-tree wood magically came flying to the site.

[3]For these springs, see p. 20, note 1, above. The stone in question is arsenolite ($AS_4 O_6$), a poisonous substance used for accelerating the growth of silkworms.

[4]'White phoenixes' – the emperor's ladies. Yeh reads 百 for 白, as does *Li Ch'ang-chi wen-chi*.

Be Sure to Take Care of Yourself
Two Poems Written When I Escorted Young Li on His Way to Mount Lu[1]

No. 1
5-character: 1 rhyme

No dish and platter in the wilds outside Lo-yang,[2]
Just a shaming old horse from a tumbledown stable.
The little goose will wing past Incense-burner Peak,[3]
Its shadow falling on the waters of Ch'u.[4]
The long boat will float moored upon clouds,
Below Stone Mirror, in the cold, autumn night.[5]
Even a man who was not sick for home
Would groan for sorrow, gazing at that moon.

[1]The title suggests a *yüeh-fu*. Ho's younger brother was going to Mount Lu, the famous Buddhist centre in Kiangsi.
[2]No ceremonial farewell meal for the traveller.
[3]One of the peaks of Mount Lu.
[4]The famous Nine Rivers of Ch'u.
[5]The Stone Mirror stood on the summit of Pine Gate Mountain, north of Hsin-chien in Kiangsi. It was a natural rock-formation, so smooth and polished it looked like a mirror.

No. 2

Irregular: 4 rhymes

WILLOWS of parting at your horse's head,[1]
On the highway, ash-tree buds like rabbit-eyes.
We are going to endure a thousand-league parting,
All this suffering just for a peck of millet![2]

Southern clouds, northern clouds,
Block off my view,[3]
My heart-threads ravelled as spring's pendant silk.[4]
Blue eaves and wheeling trees,
Moonlight floods my bed.[5]
In dreams I see a hungry lad off to the provinces.

Your elder brother is now turned twenty,
The mirror tells him how his beard is growing.
Three years ago he left our home – to come to this!
Begging rice at princes' gates,
An utter failure.

In weed-grown drains, standing water
Bright as a blade,
In old willows south of the courtyard,
Cutworms breed.[6]

[1]It was customary to say farewell under a willow.
[2]I follow Suzuki's interpretation here. Read 此 for 我.
[3]Reading 賑 for 脈 with Suzuki, Yeh and Saitō believe this stanza (lines 5–8) is spoken by Ho's mother. This seems unnecessary.
[4]Literally: 'The warp of the threads in my spirit-tower is as ravelled as the hanging silk of spring (silkworms).' 'Spirit-tower' simply means 'heart'.
[5]Yeh and Saitō take 'Blue eaves' as a reference to the mother's room.
[6]Ho is describing the dilapidation of his house.

I worry about you, young
Traveller to the River,
Over fields of the waste the evening
Horns moan sadly.[1]

Let Wine Be Brought in![2]

7-character: 2 rhymes

For a lonely failure – a cup of wine.
The host lifts his goblet, pledging our health.
'Chu-fu was too poor
To return from the west,[3]
Though his family snapped the willows
In front of the gate.'[4]

---

[1]The horns blown at sunset when the city-gates were shut, according to Yeh. Other commentators render as 'the evening wind moans sadly'.

[2]Title of an old *yüeh-fu*. *Wen-yüan ying-hua*, 336, adds the subtitle: 'Written in Ch'ang-an at the winter solstice'.

[3]Chu-fu Yen (d. 127 B.C.) was a scholar from Lin-tzu, in Ch'i, who wandered around for many years seeking employment in vain. Though recommended to the Emperor by General Wei Ch'ing (d. 106 B.C.) himself, he was not given a post until he sent up a particularly brilliant memorial. See *Shih-chi*, CXII, p. 5a. Since this allusion would imply that Ho had not yet found employment, we might well assign the poem to December 810, shortly after he had taken the selection examinations in Ch'ang-an but before he had been given an official post.

[4]His family had been leaning against the willows, waiting for him to return, for so long that they finally broke the trees down.

Long ago in Hsin-feng,
Ma Chou was a mere retainer,
Thinking heaven was desolate, earth grown old,
None knew his worth.
Yet a couple of lines
Dashed off in a moment of leisure,
Went straight to the throne
And won him imperial favour.[5]
My wandering soul has strayed away
Long past recall,
Yet at a single cock-crow
The sky will turn white.
A young man's heart should strive to reach
The very clouds,
Who heeds a man who sits and wails
Out in the cold?

[5]Ma Chou (601-48) was a retainer of Ch'ang Ho's, but this was in Ch'ang-an, not Hsin-feng (Shensi). In Hsin-feng he had astonished an inn-keeper by his capacity for drink. In Ch'ang-an, in 631, he wrote a memorial to the emperor on Ch'ang's behalf which so impressed T'ai-tsung that he summoned Ma to court. See *CTS*, LXXIV, p. 4a.

A Long Song and a Short Song[1]

5-character: 2 rhymes

LONG songs have torn the collar of my robe,
Short songs have cropped my whitening hair.[2]
The king of Ch'in is nowhere to be seen,[3]
So dawn and dusk a burning fever racks me.
I drink wine from a pitcher when I'm thirsty,
Cull ears of rice from the dike-top when I'm hungry.
Lonely and sad, I see May pass me by,
And suddenly a thousand leagues grow green.

So high those nighted peaks soar into the air,
The bright moon sinks to the very foot of the crags.
I wander about, searching along the rocks,
But the moon shines out beyond those towering crags.
Because I cannot roam round with the moon,
My hair's grown white before I end my song.[4]

[1]'Long song' and 'Short song' were the names of *yüeh-fu* ballads, both of which had for their theme the shortness of man's life. The story goes that Ho wrote this poem when he was only 7 years old. This is, of course, quite untrue. See Harada Norio's article, 'Chōka zoku tanka', in *Kyōto Joshi Daigaku Jimbun Ronsō*, 7 (November 1962), pp. 66-93. He is ill and grieving over his failure in the examinations.

[2]His hair was cut short because of his illness.

[3]At this time Emperor Hsien-tsung had retired to Ch'in; hence the allusion.

[4]Yao equates the moon with the Emperor and the high rocks which bar Li Ho from the moon with the powerful officials of the court. This seems plausible.

Song: Do not Dance, Sir![1]

7-character: 4 rhymes

Preface:
The song called *Do not Dance, Sir!* celebrates the way Hsiang
Po protected Liu P'ei. The exploits of that warrior at the feast
have won such fame that no one has bothered to write of them
again. Among the northern and southern ballads, however, there
is one song which celebrates his feat. I thought this too crude, so I
wrote another song of this title.

> FLOWERS on ancient plinths of stone,[2]
> Nine pillars in a row,
> Blood of slaughtered leopards dripping
> Into silver pots.
> Drummers and pipers at the feast,
> No zithers or flutes,
> Long knives planted in the ground
> Split the singing lute.[3]

[1]*Shih-chi*, VII, biography of Hsiang Yü, relates the story of the struggle
for empire after the fall of Ch'in between Hsiang Yü of Ch'u and Liu Pang,
Lord of P'ei, who afterwards became the first Han emperor. Liu Pang's forces
had been the first to enter the Ch'in capital, Hsien-yang, and take possession of
the strategic Han-ku Pass. Enraged at this, Hsiang Yü was about to attack
Liu's forces when he was visited by his rival in his camp at Hung-men. At
the feast that followed, Fan Tseng signalled to Hsiang Yü with his girdle-
pendant, silently asking permission to have Liu killed. When Hsiang did not
reply, Fan ordered Hsiang Chuang to perform a sword-dance in the course
of which he was to kill Liu where he sat. However, as Hsiang Chuang was
dancing, Hsiang Po, an uncle of Yü's, leapt up with his sword and joined in
the dance, 'protecting Liu with his body so that Hsiang Chuang could not
smite him'. At this juncture Liu's carriage-guard, Fan K'uai, strode into the
hall, shouldering aside the sentries, and denounced Yü for attempting to kill
his master. Thanks to the intervention of these two men, Liu was able to
escape. This episode, as recounted by Ssu-ma Ch'ien, became so popular that
it figured widely in both folk tales and plays.

Lintels hung with coarse brocade
Of scarlet woof,
Sunlight fades the rich brocade,
The king still sober.[4]
Three times Yü saw the precious ring
Flash at Fan's belt,
Hsiang Chuang drew sword from scabbard,
And stood before Liu P'ei.

'Ensign! Your rank is far too low.
You may not dance,
Our guest is kin to the gods themselves,
A red dragon's seed.'[5]
On Mang and T'ang, auspicious clouds
Coiled in the heavens,[6]
In Hsien-yang city, the royal aura
Shone clear as water.

[2]Suzuki reads 古 for 石.

[3]The lute (cheng), symbol of Chinese culture, could not survive in that barbarous, southern atmosphere.

[4]Hsiang Yü was still not drunk enough to kill Liu P'ei.

[5]Shih-chi, VI, biography of Liu Pang, says he was begotten by a red dragon.

[6]See ibid. The history recounts how the First Emperor of Ch'in heard that 'there was an emanation characteristic of a Son of Heaven in the south-west', and set out to destroy Liu Pang who fled 'and hid himself among the swamps and rocks of Mang and T'ang'. His wife, however, was able to track him down because wherever he went he was followed by the auspicious cloud mentioned above. Mang was in the old state of P'ei, in Honan. T'ang was in ancient Liang, in Kiangsu.

Iron hinges, iron barriers
Fettered the passes,
Mighty banners, five fathoms long,
Battered the double gates,[1]
'Today the King of Han possesses
The Seal of Ch'in.
Smash my knee-caps, disembowel me,
I shall say no more.'[2]

Four Poems about New Bamboo-shoots in My North Garden[3] at Ch'ang-ku

All 7-character: 1 rhyme

No. 1

BAMBOO-SKIN sloughs from the long stems
Like peeled jade.
You, sir, can see this mother-bamboo
Has the stuff of dragons.
In a single night it changes utterly,
Soaring a thousand feet,
Leaving behind it inches of mire
By the garden pool.

[1]These lines describe Liu Pang's capture of the Ch'in capital.
[2]Ho has put these words in Fan K'uai's mouth, for the *Shih-chi* does not record them. Cutting off the knee-caps, and disembowelling were ancient punishments.
[3]Bamboo-shoots are called *lung-sun* – 'dragon's grand-children'.

No. 2

I HACK away at their green lustre,
To inscribe my Songs of Ch'u.[1]
Over perfumed oils and spring powder
The black ink flies.[2]
Passionless, yet full of bitterness –
Who will ever gaze upon them?[3]
Weighed down with dew, mourning in mist,
A million branches.

No. 3

THROUGH gaps in the stones round our family well –
Two or three bamboo-shoots.
At dawn I glimpsed their hidden roots
Growing through a purple path.[4]
This year on the sands of spring
By winding waters,
I'll strip away the jade and green
From new bamboos.[5]

[1]The poet hacks away at the green skin of the bamboo until the white under-surface is exposed. On this he writes his verses. The commentators take the 'Songs of Ch'u' to refer to Ho's own poems, which he frequently compares to the *Ch'u Tz'u*.

[2]Or possibly: '... the black ink flows luxuriantly'. See *Dai Kanwa-jiten*, XI, p. 12590, 42140. 191.

[3]A highly ambiguous line. It could mean: (a) 'On this unfeeling bamboo, I who am full of bitterness at my lot write my verse.' (b) 'I have no one to love me, so full of bitterness I write my verse.' (c) 'I write verses, some of them beyond passion, some of them full of resentment.' The bamboo as it grows will carry his verses into the air, far out of the reach of men.

[4]'Purple path' – either a path in the garden or else the road itself.

[5]To make fishing-rods.

No. 4

ANCIENT bamboos whose aged tips
Tease emerald clouds.
Like Mao-ling, I've come home to rest and sigh
At my pure poverty.[1]
A gust of wind and a thousand arpents[2]
Whistling greet the rain.[3]
Birds sit so heavy on this one stem
It dips into my flagon.[4]

[1]The poet Ssu-ma Hsiang-ju retired to Mao-ling, Shensi, when he fell ill.

[2]*Shih-chi*, CXXIX, biography of Huo Chih, says: 'man with a thousand arpents (*mou*) of bamboos is on a level with a marquis with a fief of ten thousand households.' (6.6 *mou* = one acre).

[3]Or: 'When the wind blows among my thousand arpents, I greet the rain with a whistle.'

[4]Commentators explain this piece of hyperbole by saying that it must be the shadow of the birds or the bamboos that falls across his wine-cup.

She Steals My Heart[1]

5-character: 1 rhyme

Sung Yü's vain hopes have vanished in melancholy,
What a graceful beauty she is, dusted with rose.[2]
I hear her singing among dewy, spring grass,
Her gate is closed, drifted over with apricot blossom.
She rouges her mouth, a little cherry,
Pencils her brows, deep-green as cassia leaves.
At dawn by her vanity-box she makes up her face,
Night-fragrance fades from the tube in the bed.[3]
On her inlaid mirror flies a lonely magpie,[4]
On a river-view screen, waterweed is painted.
Her hair swirls up and down, a blue-black phoenix,
With golden insects quivering upon it.[5]
She is an iris brimming with clear dew,
A cattail with its clustering purple shoots.
Black eyebrows crescent-moons, unfrowning,
Her dimples red as folded flowers.
Her heavy hair curls round her like a mist,
So slender-waisted, a breeze could break her.
She writes love-letters capped with cardamoms,

[1]Presumably a poem celebrating the beauty of some singing-girl or other, with whom Ho had become involved. My translation of this highly allusive and obscure piece of verse is in several places at best tentative.

[2]Sung Yü, a poet who seems to have lived at the court of King Ch'ing-hsiang of Ch'u (*regnet* 298–265 B.C.), is the supposed author of the *Chiu Pien* (*The Nine Arguments*) of the *Ch'u Tz'u*. Tradition has it that he was a rather romantic and dissolute fellow, much given to philandering.

[3]Incense was burnt in a censer.

[4]The magpie was a common motif on mirrors. This alludes to an old story about a husband and wife who broke a mirror in two on parting, each keeping one half. When the wife proved unfaithful, her half of the mirror changed into a magpie and flew off to tell the husband.

[5]These may have been ornaments made from the iridescent elytra of the gold-and-turquoise *chrysochroa* beetle.

Laughing at 'lotus', that secret word.[6]
Do not lock up the box of purple brocade,
Nor open the basket quilted with kingfisher feathers.
Playing with her pearls she scares the southern swallows,[7]
Burning honey she entices the northern bees.
She casts red nets dappled with white,
And hangs up gins of thin, green gauze.[8]
She teaches her lovely girls to handle money,[9]
Asks her servant from Pa what medicine to buy.[10]
On her powdered cheeks a slanting line of geese,
Moving the lamp, she broods on dreams of bears.[11]
Her feelings are not tight as tied bamboo,
The flesh of her belly is suddenly taut as a bow.
At dusk new butterflies go astray in the trees,
Fading, a female rainbow longs for a vanished male.
Long ago, a bird tried to fill in the Gulf of Chihli,
Today an old man tunnels the K'ung-t'ung hills.[12]

[6]Because of the formation of its pistils, the cardamom flower symbolized love. For cardamoms, see Schafer, *Golden Peaches*, pp. 184–5. 'Lotus', (*liän*) and 'love' (*lien*) were pronounced rather alike in Ancient Chinese, both in the level tone. Here the lotus symbolizes affection.

[7]The Pearl Game, in which a plateful of pearls was skilfully juggled, was a professional entertainer's act, just the sort of diversion a singing-girl would put on for her clients. It can be traced back to the Liang dynasty (A.D. 502–57).

[8]The red nets were to catch birds, the green to catch fish.

[9]A satirical touch! The mother of the Han Emperor, Ling-ti (*regnet* 168–89), the Empress Dowager Yung-lo, was so greedy for food and money that she became the butt of a popular ballad. Ho is quoting from this. See *Hou Han-shu, Monographs*, XIII. *Wu-hsing*, I, p. 196.

[10]She instructs her maids to keep the household accounts and asks her servant-lad about what medicines she should buy. Then she undresses, retires to bed and dreams of bearing a son.

[11]Yeh interprets the geese as being jewellery worn on the temples. To dream of bears was an omen of a baby boy, as snakes were omens of a baby girl.

[12]She is hopelessly in love with someone. Yet her lover has left her and not come back, leaving her to pine away like a fading rainbow. Her efforts to forget her love are as vain as those of the *ch'ing-wei* bird that tried to fill in the Eastern Sea or Master Simple of North Mountain who set out to remove

From an embroidered rope long curtains hang,
Her silken skirt is tied at its short seam.
Like a dancing crane her heart flutters about,
Her bones are sticking out like a fallen dragon's.[13]
From the side of the well green lacquer drops,[14]
The door-rings are bound with white brass.
Hugging the flowers a rabbit-track opens,
Hard by the wall, print of foxes' feet.
The light blinds are studded with tortoise-shell,
The folding screen of glass is warm.
Her ivory bed has sides of white cypress,
Her rolled jade-mat is fragrant as water-shallot.[15]
She plays her small pipes by the curtains at dawn
On fragrant wine-lees maple-leaves fall at dusk.[16]
'Should-have-a-son' grows in the lanes of Ch'u,
Gardenias blossom around Golden Wall.[17]

Mount T'ai-lang and Mount Wang-wu. (See A. C. Graham, *The Book of Lieh-tzu*, pp. 99–101.) (Actually Ho has his stories slightly mixed up. The *ch'ing-wei* bird tried to fill in the Eastern Sea, not the Gulf of Chihli. It was the Old Man of North Mountain who put the stones and earth from the hills into the Gulf of Chihli. In any case he was successful in this, since his determination eventually led gods to move the mountains for him.) Alternatively, the lines might well refer to Ho's efforts to gain her love, which though seemingly hopeless were finally crowned with success.

[13]Lovesickness has wasted her away, so that her bones stick out like the 'dragon-bones' found in an apothecary's shop.

[14]Reading 青 for 清.

[15]Or perhaps: 'the colour of water-shallot'.

[16]Maple-leaves fall on the spot where she has been drinking.

[17]The day-lily (*hemerocallis fulva*) was also known as *yi-nan*, 'should-have-a-son'. The lanes of Ch'u were the streets in the Golden Wall quarter in the north-west of Lo-yang, where the singing-girls lived. Saitō, however, understands this line simply as: 'Gardenias blossom by a golden wall.' The gardenia was yet another symbol of love.

[18]The screen was set with jade patterned like tortoise-shell. Saitō interprets: 'She is tightly encircled by the tortoise-shell screen.' This seems forced.

The open screen is rough with tortoise-shell,[18]
Her goose-feather brush soaks up the rich, black ink,
The 'Yellow Courtyard' detains this Wei Huan.[19]
In the green trees she feeds the Han P'eng birds.[20]
At cockcrow stars hang in the willows,
Crows cry as dew drops from the plane trees.
When this yellow-painted beauty takes her seat,
Her little sisters follow in her train.
When waxen tears have fallen, fragrance vanished,[21]
With a grass broom she sweeps the ornate lattice.
She plays an old tune on her mouth-organ,
While waiting to buy wine from Hsin-feng,[22]
Sorrow thick as the grain on her short pendant,[23]
Fingers slender as chives plucking the long-stringed lute.
In the Serpentine, the ducklings are all sleeping,
In the small pavilion, the pretty maidservant dreams.
Her well-stitched mattress is sewn with double thread,
Her buckled belt has five braided tassels.[24]

[19]Wei Huan (220–91), style Po-yü (biography in *Chin-shu*, XXXVI), was a celebrated calligrapher of the Chin dynasty, renowned for the elegance of his draft script. The girl is writing a letter in a hand as vigorous as that in which Wei Huan transcribed the *Yellow Courtyard Classic* (*Huang-t'ing ching*), a well-known Taoist work.

[20]There are several versions of the Han P'eng legend, the most usual of which relates that Han P'eng, a minister of the state of Sung, had a beautiful wife. His lord, King K'ang, threw him into prison where he died, and then seized the girl, who thwarted his designs by killing herself. Furious at being thus frustrated, the king had the two bodies buried in separate graves: but from each of these there sprouted a tree, in the branches of which, interlaced over the tombs, two birds came to sing. Thus, the Han P'eng birds are symbols of undying love. For another version of the legend, see A. Waley, *Ballads and Stories from Tun-huang* (London, 1960), pp. 56–64. Yeh believes that these lines mean she detains someone – or is detained – for a banquet.

[21]The fragrant candles have burnt out.

[22]Hsin-feng was the suburb of Ch'ang-an where wines were distilled.

[23]Her jade-pendant bore a pattern of millet.

[24]Reading 係 for 綹.

M

Mist from Shu flies over the rich brocade,
Rain from the gorge sprinkles her silken nightdress.[25]
She rubs the mirror, shy before Wen Ch'iao,[26]
Flees from Chia Ch'ung in his perfumed dress.[27]
A fish lies under a jade lotus-root,
Someone is held fast by a stone-lotus.[28]
She knits her blue eyebrows, mouth full of water,
From the terrace she sprays his horse's mane.[29]
The Governor lives in a winding street,[30]
The Guardian of the Royal Tombs dwells in Lin-ch'iung.'[31]

[25]Euphemisms for love-making. *Ch'ing-yung sha* was a very fine silk from Chekiang. Here it is synecdoche for 'nightdress'.

[26]See *Shih-shuo hsin-yü*, XXVII, p. 226, *Chu-tzu chi-ch'eng* edition, for the story of how Wen Ch'iao (288–329) a minister of the Chin dynasty, sent his beautiful cousin a betrothal present of a vanity-mirror.

[27]*Chin-shu*, XL, pp. 5a–b, recounts how Chia Ch'ung (217–82), a prime minister of the Chin dynasty, had a daughter who was having an affair with a handsome retainer of his called Han Shou. Ch'ung noticed that Shou's clothes bore the scent of a rare perfume his daughter used, and so discovered who her lover was.

[28]During the Six Dynasties, certain words acquired special connotations in love-poetry. 'Lotus-root' is a symbol for girl, while 'fish' stands for pleasure. In the second line, 'stone-lotus' stands for lover, and 'man' stands for woman. The secret meaning of the lines is thus: 'Pleasure was born beneath the girl's body. The woman was held tightly by the man's hands.'

[29]Suzuki says it was the custom for singing girls to spray the mane of their lover's horse with water when he left. This was probably a magical practice designed to ensure the lover's return. An alternative translation, based on the older commentaries, runs:
    'She knits her blue eyebrows, eyes full of tears,
    On the tower she sprays her hair, a horse's mane.'

[30]*Shih-chün* was a Han dynasty title meaning 'Governor'. The line is probably a reference to the Han ballad *The Mulberries by the Path*. See J.D. Frodsham, *An Anthology of Chinese Verse* (Oxford, 1967), pp. 4–6.

[31]The poet Ssu-ma Hsiang-ju was said to have held the office of Custodian of the Royal Tomb. Presumably these two lines are spoken by the girl, who is comparing herself to the modest Lo-fu of *The Mulberries by the Path* and her lover (Li Ho?) to the romantic poet, Ssu-ma Hsiang-ju. The Governor would then be a rejected admirer. See note 34 below.

A warm ball of fragrance hangs from her cassia curtains,
From brazen incense-burners, wisps of smoke.
These long, spring days, Master Wang's ways are winning,[32]
Orioles sing, so she thinks of Hsieh's languorous maid.[33]
The jade water-clock says the Three Stars shine bright,
By the Bronze Camels the five-horse carriages meet.[34]
Rhinoceros horn banishes fear from her gall,
Mercury calms the fluttering of her heart.[35]
She uses a bracelet to tell a man's destiny,
Strums her lute and sings of good luck and bad.
'The Royal Hour occurs on the Seventh Night,[36]
Your lover has a post in the Triple Palaces.'[37]

[32]The Wang family of Lin-yi county, Lang-yeh, Shantung, was one of the most powerful of the Six Dynasties period. Suzuki believes Ho is referring to Wang Hsien-chih (344–88), a scion of this clan, who is said to have had a concubine called Peach Leaves to whom he wrote poems. Yeh and Saitō prefer Wang Tzu Ch'iao, the Immortal mentioned on p. 45, note 4. In any case, this line refers to Ho.

[33]The beautiful and talented concubine of the great Minister Hsieh An (320–85).

[34]'The Three Stars': Orion. Carriages of influential people gather in the street of the Bronze Camel in Lo-yang. Another reference to The Mulberries by the Path: 'Lord Governor came from the South country. His team of five stood waiting there.' This may well mean that the girl had rejected the advances of an influential admirer in favour of Li Ho.

[35]Rhinoceros horn was taken in powdered form during T'ang, especially as an antidote to poison. It was not used as an aphrodisiac at that time. See Schafer, Golden Peaches, p. 241. Mercury was among the most important Chinese materia medica. The girl was probably taking 'silver tallow' an amalgam of silver, tin and mercury commonly used as a sedative. See Schafer, ibid., p. 256.

[36]'Royal hour' means 'auspicious time'. On the seventh night of the seventh month the Herd-boy and the Weaving Lady meet.

[37]Heaven was said to have three palaces. Hence this line must refer to Ho's post in the Court of Imperial Sacrifices. The fortune-teller is predicting that on the seventh night of the seventh month Li Ho and the girl will meet, like the Herd-boy and the Weaving Lady.

Since I had no strength, she fed me powdered mica,[38]
Sought many prescriptions from an old medicine seller.
She sent me a blue-bird bearing an amulet,
The bag was sewn with thin, red silk.
As I passed the willows in the royal park,
Beyond the bridge the palace bells stopped ringing.
When my middle-aged maid awakes in the moonlight,
She will laugh to see my painted room is empty.[39]

[38]Mica was one of the 'superior drugs' of the Chinese pharmacopoeia. It was said to lighten the body and lengthen life. See Schafer, *ibid.*, p. 178.
[39]Ho is wending his way home just before dawn after spending the night with this girl.

Five Satires

No. 1[1]

5-character: 3 rhymes

Ho-p'u has no more shining pearls,
Lung-chou has no more 'wooden slaves'.[2]
We ought to realize the powers of Nature
Are not given solely for official use.
The wives of Yüeh had not begun their spinning,
Silkworms of Wu had just started wriggling about.
When a district official came riding on his horse,
He'd a wicked face, red whiskers like a dragon.
Now in his robe he carried a square tablet,
And on this tablet several lines were written.[3]
'If it were not for the Magistrate's anger,
Would I have come in person to your house?'

The wife of Yüeh bowed to the district official,
'The shoots of the mulberry are as yet very small.
But I promise you, if you wait till the end of spring,
The silk reels will begin to spin and spin.'

[1] A satire on rapacious officials. Since the middle of the eighth century, China had agreed to take as many horses from the Uighurs as the latter cared to send them. Since each horse cost 50 pieces of silk this placed a tremendous burden upon the silk-industry. In 809 Po Chü-yi wrote a memorial estimating that some 500,000 pieces of silk had been used to buy such horses. Po Chü-yi and other poets all wrote poems sympathizing with the peasant women who had to work themselves to exhaustion to supply the tax-collectors with silk.

[2] During the Later Han dynasty, Ho-p'u county, Kwantung, was stripped of the pearls it produced by its local officials. Lung-yang, Hunan, was where Li Meng (early 3rd century A.D.), of the kingdom of Wu, planted a thousand orange trees, telling his children on his death-bed that they now had a thousand wooden slaves to produce wealth for them. (See *San-kuo chih, Wu-chih*, 3, note to the biography of Sun Hsiu.)

[3] This was a tax notice.

The wife of Yüeh made her excuses,
Her sister-in-law prepared some yellow millet.
The district official ate it, kicked over the dishes,[4]
Then sent his petty clerks into the house.

[4]Several commentators explain 踏食 ('trampled on the food') as 'ate his fill'. Saitō believes 踏 is a loan for a rare character meaning 'to bolt one's food'.

No. 2

5-character: 1 rhyme

GENIUSES don't know what it is to be young –
How the sun's chariot limps upon its way![1]
Long years of striving for a double ribbon[2]
Left me with nothing more than whitened hair.
The bluebottles have long since ceased to whine
Round Chia Yi's grave by the gates of the capital.[3]
At the Cold Food Festival, with skies awhirl,
The angry landscape seems as bleak as winter.[4]
Of the twelve emperors of Former Han
Only one deserved to be called wise.[5]
Yet even he one evening listened to fools,
And ended his fine reputation for ever.

[1]Saitō translates: 'Even geniuses cannot remain young. How slowly the sun's chariot travels!' – explaining the second line as ironical. This misses the point. Ho is arguing – from personal experience – that geniuses, who do what they *must* (while talent does what it can), find youth has passed them by while they were immersed in their work. They are so impatient to reap success, which will only come with the years, that for them time seems to crawl along. Yeats thought much the same, as is evident from his poem 'What then?' See *Collected Poems* (London, 1952), p. 347.

[2]Of high office.

[3]Chia Yi (201–168 B.C.) was a brilliant, young writer who lost favour with Emperor Wen when he was slandered by his envious contemporaries and later died tragically. 'Bluebottles' could stand for 'slanderers', as in *Song* 219. Alternatively, as Saitō points out, it could mean that bluebottles, whining round the corpse, were the only mourners for Chia Yi.

[4]The Cold Food Festival was held on the 105th day after the winter solstice, just before the Ch'ing-ming Festival. Ho visits Chia Yi's grave during the Ch'ing-ming Festival, as was the custom, and sees the landscape mirror his mood.

[5]Emperor Wen, who was stupid enough to listen to the calumnies of fools.

No. 3

5-character: 1 rhyme

THE melancholy of the Southern Mountain,[1]
Where ghostly rain falls spattering on dead grass!
Back in Ch'ang-an, this autumn midnight,
How many men have withered in this wind?[2]
I lost my way on these paths in the yellow twilight,
Blue chestnut-oaks are tossing by the road.
Moon at her height, tree-shadows dwindled away,
The entire mountain bathed in a white dawn.[3]
Lacquer torches are out to welcome newcomers,[4]
As fireflies dance over these lonely tombs.[5]

[1]Mount Chung-nan was the site of many graveyards.
[2]Some editions read: 'Spring's beauty ages under the wind's shears.'
[3]Yao believes this is a reference to Shun-tsung's accession.
[4]'Lacquer torches' – will-o'-the-wisps, generally called 'ghost fires'. 'Newcomers' – those newly buried.
[5]Yao interprets this poem as a lament for Lu Chih and Yang Ch'eng, two acquaintances of Ho's who had died in exile before the pardon granted to them by Emperor Shun-tsung (*regnet* 805) could reach them. If this poem was in fact written in 805, it must be one of Ho's earliest works.

No. 4

5-character: 1 rhyme

By now the stars have faded, heaven is high,
All nature knows another day is dawning.
Born into this world, I have to feed myself,[1]
So out of my gate I go, with burdened back.
Chün-p'ing was long gone and did not return,[2]
K'ang-pai ran away on the state highway.[3]
'What a rowdy place this is!' I think at day break.
Round the market gates, a thousand chattering men.[4]

[1]Read 已養 for 已養 with Suzuki.

[2]Yen Tsun, style Chün-p'ing, was said to have been Lao-tzu's teacher. He lived in Ch'eng-tu, Szechwan, where he told fortunes in the market-place for a living, always shutting up shop for the day when he had gained a hundred cash.

[3]Ho meant to refer not to Han Pai, style K'ang-pai (332–80), of the Eastern Chin dynasty, but to Han K'ang, style Pai-hsiu, of the Later Han. He sold medicines in the market place at Ch'ang-an, gaining such a reputation for honesty that the Emperor himself finally sent for him. K'ang, however, managed to escape on the way.

[4]Outstanding men have fled from the workaday world, leaving only a crowd of noisy nonentities behind them.

No. 5

5-character: 1 rhyme

AT the rocks' foot, bright autumn water,
At the rocks' side, thin autumn grass.
Fragrance of wild bamboo pervades my clothes,
Countless leaves drooping luxuriantly.
Over the peaks the moon returns,
Toad-light hung in a lovely sky.[1]
The fairy maid watches dew from her cassia[2]
Fall in twinkling droplets under the clouds.[3]
Chill and lonely, the gardenia drops its seeds,
A mountain crevice weeps with crystal tears.
Down below Chang Chung-wei is living,[4]
When he sits down to study, his desk falls apart.

[1]A toad was supposed to live in the moon.
[2]Ch'ang-o, goddess of the moon, with her cassia tree.
[3]Or perhaps: 'The fairy maid watches her dewy cassia,
           The lowering clouds gradually descend.'
[4]A scholar-hermit of the Later Han. Ho is referring to his own loneliness and poverty.

In the Third Month I Pass by the Imperial Travelling Lodge[1]

7-character: 1 rhyme

MOAT water, vexed with red,
Isolates the palace.[2]
Little leaves flirt with the breeze,
Mimicking palace girls.
How many springs have they watched growing old
Hidden by hanging blinds,
Locked up here for a thousand years
Of long, white days?

[1]When Emperor Hsüan-tsung stayed at the lodge, several girls had been brought in for him to spend the night with. After his departure, the girls were commanded to remain immured in the lodge for ever, even though the emperor would never return there.

[2]Yeh reads 荘 for 紅 and 蘩 for 繁.
'The palace is surrounded by a moat where prince's feather and artemisia grow.' Saitō follows this.

Following the Theme of Ho and Hsieh: Singing-girls in the Brazen Bird Tower[1]

5-character: 1 rhyme

A lovely girl pours out a bowl of wine,
The autumn landscape stretches a thousand leagues.
Stone horses slumber in the early mist,[2]
There are no words to fit such melancholy.
Faintly their singing wafts upon the wind
That rustles in the trees upon his tomb.
The tower is crushed by their long skirts,[3]
Their tearful eyes gaze at the flower-filled table.[4]

---

[1]Li Ho is here following a theme already treated by two earlier poets, Hsieh T'iao (464–99) and Ho Hsün (d. *circa* 527), during the Six Dynasties period. (See J. D. Frodsham, *An Anthology of Chinese Verse*, p. 185, for a translation of Ho Hsün's poem.) The Brazen Bird Tower in Yeh (Lin-chang county, Honan) had been built by Ts'ao Ts'ao, first Emperor of the Wei dynasty, in A.D. 210. When he died, he left instructions to his sons that all his concubines were to be immured in the mausoleum tower. Morning and evening, the girls had to bring food and wine to his bed, which stood with drawn curtains upon the topmost storey. On the first and fifteenth days of every month, the girls had to dance and sing before his bed, just as though he were still alive. Yao believes that Ho's poem is a satire upon a cruel and dissolute contemporary of his, a certain T'ien Chi-an. This seems doubtful.

[2]Stone horses lined the path to the royal tombs, which lay west of the tower. Wang understands mist as 'grass'.

[3]Because the girls are so numerous.

[4]The sacrificial table on which offerings to Ts'ao's spirit were laid.

Seeing off the Banquet Officer Ch'in
on His Military Expedition to the North[1]

5-character: 1 rhyme

MELTING our bow-glue, we fight northern nomads,[2]
On autumn sands at dawn, the din of drums.
Bearded tribesmen violate our borders,
Arrogant as rainbows arched on heaven.
Warships bear soldiers over Pa river,[3]
At Little Willow, our camp-gates open wide,[4]
The general gallops round on his white horse,
His gallant men display their virile mettle.
Their arrows shoot down threatening comets,[5]
Banners soar higher than the sun or moon.
Where mountains loom through bare-branched elms,[6]
Horses are whinnying, loaded down with armour.
Starlight fades from the far-off sky,
The short grass hugs the level sand.
Wind howls around the cloud-swathed beacons,

---

[1]Ch'in's identity is unknown. He held a post in the Office of Imperial Banquets (*Kuang-lu ssu*).

[2]*Han-shu*, LXIX, p. 16a, states cryptically: 'He who wishes to establish his power, must begin by melting glue.' Su Lin's commentary explains that glue for sticking together the sections of composite-bows was made in autumn, when the nomads attacked. *Ch'i-min yao-shu*, XC, p. 71 (*Wan-yu wen-k'u* edition, Shanghai, 1930) says: 'Glue-making ought to be carried out in the second, third, ninth and tenth months: success cannot be assured in other months.' The commentary goes on to explain that glue cannot be made successfully if the weather is either too hot or too cold. See also *Chou-li*, XLII (匠 人): 'When the bowyer makes his bows, he must select his six materials in their due seasons.'

[3]The river Pa flows through Shensi, east of Ch'ang-an.

[4]During the Former Han, Chou Ya-fu (d. 143 B.C.) had encamped at Hsi-liu (Little Willow), north-west of Ch'ang-an, while on a punitive expedition against the nomads.

[5]Comets were portents of war.

[6]Elms planted along the Great Wall.

Mud fouls the snows that fall upon Jade Gate.[7]
Many a nomad khan he has beheaded,
And planted fire in many a traitor's belly.[8]
The *T'ai-ch'ang* still enjoys his former honours,[9]
Yet has been raised to the rank of Banquet Officer.
On his precious ring a unicorn starts up,
On arrow-jars of silver, baboons howl.
Out he rides, his horse dappled with peach-blossom,[10]
Ornate silks beating against his saddle.
His arm weighed down with a dangling, gold seal,
He moistens his lips from a wine-jar of jade.
He dined on clear cheese and ant-froth wine,[11]
Washed down the purple fat with brimming cups.
His horse caparisoned with tiger-skins,
His Fish-gut sword could cleave a rhino's hide.
His fleet-foot hounds come from the Western Jung,
His slant-eyed slaves, captives from Northern Ch'i.
Dogs guard his tent where evening incense fumes,
Slaves watch his falcons through the weary night.[12]

[7]Jade Gate is a strategic point in Kansu, west of Tun-huang.

[8]Towards the end of the Later Han dynasty, the corpse of the rebel Tung Cho (d. 192) was left in the market-place with a fire burning in the fat of its belly, (*TCTC*, p. 1934). Hence our line reads literally '. . . planted fire in Tung Cho's navel'.

[9]*T'ai-ch'ang* – an officer of the Court of Imperial Sacrifices.

[10]Peach-blossom markings were a sign of a fine horse.

[11]Read 酥 for 蘇. A reference to the farewell banquet given to him by the emperor, in connection with his new appointment.

[12]All these were presents bestowed on him by the emperor. 'Fish-gut' was the name of a famous sword of antiquity. Sticks of incense were burnt to mark the watches of the night. Falcons were kept awake at night to make them hungry and fierce.

Journeying to Yellow Dragon he parted from his mirror,[13]
At Green Grave his thoughts turned to Sunny Terrace.
As Chou Ch'u slays the dragon at Long Bridge,
Hou T'iao plays mournful tunes upon her harp,[14]
He took two phoenix-wings from Ch'ien-t'ang,[15]
His wife presented him with simurgh-hairpins.
His lady plucked a branch from a jewelled tree,
A nomad boy played the tune called 'Falling Plum'.
This morning he departed, sword in hand.
Oh, when will he return, the dragon slain?[16]

[13]The last ten lines have vexed the commentators into disagreement. Presumably this couplet means that he parted from his wife when he set out for Yellow Dragon Fort in Liao-tung, and on the way took a concubine at Ch'ing-meng (Green Grave) in Inner Mongolia, south of present-day Huhehot. A broken, bronze mirror is the symbol of the parting of husband and wife. 'Sunny Terrace' refers to a line from the *Kao T'ang fu*, a poem attributed to Sung Yü, where the goddess with whom the king has spent the night mentions this spot on Mount Wu. Hence our line may allude to a clandestine love-affair. Saitō, however, believes that the line simply means that Ch'in was thinking of his wife while on his journey.

[14]While he defeats the nomads ('slays the dragon') his wife laments his absence. Hou T'iao was supposed to have invented the vertical harp at the instigation of Han Wu-ti.

[15]Presumably a reference to his taking his sons with him. But some commentators believe this refers to singing-girls from Ch'ien-t'ang, a city famous for its courtesans. Read 偕 for 階. Saitō points out that the poem has defeated all the commentators. He himself believes that it is either incomplete or else full of mistakes.

[16]Wu Cheng-tzu believes this refers to the story in *Huai-nan-tzu* about Tz'u Fei slaying the water-dragon. But Wang thinks it refers to Chou Ch'u, who slew a dragon at Long Bridge.

Written in Reply

Both 7-character: 1 rhyme

No. 1

YOUNG gentleman with the golden fish[1]
And long lined gown,
Embroidered robe, leather belt
And square-holed jade.
The spring wind follows your horse's tail
All the way,
Willow floss beats against
The palace-lady's perfume.[2]

No. 2

MARCH in Yung-chou – spring has come[3]
To the plum-blossom pool.
By the royal canal night-herons stand
In warm, white duckweed.[4]
We may well ask: 'Who is that man
Plucking flowers this morning,
Singing and beating time
Down by the wine-shop?'

[1]Officials of the third degree and upwards wore golden-fish purses at their belts.
[2]Perfume made and given to him by a palace lady.
[3]'Yung-chou': the district round the capital.
[4]The night-heron was commonly kept as a pet since its presence was supposed to avert fires.

On a Painting of the Walls of Yung-tung[1]

5-character: 1 rhyme

WHEELING, the River of Heaven, day breaking bleakly,
Crows flying up from lofty battlements.
Distant sails signpost the shores of Yüeh,
From the cold ramparts hang the swords of Wu.
Mussels are born in the chill sunshine,
Fish-eggs spurt into the white waves.
As water-flowers spray their head-bands,
With drums and flags they welcome the night tide.[2]

[1]Reading 甬東 for 角東. Yung-tung is a well-known port in Chekiang.
Since both a dawn scene and a night scene are depicted, Ho may be describing
two paintings.

[2]Sea-spray ('water-flowers') wets the head-bands of the soldiers, who are
welcoming the spirits of the tide with banners and drums.

*Bachelor Hsieh Had a Concubine by the Name of Kao-lien
Who Deserted Him for Another Man. Hsieh Tried to Make
Her Stay with Him, but Was Unsuccessful. Later She Grew
Sentimental about Him. Those of Our Party Wrote Poems
Satirizing and Vilifying Her. Later I Added Four Poems of
My Own.*[1]

All 5-character: 1 rhyme

No. 1

WHO'D ever guess that mud could dream of clouds![1]
Her hopes are dashed, the pear-blossom spring is over,
She weaves glossed silk of lotus on her loom,
Cuts out a skirt patterned with lotus leaves.
In the bright moonlight my elder sister is weeping,[2]
Thinking she meets her love by a guttering lamp.
All this even though her present husband
Has a golden fish hanging from his belt.[3]

[1]'Mud' stands for the girl; 'clouds' for her first husband.
[2]'Elder sister': the girl in question, who was, of course, no relative of Ho's.
[3]Insigne of high office.

No. 2

By a bronze mirror stands a blue-green simurgh,[1]
She puts on rouge from Yen with a purple brocade.[2]
Her blossoming cheeks are brushed with dusky powder,
Cold tears invade the corners of her eyes.
Once Emerald Jade had split the melon
Her lute of jade was played by another hand.[3]
Today things aren't the same as in the past,
What man is there dare look her in the face.[4]

[1]Suzuki believes that 'simurgh' here stands for the girl. It is more likely that her vanity-mirror was cast in the form of a simurgh.

[2]See p. 27, note 4, above.

[3]Reading 破 瓜 後 for 破 不 復 with Sung ed. A prince who had a concubine by the name of Emerald Jade was so infatuated with her that he wrote her a *yüeh-fu* beginning: 'When Emerald Jade split the melon . . .' The expression *p'o-kua* ('to split a melon'), when used of a girl, means 'to reach her sixteenth year', since the character for 'melon' can be split up into two characters which look like the graph for 'eight'. But in the strongly satirical context of our poem, the phrase also suggests the expressions *p'o-shen* and *p'o-chen*, both of which mean 'to be deflowered'. The next line of the couplet carries on this suggestion.

[4]Because the rank of her new master was so exalted. But the line might also mean: 'What man dare she look in the face (after such infamous conduct)?'

No. 3[1]

IN sequestered chamber her thoughts unchecked
Do as the bee does in the hearts of flowers.[2]
Ash lies warm by the crumbling incense-stick,[3]
Her hair spreads cool beneath blue insect-pins.[4]
As night wears on, the lamp-flame gutters low,
Soundly she sleeps in the depths of a little screen.
How sweet to dream of coupled mandarin ducks![5]
South of the walls they have stopped pounding the blocks.[6]

---

[1]This poem has been brilliantly translated by Schafer, *Golden Peaches*, p. 116.

[2]She is thinking of her former husband with as much ardour as the bee shows when honey-gathering.

[3]Aromatic candles were popular in well-to-do households. But since the lady already has a lamp in her room (line 5), the incense-stick here was presumably for sweetness rather than light.

[4]See Schafer, *Golden Peaches*, pp. 115–16, for a discussion of the *chrysochroa* beetle, whose wing-cases were used as ladies hair-ornaments and love-talismans. Yeh thinks this line shows she was not yet in bed.

[5]Mandarin ducks – ironically in this context – are a symbol of faithful love.

[6]The sound of the pounding of washing-blocks with batons had reminded her of the days of her poverty and so prevented her from sleeping. It was not so much the noise as her conscience that was troubling her!

No. 4

As a rule, she despised Sung Yü,[1]
Today she is the wife of this Wen-ying.[2]
Halberd-handles top his dragon-stands,[3]
By the cassia window he toys with a ring-handled knife.[4]
He welcomes his guests wearing a short-sleeved gown,
While sitting upright on a folding chair.[5]
Her red silk kerchief is drenched with tears,
She watches a crow perched on the painted beams.[6]

[1]Sung Yü (see p. 106, note 2) here stands for Bachelor Hsieh.
[2]Wen Shu, pet-name Wen-ying, son of Wen Ch'in of the Wei dynasty, was a general at eighteen. Kao-lien had obviously married a military man.
[3]The tops of the frames which held musical stones, drum and so on were often shaped like the handles of halberds. The uprights of such stands were ornamented with dragons.
[4]A 'cassia window' is a window with a cassia tree growing across it.
[5]To welcome guests in such a way was the height of vulgarity.
[6]Yeh's interpretation. On the beams, customarily ornamented with dragons and phoenixes, she sees only a crow, symbol of her present husband.

While Studying in Ch'ang-ku, I Showed This Poem to My Servant-lad from Pa.[1]

5-character: 1 rhyme

INSECTS were singing and the lamplight was wan,
The cold dark heavy with fumes of medicine.
You pitied the one with drooping pinions,[2]
And through his suffering went on serving him.

The Servant-lad from Pa Replies

My great nose goes with my mountain dress,
Your beetling brows suit your bitter songs.[3]
If you didn't chant those ballads of yours,[4]
Who'd know how much you hated autumn?

[1]Pa was the name of the ancient state which occupied present-day Pa county, Szechwan. The boy belonged to the Lao people. Suzuki thinks this lad may have been the boy who accompanied Ho when he wandered round the countryside writing poems.

[2]Disappointed and ailing after failing to obtain his doctorate, Ho sees himself as a defeated fighting-cock, nursing its wounds.

[3]P'ang might possibly mean 'grizzled' rather than 'beetling' or 'bushy'. Anyway, the term suggests old age. Cf. the common expression, 'P'ang-mei hao-fa' ('Beetling eyebrows and white hair'), used of old men.

[4]An allusion to Ho's 'new yüeh-fu' criticizing the government and the times. Ho seems to be hinting that writing these ballads has ruined his career.

I Take Ts'ui's Place in Seeing off a Traveller

5-character: 1 rhyme

A TRAVELLER's awning under misty willows,
Horses' hooves trampling in white.
I'm afraid my friend will suddenly disappear –
How can he bear to use his whip again?[1]

Leaving the City[2]

5-character: 1 rhyme

SPARSE cassia blossom under snow,
A crying crow, struck by a bolt, came home.
In a pool by the Pass, shadow of donkey and rider,[3]
His hat and belt hung on the Ch'in wind.[4]
It felt so good to be back home again.[5]
Yet he could only grieve he bore no seal.[6]
The woman he loved asked him no questions[7] –
But in the mirror he glimpsed her falling tears.

[1]The mist is so thick that the slightest movement of their horses will make them lose sight of each other. Read 隨 for 迄 with Suzuki.

[2]This poem was written in 810, after Ho had been refused his doctorate.

[3]The Han-ku Pass.

[4]The wind was blowing him in the direction of Ch'ang-an.

[5]Reading 誠 重 for 試 萬 里 with Suzuki.

[6]He had no official position.

[7]Ch'ing-ch'ing 卿 卿 would refer to a mistress rather than a wife. There is no indication that Ho was married.

Plant no Trees

5-character: 1 rhyme

PLANT no trees in your garden,
Trees fill the four seasons with sadness.
Sleeping alone, the moon at my southern window,[1]
This autumn seems all autumns past.

Setting out

5-character: 1 rhyme

MATS from my eastern bed are rolled away,
I'm just a misfit off on another journey.
Autumn whitens the infinite heavens,
Moon bathes the highroad running past my gates.[2]

[1]Several versions read '. . . the moon over my southern couch'. This seems poetically less evocative.
[2]Some editions read 日 for 月.

Four Poems Written after Looking at a Painting of the Chiang-t'an Park

All 5-character: 1 rhyme

No. 1

VIRIDIAN dawn in the park at Wu,[1]
And palace ladies clad in gosling-yellow,
(Switches of false hair, a touch of rouge and powder)
On horseback with pearls dangling from their belts.
On the road they point to the distant T'ai-ch'eng palace[2] –
Such fragrance from their sendal riding-skirts!
Journeying clouds drench the kingfisher carriage,[3]
Today you'd swear you saw King Hsiang himself.[4]

---

[1]The Chiang-t'an Park, 20 *li* south-east of present Nanking, had been established by Emperor Wu of Liang in A.D. 543. Anciently, this territory had belonged to the state of Wu.

[2]The T'ai-ch'eng palace was built by Emperor Ch'eng of Chin in A.D. 332. It stood near the Chi-ming temple in modern Nanking.

[3]The imperial carriage was decorated with kingfishers' wings.

[4]King Hsiang of Ch'u was notorious for his love of women and pleasure. Yeh thinks this line is a thrust at Emperor Hsien-tsung.

No. 2

JEWELLED slips under thin chrysanthemum gowns,
Banana-flowers cold with clustering dew.[1]
Hair shining like water, glossy as orchid leaves.
Heavy belts patterned with knife-money.[2]
Once the horn is warm, it's easy to draw the bow,[3]
Wearing long boots makes riding difficult.
Last night their bed-curtains were wet with tears,[4]
Now powdered faces are mirrored in golden saddles.

No. 3

YOUNG goshawks, in slanting line, with scissored wings,
Jessed to swivels of ornamented jade.[5]
Bridles dangling, filigree-patterned with millet,
Quivers studded with carved ivory.
Baboons screaming deep in the bamboos,
Night-herons standing venerably on wet sand.[6]
As palace servants light the hunting fires,[7]
Flying ashes sully lead-powdered faces.

[1]This poem continues the description of the palace ladies, who are wearing red-flowered slips under yellow gowns.

[2]Money shaped like knives was used in parts of North-east China in ancient times.

[3]Bows were decorated with horn.

[4]The ladies have been weeping because the emperor did not spend the night with them. In spite of their gorgeous attire, they are all deeply unhappy. Another thrust at the emperor?

[5]In this *vignette* the palace-ladies are seen as austringers hunting hares, pheasants and partridges with goshawks. 'Scissored wings' is puzzling. I suggest their wings look like the open blades of scissors. Jesses are straps fixed to the hawk's feet. They are attached to the leash by a swivel. See E. H. Schafer, 'Falconry in T'ang Times', *T'oung Pao*, 46 (1958) pp. 293–338, for an excellent treatise which includes a glossary of falconers' terms.

[6]See p. 124, No. 2, note 4.

[7]Suzuki amends 蠟 to 獵 on the grounds that candles would not blow ashes onto the ladies' faces.

No. 4

TEN riders clustered together like lotuses,
A red platoon all clad in palace dress.
Their scent has perfumed the Sung magpies[1]
As they tramp Black Dragon looking for their arrows.[2]
The banners are drenched, their gold bells heavy,
Over dry frost jade stirrups dangle empty.[3]
Today they painted in their brows at dawn,
Not waiting for the bell from Ching-yang tower.[4]

[1]These were black and white hounds known as 'Sung magpies'.
[2]Black Dragon Mountain (Lu-lung shan), now known as Mount Shih-tzu, stood very close to Nanking.
[3]The ladies have dismounted to search for their arrows.
[4]Emperor Wu of the Southern Ch'i dynasty (*regnet* 482–93) found that his harem could not hear the palace drum which told the hours, so he set up a bell in the Ching-yang tower to let them know when it was time to get up.

While Recovering from a Drinking-bout in the Elder Chang's House in Lu-chou, I Sent This Poem to My Fourteenth Elder Male Cousin through the Agency of a River Messenger.[1]

5-character: 1 rhyme

ONLY when autumn comes to Chao-kuan,
Will you know how cold it is up here in Chao.[2]
I tied this letter to a short-feathered summons,[3]
Cut out a long screed for a recital of woes.
Through the clear dawn I slumbered in my sickness,
While the sparse plane-trees cast fresh emeralds down.
The city crows cried from white battlements,[4]
Military bugles saddened the mist in the reeds.[5]
With turban askew, I lifted the silken curtains,[6]
In dried-up pools the broken lotus lay.
On the wooden window, traces of silver picture,[7]
On the stone steps water had left its coins.[8]

---

[1]Li Ho wrote this poem at the end of his life, while he was staying with his friend Chang Ch'e in Lu-chou. At this time hostilities had been recommenced against the rebel general, Wang Ch'eng-tsung. This explains the presence of the River Messenger, a military courier who travelled in the region south of the Yangtze bearing urgent messages.

[2]Chao-kuan was in the south: in Ho-chou, west of Han-shan county; Lu-chou was up north, in the ancient territory of Chao. Hence the marked difference in climate.

[3]A traditional name given to urgent military despatches.

[4]The battlements were white with mist.

[5]A reference to the military situation. It is possible that Ho even held a position on Chang Ch'e's staff, a fact which would explain his three-year sojourn in Lu-chou.

[6]His 'turban' was a night-cap.

[7]'Silver': perhaps traces of frost. Suzuki suggests it was the remains of a picture done with silver paint.

[8]'Coins': round patches of moss, looking like copper coins covered with verdigris were growing on the steps of the artificial hill in the garden.

The traveller's wine caught at my ailing lungs,[9]
While songs of parting rose from languid strings.
I sealed this poem with a double string of tears,
And culled a single orchid wet with dew.
The sedge is growing old, the cricket weeping,
While broken gargoyles peer from withered pines.[10]
Waking, I sit astride a horse from Yen,[11]
Dreaming, I voyage on a boat through Ch'u.[12]
Pepper and cinnamon poured above long mats!
Perch and bream sliced up on tortoise-shell![13]
Surely you can't forget the roads leading home,
To spend your youth on river-girdled isles?[14]

[9]'Traveller's wine': the wine he had been drinking while travelling. Note the allusion to his lung complaint.

[10]A little evergreen bush often found growing on the roofs of old Chinese houses, where it finds a footing in the dirt that accumulates between the ridge-shaped tiles, is known as 'roof-pine' (wa-sung). Emperor Ming of the Wei dynasty was so fond of these bushes that he had them planted on the roofs of Lo-yang. The 'tile-animals' were highly coloured ceramic beasts placed on roofs to ward off evil influences.

[11]Yen was the old name for the territory in the north next to Chao. It was famous for its horses.

[12]Chao-kuan was in former Ch'u territory.

[13]Wine flavoured with pepper or cinnamon was a southern delicacy, as were perch and bream. See Ch'u Tz'u, The Nine Songs, The Great One, Lord of the Eastern World, p. 36: And libations of cinnamon wine and pepper sauces'!

[14]Island in the Yangtze, i.e., in the south. Ho is half-playfully asking his cousin whether the delights of the south are going to prevent their reunion.

Song: Hard to Forget

5-character: 1 rhyme

LINING the road, gate after open gate.
Weeping willows droop over painted halberds.[1]
Shadowing blinds, pattern of bamboo flowers,
Somebody playing a flute in a sunny spot.
As bees go buzzing round her vanity mirror
She paints on her brows, emerald as hills in spring.
Twigs of sweet daphne, intricately interlaced,
Cover the balustrade, flowers turned to the sunset.[2]

[1]During T'ang, officials from the third rank upwards stuck painted halberds before their gates. The girl in question is clearly of good family.
[2]Sweet daphne was a symbol of constancy in love. Yeh interprets this poem as a satire on rich families and their many concubines. This seems doubtful.

The Noble Son-in-law of Chia Kung-lü[1]

5-character: 3 rhymes

IN full court-dress (robes none too long),
Flower nodding to flower on his stitched gown,
He rides his tinkling white horse,
Its head bowed down with golden trappings.

This morning perfume sickens him,
His coral pillow feels too rough,[2]
He's longing for a playful girl,
Drunk on warm sand among the reeds.

Chattering swallows tread the curtain-hooks,
A sunny rainbow emeralds the screen.[3]
When Governor P'an is in Ho-yang,
No girl puts death before dishonour.[4]

[1]For the story of Chia Ch'ung, style Kung-lü, who married off his errant daughter to Han Shou, see p. 110, note 27, above. This poem is evidently pure satire. A rich, young man, tired of his well-born wife, is off to spend the day with a singing-girl.

[2]A coral pillow was the height of luxury. The perfume that sickened our hero must have been the rare scent used by his wife, with whom he shared the pillow.

[3]Literally: 'A sunny male-rainbow . . .' The rainbow was a sexual symbol for the Chinese. The line means that the man was closeted with the girl.

[4]P'an Yüeh (d. A.D. 300) was so good-looking that women found him irresistible. He once held the rank of Governor of Ho-yang county.

Song: Drinking All Night, Asleep All Morning[1]

7-character: 2 rhymes

FLUSHED with wine she leaves her seat,
As the east grows light.
The sash at her waist is half-untied,
Under weary stars.[2]

In the willow-garden crows are cawing;
A drunken princess!
Flowers bow down beneath light dew,
Melilote's breath.
Windlass of jade and rope of silk,
Draw the dawn water,
Her powdered face, like purple carnelian,
Hot and fragrant.[3]
Drinking all night, asleep all morning,
Not a care in the world,
Beneath her curtains of southern silk,[4]
Sleeps the Emperor's child.

[1]Yao contends, rightly I think, that this ballad is a satire on the marriage of the Princess of P'u-ning, daughter of Hsien-tsung (*regnet* 805–20), to Chi-yu, dissolute son of the powerful Yü T'i. This alliance was contracted in spite of the protests of many of the more upright officials of the court. Ho is obviously hinting that the princess will be corrupted by her husband's licentious behaviour.

[2]Suzuki reads 醒 for 星 and would thus translate: 'Worn out with drinking'. This is ingenious, but unnecessary.

[3]The warmth of her face, heated by wine, brings out all the fragrance of the powder.

[4]Literally: 'silk from Ch'u', an allusion to her marriage with the son of a governor of a circuit in this region.

Written by the Tomb of Wang Chün[1]

5-character: 1 rhyme

No more Little Tungs left in the world today –
Yet still we sing of 'Dragons in the Water'.[2]
White grasses, dead beneath invading mist,
Red coils of autumn goosefoot on the earth.
Ancient writing effaced from the black stones,
The green bronze spirit-sword is broken.[3]
Ploughlands rising like scales of a fish,
Tomb's slope sharp as a horse's mane.[4]
Petals of chrysanthemum drooping, wet with dew,
Dry wormwood lying on the date-tree path.
Poignant, the harsh fragrance of pine and cypress,
How many nights wind moaned these southern fields![5]

[1]Wang Chün (206–85) played a major part in helping the Chin dynasty overcome the kingdom of Wu in A.D. 280 and thus briefly unify China. He was buried in his native place, on Mount Pai-ku, Shensi, in a magnificent tomb surrounded by a wall 15 miles long, with four entrances flanked by lines of funereal pine and cypress.

[2]'Little Tung' was Wang Chün's pet-name. Yang Hu (221–78), Prime Minister of Chin, heard a popular song about Little Tung which said that he:

'Did not fear the tigers on the shore
But only feared the dragons in the water.'

This led Yang to give Wang high office.

[3]The writing on the funeral inscription has worn away, while Wang's sword, buried with him, has rusted.

[4]The tomb and the ground around it have been ploughed over.

[5]The fields south of the tomb.

o

The Traveller[1]

5-character: 1 rhyme

An aching heart for a thousand leagues,
Sunshine warm on the rocks of South Mountain.[2]
I could not stay in the Ch'eng-ming Lodge,[3]
Growing old I'll be a guest of Lord P'ing-yüan.[4]
Four seasons away from my ancestral temple,
Three years gone by since I left my native place.
Often I sing a traveller's song, beating my sword,[5]
Sometimes, on a strip of silk, I say I'm coming home.[6]

[1]Suzuki believes this poem was written when Ho was travelling to Ch'ang-an.
Wang thinks Ho wrote it in Lu-chou. Line 4 makes this seem most likely.

[2]Probably Mount Chung-nan, near Ch'ang-an.

[3]The name used during the Han dynasty for the place where high officials
stayed while awaiting audience with the emperor.

[4]See p. 47, note 7, above. Lu-chou was situated in the ancient territory of
Chao. The Lord of P'ing Yüan, Chao Sheng, was the son of a feudal lord of
Chao.

[5]During the Warring States period, Feng Hsüan, a retainer of Lord Meng
Ch'ang of Ch'i, expressed his dissatisfaction with his lot by beating time with
his sword and singing: 'Long sword, why don't we go home?' See *Chan-kuo
ts'e*, XI, (Ch'i) 4.

[6]Letters were sometimes written on strips of silk.

After Days of Rain in the Ch'ung-yi District[1]

5-character: 1 rhyme

WHO can he be, this sad and lonely man,
Who's come to suffer autumn in Ch'ang-an?
As a young man I knew a traveller's sorrow,
Wept in my sleep until my hair turned white.
I feed my skinny nag on mouldy hay,
As gusts of rain splash in the chilly gutters.
The Southern Palace is darkened by ancient blinds,
Its sundials blank beneath a watery sun.[2]
My mountain home's a thousand leagues away,
East of here, at the very foot of the clouds.[3]
Sleeping in sorrow, my sword-case as my pillow,
In this makeshift room I dream of a marquisate.[4]

[1]This poem was written between 811 and 814, when Ho was working in the Office of Rites. The Ch'ung-yi district was the second street east of Vermilion Bird Gate, in the ninth sector of Ch'ang-an.

[2]A reference to the Department of State Affairs (the Southern Palace), which was responsible for the examination. These two lines must be understood as criticizing the blindness and stupidity of the examiners who had refused to let him sit for his doctorate.

[3]Ch'ang-ku lay to the east of Ch'ang-an.

[4]Once again Ho is hinting that he would like to give up scholarship and gain fame as a soldier.

Feng Hsiao-lien[1]

5-character: 1 rhyme

AT a bend in the river I saw Hsiao-lien
And asked her to play for me on her lute.
Though she dispelled my love-lorn melancholy,
How very little I paid her today.[2]
Her skirt hangs from a belt of bamboo leaves,[3]
Mist-hung apricot-blossom soaks her hair.
The jade feels chill, the red strings heavy,[4]
She has saddled her horses and left the palace of Ch'i.[5]

[1]Feng Hsiao-lien was a skilful *p'i-p'a* player and dancer who rose from being a bondmaid to become the favourite of Hou-chu (*regnet* 565-77) of the Northern Ch'i dynasty. After the fall of the dynasty, she fled and hid herself among the common people. But Emperor Wu (*regnet* 560-78) of the Northern Chou dynasty captured her and gave her to one of his princes. This poem must describe her plight while in hiding.

[2]Saitō and Suzuki render this as though the girl was speaking: 'For dispelling the spring-wind (=love) melancholy of others, how much have I earned since this morning?'

[3]A belt with a bamboo-leaf pattern.

[4]This almost certainly refers to her *p'i-p'a*, though Wang and Yeh contend she is talking about her whip.

[5]Read 鞍 for 鞭.

Presented to Ch'en Shang[1]

5-character: 3 rhymes

In Ch'ang-an city lives a lad of twenty
Whose heart's already so much rotten wood.
The *Lanka* sutra heaped upon his table,[2]
The *Songs of Ch'u* piled up beside his elbow.
All his life he's bowed beneath his troubles,
When twilight falls he sips a little wine.
He knows by now the way is blocked to him,
No need to wait until his hair turns white.

Ch'en Shu-sheng! – you too are poor and wretched,
Shabbily clad, toiling at rites and music.[3]
You imitate the style of Yao and Shun,
Despising your fellows for writing decadent prose.[4]
By my brushwood gates, the carriage-ruts ice over,
Elms fling gaunt shadows as the sun goes down.
You come and visit me in the yellow dusk,
Bitter seasons have etched your face with lines.[5]

[1]Ch'en Shang, style Shu-sheng, was a fifth-generation descendant of the royal house of Ch'en (*regnet* 557–89). Though he and Ho were not intimate friends, we may assume that their royal blood gave them a feeling of kinship. Ch'en was more fortunate in his career than Ho, gaining his *chin-shih* degree in 814 and later rising to high office as a Vice-President of the Ministry of Rites and Director of the Imperial Library. He became prominent in the literary circle around Han Yü. This poem was evidently written between 811 and 814, when Ho held the post of Secretary-Director of Rites.

[2]The *Lankāvatāra-sūtra* is one of the most important classics of the Ch'an (Zen) sect.

[3]Literally: 'you hoe among the sacrificial dishes'. 'Ch'u' 鉏 must mean 'work with great labour'. Suzuki says the line means Ch'en is undergoing great hardship while studying rites and music.

[4]Ch'en was an enthusiastic partisan of Han Yü's *ku-wen* movement, which aimed at driving out parallel prose and replacing it by a more classical style. Ch'en seems to have carried this to such lengths that even Han Yü complained that his style was too antique for clarity.

[5]'Ch'ing-yang' 青陽, a term for spring, here stands for Ch'en's face.

Mount T'ai-hua soars up forty-thousand feet,[6]
Sundering the earth, it towers above us all.
Not a foot of flat anywhere around it,[7]
It strikes the Ox and Dipper in a single bound.[8]
Though high officials may not sympathize
They cannot put a padlock on my mouth.
For I have taken T'ai-hua as my master,
Ensconced myself there to gaze at the white day.
Frost has warped me into a stunted oak,[9]
Whom kinder weather would make a willow in spring.
The Office of Rites has forced me from my true nature,
I look haggard and worn, like a straw dog cast aside.[10]
In wind and snow, I serve at the Altar of Fasting,
My black belt threaded through a brazen seal.[11]
The work I do is fit only for slaves and bond-maids
Who want no more than to wield a dustpan and brush.
Whenever will the eyes of Heaven be open,
And these antique swords together give a roar?[12]

[6]Mount T'ai-hua, used as a symbol for Ch'en Shang, is one of the five sacred mountains of China.

[7]Three editions read 旁古: two editions read 旁苦. Suzuki amends to 旁若 'around'.

[8]Two constellations.

[9]Literally: '. . . into a p'u-su'. This is *quercus dentata*, Th., the big-leaf oak, a tree considered useless for any purpose.

[10]Straw dogs were used for sacrificial purposes and then discarded.

[11]During T'ang, only officials of the fifth degree were authorized to wear black belts. Ho must be referring to a Han dynasty practice.

[12]Ancient swords were believed to have magical powers, among them those of flying in the air and roaring like tigers. Ho sees Ch'en and himself, with their talents unused, as priceless swords locked away forever in a box, forgotten by all. If we understand '*yung*' 庸 as 'always', we must translate: 'The antique swords are always roaring.'

Fishing

5-character: 1 rhyme

FISHING in a red canal at the autumn floods,[1]
I hoped to catch the Fairy's white silk letter.[2]
My lone cocoon tangled in water-chestnut thread,[3]
Beneath wild paddy a couple of fish lay low.[4]
Dangling a bamboo rod by a clear pool,
I let my long line trail through its emerald void.
A spring newt swung upon my bait
And pulled the little frog from off my hook.[5]
Fishing filled Master Chan with boundless joy,[6]
But plunged the Lord of Lung-yang into despair.[7]
I thought I saw upon the mist-wreathed shore[8]
A girl from Ch'u whose tears had soaked her dress.

[1] A canal red with silt from the fields, or red with flowers.

[2] The *Lieh-hsien chuan* tells the story of one Ling-yang Tzu-ming who caught a white dragon while out fishing. He was so frightened that he promptly let it go; whereupon, in gratitude, it let him catch a white fish, in whose belly he found a silken letter which contained the recipe for the elixir of life.

[3] 'Lone cocoon': silk from a single cocoon.

[4] 'Wild paddy': Indian rice (*zizania aquatica*).

[5] Following Suzuki. Yeh thinks both the newt and the frog were used as bait.

[6] Chan Ho, a character of the time of the Warring States who is mentioned in *Lieh-tzu*, was an expert fisherman, who could catch a fish as large as a cart with a single strand of silk, half a grain and a hook made from a beard of wheat. See A. C. Graham, *The Book of Lieh-tzu*, p. 105.

[7] The *Chan-kuo ts'e* carries the story of the Lord of Lung-yang, a handsome favourite of the King of Wei, who caught a dozen or so fish while out fishing, only to burst into tears. He was afraid that just as he had wanted to throw away the first fish he had caught once he had caught even bigger ones, so the king would one day wish to discard him.

[8] His own momentary disappointment at his failure to catch anything – symbol of his failure to achieve his ambitions – vanishes at the sight of the weeping girl, whose sorrows are greater than his.

Poem Presented to My Second Elder Cousin (Its
Rhymes Harmonizing with a Poem of His) When He
Stopped Being a Messenger, Sent Back His Horse and
Went Home to Yen-chou[1]

5-character: 1 rhyme

To no avail you kept your yard-long blade,
They could not use your single ball of mud.[2]
Your horse has gone back to its sandy plains,
You have come home to your native land again.
Once your sad flute played the Lung-t'ou song,[3]
Spring ashes now filter our joyful wine.[4]
Your baldric no longer startles wild-geese,
Your spur on fighting-cocks in your silken robes.[5]
Long months have passed since you returned to Wu,
But do not fret, for you'll enter Ying again,[6]
You're a peach-tree in flower, a blossoming plum!
Be sure that they will beat a path to you.[7]

---

[1]Yen-chou lay some 210 miles north-east of Ch'ang-an. Ho wrote this poem
to console his cousin at his loss of office.

[2]His talents were not used. Wang Yüan of the Later Han dynasty, once
offered 'to block up the Han-ku Pass with a ball of mud'.

[3]For the Lung-t'ou song, see J. D. Frodsham, *An Anthology of Chinese Verse*
p. 106; also p. 188, note 4, below.

[4]Lime-water was dropped into heated wine to clear it. This was called 'ash-
wine.'

[5]His cousin no longer goes hunting wearing his official robes, but watches
cock-fights at home.

[6]'To return to Wu' means 'to retire from office'. 'To enter Ying' (ancient
capital of Ch'u) means 'to assume office again'.

[7]A reference to the saying: 'Peach-tree, plum-tree do not say a word, yet
people beat a path beneath them.' Though he is living in retirement, his bril-
liance will make people seek him out.

Presented in Reply[1]

5-character 1 rhyme

You, sir, are Chang Kung-tzu himself,[2]
This lady long ago was called 'Green Flower'.[3]
Rich incense fumes in little elephants,[4]
Cawing crows pair off upon the willows.
Dew lies thick on gold-spangled dresses,
A jade tree sprawls among the empty goblets.
The man selling wine in his Lute Hall
Has just bought a flower for his back garden.[5]

[1]Suzuki believes Ho wrote this poem for a lady (the 'Green Flower' of line 2) to present to someone whose identity we do not know.

[2]Chang Fang, Marquis of Fu-p'ing, used to accompany Emperor Ch'eng of Han (regnet 33–7 B.C.) when the latter roamed round in disguise. See Han-shu XCIII, p. 9b, Po-na edition.

[3]In A.D. 359, a Fairy called Ngo Lü-hua ('Green Flower') is said to have visited the house of one Yang Ch'üan and presented him with a poem.

[4] Read 象 for 像.

[5]Ssu-ma Hsiang-ju once sold wine for a living. Later he built himself a Lute Tower. Presumably Green Flower had just become the concubine of Ho's friend, who has got drunk (the jade tree sprawled among the goblets) to celebrate.

Written on the Wall of Chao's House[1]

5-character: 1 rhyme

YOUR elder wife burns bamboo roots,
Your second wife pounds jade to powder.[2]
For winter warmth, you gather sticks of pine,
A thin haze, half-discerned, across the sun.[3]
Plane trees green with moss,
Plash of water from a stony spring.[4]
Sun on your back, you sprawl in the eastern pavilion,
Peach-blossom covering your flesh and bones.[5]

[1]Chao seems to have been a friend of Ho's who was living pleasantly in retirement.
[2]One cooks, while the other pounds rice to make flour.
[3] Reading 生 for 坐 with Suzuki.
[4]The Wu edition reads 'stone well'.
[5]Chao's skin was a healthy, peach-blossom colour.

Spring Melancholy

5-character: 1 rhyme

THE warm sun leaves me lonely and depressed,
Blossoms only sadden this Pei-kuo Sao.[1]
Elm-seeds eyed like plough-money,[2]
Willows fragile as a dancing-girl's waist.
Our baldaquins welcome the holy swallows,[3]
With flying silk we see off the shrike.[4]
Today my northern lute grows rancorous,
Quick-tongued its body of red sanders.[5]

[1]Mentioned in the *Lü-shih Ch'un-ch'iu*, XII, as supporting his widowed mother by weaving nets and making sandals. Ho also supported his own widowed mother by what he considered menial employment.

[2]In A.D. 465 a Liu Sung emperor cast irregular shaped and unpolished coins worth one-twelfth of a tael. Read 朱 for 萊. Even the elms remind Ho of his poverty.

[3]*Li-chi*, *Yüeh-ling*, 2, records that it was anciently the custom to welcome the returning swallows in the second month of spring with a sacrifice to the tutelary spirit of births and marriages. See S. Couvreur, *Li Ki. Ou Mémoires sur les bienséances et les cérémonies*, 2 vols. (Ho Kien Fou, 1913), I, pp. 341–2.

[4]A reference to a custom about which the commentators know nothing. Yeh interprets 'flying silk' as 'gossamer'. Since the shrike was a bird of ill-omen, it is not surprising to find it chased away.

[5]'Northern lute' (*hu-ch'in*) here refers not to the modern *hu-ch'in* but to an instrument like the *p'i-p'a*. This was made of red sanderswood studded with mother-of-pearl.

Immortals

5-character: 1 rhyme

STRUMMING his lute, high on a crag of stone,
Sits an immortal sylph flapping his wings.
White tail-plumes of a simurgh in his hand,
He sweeps the clouds at night from the Southern Hill.
Deer should drink down in the chill ravines,
Fish swim back to the shores of the clear sea.
Yet during the reign of Emperor Wu of Han
He sent a letter about the spring peach-blossoms.[1]

Song of Ho-yang[2]

Irregular: 3 rhymes

WHEN you dye silk clothes
Autumn blue is a difficult shade to get.[3]
Like that man from Lin-ch'iung[4]
I am not without a heart.

[1] Yao believes this poem is a satire on the self-styled Immortals who thronged Hsien-tsung's court, all promising him eternal life. Ho is pointing out that no real Immortals would ever come to court, for their place is far from the haunts of men. During Han Wu-ti's reign, those who came to court claiming that they knew that the Magic Peaches of the Mother who is Queen in the West were ready to ripen were legion. Yet they were clearly frauds, for these peaches ripen only every three thousand years.

[2] I follow Suzuki in understanding this as a poem about two singing-girls whom Ho had evidently met some years previously while passing through Ho-yang county, Honan. Yeh interprets rather differently. Ho may well have written this poem while on his way to Lu-chou in 814.

[3] 'Autumn blue' is a blue-black colour. Yeh believes the lines mean that Ho considers himself too old for a love-affair with a young girl.

[4] Reading 臨 for 藝. The poet Ssu-ma Hsiang-ju was once Magistrate of Lin-ch'iung, Szechwan.

Blossoms burn in Chung-tan city,[5]
But Master Yen is old by now.[6]
I'm sorry I let those two young girls
Pluck my heart like a spring flower.

Today, I noticed their silver plaques,[7]
Tonight, they'll beat jade pendants at a feast.
Ox-heads, a foot high![8]
You could hardly miss them, sitting there apart.
Moon rising east,
Wine circling east.[9]
Greedy mouths red on the flagons.[10]
A thousand beeswax candles shining.

[5]In Ho-yang. 渾 is here read 'tan'.
[6]Suzuki believes this might refer to Yen Hui, the favourite disciple of Confucius, whose hair turned white while he was still young. Other commentators refer to Yen Ssu, who was asked by Emperor Wu of Han why he still held the junior post of Gentleman (郎) though his hair was white. Yen explained that he had failed to find favour with either Emperor Wen (regnet 180–157 B.C.) or Emperor Ching (regnet 157–141 B.C.) Emperor Wu, touched by his story, finally promoted him. Ho sees himself as old before his time, a white-haired menial.
[7]A licensed singing-girl wore a silver plaque at her belt, inscribed with her name.
[8]Probably a reference to their hair-styles, rather than to their goblets.
[9]The host sat on the east side of the room.
[10]Wang suggests reading 沃 for 飫. 'Wet mouths red on the flagons.'

Song: An Outing among Blossoms[1]

5-character: 1 rhyme

Preface:

   On the day of the Cold Food Festival,[2] several princes accompanied by singing-girls, went on a picnic. I was one of the party. I wrote a song called *An Outing among Blossoms* which harmonized with a poem of Emperor Chien-wen of Liang (*regnet* 549–51) and gave it to the girls to play and sing.

SPRING willows on the southern path,[3]
Cold flowers degged with chilly dew.
This morning, drunk outside the city walls,
Rubbing our mirrors, we brush on our rich brows.
In drizzling mist we fret in clumsy carriages,
Red oil-cloth covers up our painted clothes.
These dancing-skirts, though perfumed, are not warm
Our faces flush but slowly from the wine.[4]

[1]'Blossoms' refers to the girls as well as the flowers.
[2]The Cold Food Day, when nothing hot was eaten and no fires were lighted, fell on the eve of the Ch'ing-ming Festival at the end of the second or beginning of the third lunar month, in early spring.
[3]Willows are traditionally connected with Ch'ing-ming Festival.
[4]Because of the cold.

Spring Morning[1]

Irregular: 1 rhyme

IN Vermilion City[2] they announce the spring
As the water-clock turns.
A sunny breeze stirs the lotuses
As it blows through the little palace.
Thin grass can just bear a comb,
Willows long as silk threads.
The Emperor of Ch'in rolls up the clothes,[3]
Swallow of Chao brushes on her powder.[4]
Sunshine caught in painted drapes,
Bees lighting on silken mats.
Flowers on the P'ing-yang rockery,[5]
Flowers in Ho-yang county.[6]
Wives of Yüeh propping up their looms,[7]
Wu silkworms spinning cocoons.
Water-chestnuts girdle the shores
Girls with fans recline by lotus-pools.
South of the Yangtze all is joy,
North of the Passes, boundless lands.[8]

[1]Lines 1 to 10 describe spring in the palace; lines 11 and 12 describe spring among the nobility; lines 13 to 16 describe spring among the people.

[2]'Vermilion City' – the palace.

[3]A reference to an old *yüeh-fu* which tells how the First Emperor of Ch'in rolled up clothes which he presented to the palace beauties.

[4]Flying Swallow of Chao (Chao Fei-yen).

[5]During the Han dynasty, the Princess of P'ing-yang built a famous rockery in her garden.

[6]P'an Yüeh, when Magistrate of Ho-yang in Honan, planted flowers and fruit-trees everywhere in the county.

[7]Placing stones on the base of their looms to keep them steady.

[8]Some editions read 恨 for 限.

The Palace of Peace and Joy[1]

5-character: 1 rhyme

By the deep well, crows rise from the plane-trees,
As the Wardrobers draw up the crystal water.[2]
Before the Prince of Shao-ling had washed his face,[3]
Long, azure waves were stirring in the vase.
When the Palace of Peace and Joy was newly built,
Its roofs were like the phoenix's outspread wings –
Circling songs, click of waxed castanets,
Tso Kuan himself to act as cup-bearer.[4]
Now green wormwood saddens these winding waters,
As mountain dogwood parts with its autumn fruits.[5]

[1] An old *yüeh-fu* ballad of this title dates from the sixth century. The An-lo Palace ('Palace of Peace and Joy') built in A.D. 223 by the Emperor of Wu, stood in north-west Wu-ch'ang county, Hupeh, south-east of Ch'ang-an. It was pulled down in 250 to provide material for building palaces in the capital, Chien-yeh. Wang's reading of this poem is greatly at variance with Suzuki's interpretation, which is based on Wu Cheng-tzu's commentary.

[2] Reading 服 for 復 with Suzuki. The Wardrobers (*shang-fu*) were ladies in charge of the royal wardrobes.

[3] Reading 王 for the erroneous 瓜 of the Wu edition. *Li Ch'ang-chi wen-chi* supports this. Hsiao Lun, Prince of Shao-ling (*circa* 507–51), was a son of Emperor Wu of Liang. If we follow Wang and Saitō, we must translate: 'Shao-ling melons, not yet washed, are swaying in the long, azure waves of the jars.'

[4] Tso Kuan was a high ranking official during the reign of Emperor Huan of Later Han (*regnet* 146–68) and hence could never have seen this palace. The line simply means: 'Even high-ranking palace officials were happy to serve in a menial capacity just to be present at these banquets.'

[5] 'Wormwood' is beach wormwood (*artemisia stelleriana*, Bess.). Mountain dogwood (*cornus officinalis*, S. et Z.) was planted near wells so that its leaves could fall into the water. This was held to keep the water fresh and pure.

Butterflies Dancing

7-character: 2 rhymes

WILLOW flowers beat at the curtains,
Under sweltering spring clouds.
Sheltered from wind by tortoise-shell screens,
His drunken eyes are dazzled by the flowers.[1]

Butterflies from the eastern neighbour
Come fluttering to the west.
Today the young man has returned,
Riding his white steed.

[1] I adopt Suzuki's interpretation of this line.

P

A Young Nobleman of Liang[1]

5-character: 1 rhyme

HE bears the stamp of the Hsiao family,
As handsome as that bullrush flower.[2]
In South Pool lotus seeds ripen,[3]
Along the Yangtze sands he waters his horse.
On royal notepaper, cold lines of silver,[4]
Coiled phoenixes across his bamboo mats.
T'ao K'an's willows shade the camp[5]
Where he writes his letters to a singing-girl.[6]

[1]Probably a satire on some young general of noble birth, notorious for devoting his time to singing-girls, rather than to military matters. The nobleman in question may have been a descendant of the royal house of Liang (502–57). It is possible, however, that he was a member of the T'ang royal house. If so, Ho would be availing himself of a literary convention to protect himself from a charge of *lèse-majesté*.

[2]Hsiao was the surname borne by the house of Liang. While pregnant with Emperor Wu of Liang (*regnet* 502–49), his mother had a vision of a supernaturally beautiful bullrush flower, which she promptly swallowed.

[3]A veiled allusion to his love-affair.

[4]A type of expensive, ornamental paper, mottled with silver, similar to the present-day *leng-chin chien* 冷 金 牋 used in calligraphic scrolls.

[5]During the Chin dynasty, the great general T'ao K'an (259–334) planted willows all over Wu-ch'ang district, Hupeh. The camp was presumably in this locality. The reference to T'ao K'an is highly ironic. Our young fop playing at soldiers, is contrasted with one of China's finest soldier-statesmen, a man noted for his integrity and austerity.

[6]Literally: 'The girl from the Kuan-wa palace' (in Wu). Here the expression means simply, 'a beautiful girl'.

Song: Planting Tree-peonies

7-character: 3 rhymes

WHEN lotus stalks are but half-grown,
Thoroughwort and asarum fading,[1]
Riding our horses, laden with gold,[2]
We're off to hoe peonies.
Water drenches fragrant mud
In their crescent pots,
After one night their green chambers
Greet the white dawn.

Lovely girls chatting tipsily,
Mist-hung gardens.
Evening petals scattered by now,
Butterflies fade.
The Prince of Liang grew old and died,
Sendal robes remain,[3]
Waving their sleeves as the breeze plays
'Zithers from Shu'.[4]
Wavering mists return in tatters,

[1]Chinese thoroughwort (*eupatorium chinense*) and *tu-heng* (*asarum blumei*).
[2]During T'ang, tree-peonies were greatly prized and very costly. The gold is for buying these flowers.
[3]Wang thinks this line means: 'The two singing-girls named Liang and Wang have grown old and departed but Silk Robes (another singing-girl) is still here.' This is forced and quite unconvincing. Ho has several poems which mention a 'Prince of Liang' – here he is clearly referring to some nobleman or other who was fond of peonies. Yeh suggests that 'Prince of Liang' was the name of a variety of peony. If so, the line would be intentionally ambiguous. 'Sendal robes' would then mean both 'silk-clad dancing girls' and 'peony leaves'.
[4]Name of a *yüeh-fu* ballad. Note how the peonies are seen as dancing girls – expensive beauties whose loveliness is all too fleeting.

Broidered awnings in shadow,[1]
Bewitching reds tumble to dust
Favoured no more.

Master T'an and the Hsieh girl[2] –
Where are they sleeping?
Moon shines bright on terrace and tower,
Swallows chatter all night.

Song: Digging a Well in the Back Gardens[3]
Irregular: 2 rhymes

OVER the well a windlass turns
Upon its bed.
Slapping of water,
Faint murmur of a lute.
What sort of love am I seeking?
That of Hsün Feng-ch'ien.[4]

O sun above the city wall,
Forever stay above the city wall!
Let a single day be as a thousand years,
And never sink to rest.

---

[1] Reading 披 for 帔. The broidered awnings, which were probably used to shade the peonies, were made of patterned silk from Shu. Yeh thinks they were made of Shu paper.

[2] The poet P'an Yüeh, whose minor name (*hsiao-tzu* 小字) was T'an-nu, is another of Ho's favourite characters. The Hsieh girl is not the fourth-century poetess Hsieh Tao-yün, but the renowned singing-girl who belonged to the great statesman Hsieh An (320–85).

[3] The title is taken from an old *yüeh-fu* ballad, dating from the Chin dynasty, whose theme is much the same as this. Love between husband and wife must be deep and inexhaustible as the well which is being dug in the back gardens of the palace.

[4] Hsün Ts'an, style Feng-ch'ien (*floruit* 3rd century A.D.) married General Ts'ao Hung's daughter because he admired her for her beauty alone, paying no attention to her character. Yet when she died he pined away for grief in just over a year. The girl wants a husband like this.

Song: Throwing off My Sadness
Written under Mount Hua

7-character: 3 rhymes

AN autumn wind blows over the earth,
The grasses die,
Mount Hua becomes a sapphire shadow
In the chill of dusk,[1]
Though I have reached my twentieth year,
I've missed my goal.[2]
My whole heart sad and withered
As a dying orchid.

Clothes like the feathers of a flying quail,[3]
Horse like a hound,[4]
Where the road forks I beat my sword
With a brazen roar.
Dismounting at a tavern I shed
My autumn gown,[5]
Wishing to pledge it for a jar
Of Yi-yang wine.[6]

---

[1]Mount T'ai-hua in Hua-yin county, Shensi, between Hsi-an and Lo-yang.

[2]Suzuki dated this poem at A.D. 810. The line would thus refer to Ho's rejection as a *chin-shih* candidate.

[3]*Hsün-tzu*, XIX, p. 22b. 'Tzu Hsia was so poor his clothes were [like the feathers of] a hanging quail. Someone said: "Why doesn't he look for an official post?" he said: "The feudal lords look down on me, so I cannot become a minister!"'

[4]It was said of Chu Chen of the Later Han that he was so poor 'his carriage was like a bird's nest, his horse like a hound'. See *Hou Han-shu*, XCVI.

[5]The 'beflagged pavilion' here refers to a tavern, not to the market-place, as some commentators would have it.

[6]Yi-yang was the old name for the county where Li Ho's family lived. It lay about 120 miles east of Mount Hua.

Deep in the jar I called on Heaven –
No clouds rolled back,[7]
The white day stretched a thousand leagues,
Cold and forlorn,
My host urged me to cultivate
Both body and soul,[8]
Nor care at all if the vulgar crowd
Made mock of me.[9]

[7]Arai thinks this refers to the story of the Immortal Shih Ts'un who jumped into a wine-pot, made it his universe and called it 'the wine-pot Heaven'. Saitō interprets this as a reference to the story of Fei Ch'ang-fang of the Later Han who met an old man with a magic wine-jar, from which the two of them could drink all day without emptying it. Fei followed the old man into the jar and learnt the arts of immortality. See *Hou Han-shu*, CXII.

[8]Arai interprets 'to cultivate heart and bones' as meaning 'to cultivate mental energy'.

[9]The character *hui* appears for the first time in this line, with the meaning 'strike at: clash'. Wang equates *t'ien-hui* (to vex) with *ch'en-hui* (to ridicule) Arai suggests *hsüan-hui* 喧 豗 (noisy).

Chʻin Kung

7-character: 5 rhymes

Chʻin Kung of the Han dynasty was a favourite slave of General
Liang Chi. He was also granted the favours of Liang's wife and
so gained the reputation of being arrogant and haughty. I looked
into this old story and wrote a long poem on this subject comparing Chʻin Kung with Feng Tzu-tu. It is also said that long ago
another poem on this subject was extant.[1]

WAVING sleeves of his Yüeh sendal gown
Greet the spring wind,
He wears a red belt figured with jade
And patterned with unicorns.
A party on top of a palace tower,
Immortals talking,
Mouth-organs playing under awnings
In thick, scented mist.[2]

Warm wine drunk at leisure,[3]
Spring spreads everywhere,
Flowering branches stray through screens,
The long, white day.
By the high windows of the double gallery
They count the cups they quaff,[4]
At midnight in the brazen bowls
Candles burn yellow.

[1]For Liang Chi see p. 199, note 1, below. Feng Tzu-tu was the favourite
slave of the Han general, Ho Kuang (d. 68 B.C.) See the poem attributed to
Hsin Yen-nien in J. D. Frodsham, *An Anthology of Chinese Verse*, p. 14. After
Ho's death, Feng took his late master's wife as his mistress.
[2]'Scented mist' – incense-smoke.
[3]Read 閒 for 間.
[4]Tallies were used at drinking-parties to keep track of how many cups each
person had drunk; so nobody could refuse another goblet on the grounds that
he had already had too many.

Wearing a short-sleeved, low-cut robe
He's teaching a parrot to talk,
In purple brocade and flaxen shoes
He treads on a roaring tiger.[5]
Burning cassia in golden braziers
He prepares for a banquet at dawn,
Up till midnight boiling clear cheese
From rare, white deer.[6]

In eternal galleries of flowering *t'ung*
He tries out a new horse,[7]
Great screens in the inner rooms
Adorned with living pictures,
He opens the gates and squanders the gold
From the emperor's private purse,
He rolls up this Yellow River,
And pours it over himself.[8]

Even high heaven was once unlucky
And split and broke.[9]
But Ch'in Kung spends his whole life
Under the flowers.
He goes off with her simurgh tooth-comb,
Nor will he give it back,[10]
Sleeps drunkenly on the Persian rugs
In the moonlit hall.

[5]Saitō points out that Liang Chi had a private zoo in his garden. Hence it would have been Ch'in's duty, as Steward of the Household, to supervise the rearing of these animals.

[6]Deer were supposed to turn white when they reached the age of 1,500 years.

[7]'Eternal galleries' – long galleries in the imperial palace. Liang Chi had free access to the palace.

[8]'Yellow River' – a river of gold from the imperial treasury.

[9]*Chin-shu*, XII, p. 12a (*T'ien-wen*) records that in A.D. 292, 303 and 361 the sky split open, due to a deficiency of the Yang element. This meant that women were playing too great a role in the government.

[10]A reference to Ch'in's intimacy with his master's wife, Sun Shou – whose comb he takes as a love-token.

'Ballad on the Boys by the Walls of Ancient Yeh'
An Imitation of Wang Ts'an's Satire on Ts'ao Ts'ao[1]

3-character: 4 rhymes

In the city of Yeh
Dust rises at dusk.
Those drawing black balls
Behead civil servants.[2]

Brambles for whips,
Tigers for horses,
Running in packs
Under Yeh's walls.

Swords to cut jade,
Sun-shooting bows,[3]
Presented to whom?
Why, to the Minister.

[1]Yeh (in Honan) was the capital set up by Ts'ao Ts'ao.

[2]*Han-shu*, XCV, Biography of Yin Shang:
'In Ch'ang-an . . . gangs of young men from the villages killed officials.
They were bribed to avenge grievances and held meetings at which they
drew lots with pellets. Those who drew red pellets killed military officials,
those who drew black pellets killed civil officials, those who drew white
pellets looked after the funeral ceremonies (for those of their number who
were slain). Within the walls dust rose at evening. People surged about,
robbing and looting. Dead and wounded lay around the streets.'
In 815 rebellious generals had sent assassins to Ch'ang-an who had murdered
the Chief Minister, Wu Yüan-heng. This poem probably refers to the murder.

[3]*Lieh-tzu*, V, p. 21a, mentions a sword which could cut jade as if it were
mud, which the Western Jung presented to High-king Mu of Chou.
Huai-nan-tzu, VIII, p. 5a, tells of the bow with which the legendary archer
Yi shot down nine suns.

Propping his chariot-hubs
Boys from west of the Pass.
Sweep the roads with perfume!
The Minister comes home![4]

[4]Just as the Chief Minister Ts'ao Ts'ao gained power at the expense of the Emperor, so men like Huang-fu Po gained power at the expense of Hsien-tsung.

Singing of Yang's Purple Inkstone with a Green Pattern[1]

7-character: 2 rhymes

STONE-CUTTERS of Tuan-chou, subtle as spirits,
Trod the sky, hewed purple clouds with polished knives.
How true they trimmed the well of stone
That brims to its lips,
Darkly soaked with cold stains –
Blood of Ch'ang-hung.[2]

Silken curtains warm in daytime,
Ink-flowers in spring,
A floating froth in airy bubbles
Fragrant with pine and musk.[3]
Ink dry or oily, thick or thin,
Its feet stand firm.[4]
Just a few inches of autumn sunshine
That dusk cannot touch.
Often the round brush whispers on
The stone, forever new.
Master K'ung's ink-stone, broad and stubborn,[5]
Was no match for this.

[1]The mountains of Tuan-chou, in present Kao-yao county, Kwangtung, produced a famous purplish stone, veined with green, used for making fine inkstones. Arai argues, unconvincingly I think, that the title should read 'Egg-shaped Inkstone' for 'Purple Inkstone'. We do not know who Yang was.

[2]The green stains on the stone remind the poet of Ch'ang-hung's blood, which turned to emerald jade. See p. 49, note 8, above.

[3]Ink was often made with pine-soot mixed with musk.

[4]Chinese ink is in block form and has to be rubbed on the stone, which must therefore be firm enough to cope with all types of ink. See R. H. van Gulik, 'A Note on Ink Cakes', *Monumenta Nipponica*, XI, 3 (1955), pp. 84–100.

[5]An inkstone, said to have belonged to Confucius, was preserved in the sage's tomb-temple in Shantung.

Thoughts in Her Chamber[1]

5-character: 2 rhymes

NEW cassia-crescent like a lady's brow,[2]
The autumn gusts blowing down little emeralds.
Sound of the traveller's wheels leaving our gate,
Jade simurgh-bells tinkling intermittently.[3]

Wind-blown dew drops on the moonlit verandah,
The courtyard bleak and lonely in the dawn.
Who could endure such loneliness?
Lying awake, I listen to the crickets' tears.[4]

Dawn in Shih-ch'eng[5]

Irregular: 3 rhymes

THE moon is setting over Great Dike,[6]
Up from the parapet fly the roosting crows.
A fine dew soaks the crimson spheres,[7]
Their cold scent clears the drunken fumes of night.

[1]Ostensibly the poem deals with a lady, lying awake in her room alone and neglected, as her husband sets out on a long journey. Yao considers these verses a comment on Li Ho's own unhappy position.

[2]Literally: 'New cassia like moth-eyebrows'. Wang believes that this refers to the new leaves of the cassia tree. But what is a cassia doing budding in autumn? The cassia must be the cassia-tree in the moon. Yeh points out that the line also means: 'The lady's moth-eyebrows are like new cassia.'

[3]Bells in the form of the mythical simurgh were attached to horses' bridles.

[4]'Crickets': *holochlora brevifissa*.

[5]The whole atmosphere of this poem suggests a *tz'u*. Mo-ch'ou, heroine of many a southern folksong, lived in Shih-ch'eng, in Chung-hsiang county, Hupeh.

[6]Perhaps the Great Dike mentioned on p. 28 above.

[7]'Crimson spheres': flowers.

Lady and Herd-boy cross the River of Heaven,[8]
Misty willows cover the coign of a wall.
A noble guest lingers, tears off his satchet[9] –
She knits the emerald smudges of her brows.

Spring curtains of cicada-wing gauze,[10]
Half-seen,
The bed awaits, vaguely patterned,
With golden braid.[11]
Goose-down flying in front of the curtains,
Light willow-fluff,[12]
There are no words for spring sorrow,
Try as you may.

[8]At dawn on the seventh night of the seventh lunar month the Weaving Lady and the Herd-boy must part again, after their brief tryst.

[9]Older commentators believed this referred to the story of a guest of King Chuang of Ch'u, who was imprudent enough to dally with one of the King's ladies when the candles blew out during a banquet and had his cap-strings torn off. The King then ordered all his other guests to tear off their cap-strings before the candles were lighted again, so as not to disgrace the man. Saitō adopts this explanation. But this story has nothing to do with our poem, as Wang points out. The girl's lover, leaving her at dawn, has given the girl his scent-sachet as a keepsake.

[10]'Spring curtains': curtains aglow with spring sunlight.

[11]Yin t'i hua: 'bearing an indistinct pattern' rather than 'patterned in a transparent medium'.

[12]Wu edition reads 鶒. Li Ch'ang-chi wen-chi reads 鶒.

Lament That the Days Are So Short

Irregular: 3 rhymes

FLYING lights, flying lights,[1]
I pledge you a cup of wine.
I do not know if the blue heavens are high,
The yellow earth is rich,
I only see cold moon, hot sun,
Both come to plague us.
Eat bears and you'll grow fat,
Eat frogs and you'll grow thin.[2]
Where is the Spirit Lady?
Where the Great Unity?[3]

East of the sky stands the Jo tree,[4]
Under it a dragon with a torch in its mouth.[5]
I'll cut off the dragon's feet,
And eat the dragon's flesh.[6]
The morning will not come back again,
Night will not stay.
So old men will not die,
Nor young men weep.
Why should we swallow yellow gold,
Or eat white jade?[7]

[1]Sun and moon.

[2]Bears' paws were a rich man's delicacy: frogs were eaten by the poor.

[3]The Spirit Lady was worshipped by Han Wu-ti. See *Shih-chi*, XXVIII, p. 46. The Great Unity was the supreme deity of the Taoist pantheon.

[4]The Jo tree is a mythical tree in the far west (not the east) the foliage of which gives off a red glow at sunset. See *Shan-hai ching* XVII, p. 4b.

[5]*Ch'u-tz'u*, *The Heavenly Questions* (*T'ien-wen*), p. 49: 'What land does the sun not reach to? How does the Torch Dragon light it?' Wang points out that Ho was mistaken in these allusions, since the Jo tree was not in the east, nor the dragon beneath the Jo tree, but in the gloomy abyss of the north-west.

[6]Perhaps the feet of the dragon that drew the chariot of the sun?

Who is Jen Kung-tzu
Riding a white donkey through the clouds?[8]
Liu Ch'e lies in the Mao-ling tomb,
Just a pile of bones.[9]
Ying Cheng lies in his catalpa coffin –
What a waste of abalone![10]

Second Year of Chang-ho[11]

Irregular: 4 rhymes

COILED clouds above our fields,[12]
A soughing wind.
Ears of wheat like brushes,
Millet like corn.[13]

For every old man in the Pass
A hundred jackets,
Officials east of the Pass
Never shout for taxes.

---

[7]Elixirs of life.

[8]Not the Jen Kung-tzu of *Chuang-tzu*, XXVI, but some other unidentifiable Immortal.

[9]Emperor Wu of Han, an assiduous seeker after immortality, was buried in the Mao-ling tomb. Liu was his family name, Ch'e his personal name.

[10]Ying Cheng, another ardent searcher for immortal life, was the notorious First Emperor of Ch'in. He died while on a journey, so his attendants, anxious to conceal his death until they returned to the capital, filled the carriages with abalone to hide the smell of the corpse.

[11]An old *yüeh-fu* title. The second year of the *Chang-ho* period (A.D. 88) was an unusually prosperous one. This poem is an idyllic picture of peasant life, so far removed from the brutal realities of Ho's own time that I suspect his intent was satirical.

[12]'Coiled clouds' – auspicious five-coloured clouds.

[13]The seeds on the panicled millet (*shu*) are as numerous as those one finds on ordinary millet (*su*).

Strong, young oxen plough in spring
The rich, black earth.
Bullrushes grow in thick clusters
By veins of water.
Since they have courteously
Returned our land-tax,[14]
We can spend a hundred cash
On strolling lute-players.
We roam in springs' radiance,
White flowers on the hillsides,
Burn incense in the wild woods,
Call spirits down to the mats.

We worship the spirits to win long life
For the Emperor,
Till the thread of the Seven Stars snaps
And the Moon Goddess dies.[15]

[14] I follow Wang. Suzuki reads 鉏 for 租. 'Other people come to help us plough our fields.'

[15] A characteristically disturbing image which one would have difficulty in finding in any other Chinese poet. The Seven Stars (the Plough) and the Moon Goddess (here called Heng-o) will perish in their turn. Ho's cosmology is markedly Buddhist.

Returning to Ch'ang-ku in Spring[1]

5-character: 3 rhymes

I STARTED studying when I reached my teens,[2]
Regretting I had left my plans too late.
Before Chang Chün earned his official carriage
This Yen-tzu's hair turned prematurely white.[3]
The net of Heaven, though truly wide and high,[4]
Trammelled this stubborn man in endless trouble.
My eyes had feasted upon sweet delights
My homeless heart found bitter as the smartweed.
Then came the fiery clouds of March and April,
Their peaks and crags whelming and toppling.
Who hung on high that bowl of crimson jade,
Flooding the eastern sky with reddest fire?
In that hot spring I raised my parasol,
Buds on the roadside elms still rabbit-eyes,
My brain on fire, my sickness on my face,
Gall filled my mouth, cramp twisted my guts.
There in the capital my heart was shattered,
Even in dreams I rarely saw my home.[5]

[1]This poem, written when Ho had returned to Ch'ang-ku after his examination failure, falls into three sections. The first deals with his life in Ch'ang-an; the second with his journey home; the third with his sojourn in Ch'ang-ku. Stylistically, the poem is very close to some of Han Yü's verses, as Yeh points out.

[2]Literally: '. . . when my hair was bound up'.

[3]During the reign of Emperor Wu of the Former Han, Chang Chün became an official at the early age of eighteen – just the age when Ho failed to enter the bureaucracy. Yen Hui, a disciple of Confucius, found his hair had turned white when he was still young. Hence the couplet reads: 'Before I had a chance to become an official at eighteen, my hair had turned prematurely white.' Suzuki reads 聲 for 髮.

[4]'Net of Heaven' – the examination system.

[5]He must have lingered on in the capital till the spring of 810, probably recovering from his sickness. Then a spell of unseasonably hot weather drove him to seek the shelter of his home, in the cool of the country-side.

My brakes released outside the Eastern Gate,
Sky and earth stretched infinite before me.
Green trees were burgeoning atop Mount Li,[6]
A flowery wind invaded the Ch'in roads.
The palace towers, in dazzling disarray,[7]
Unfurled in painted scrolls on peaks and crags.
Tender, green leaves, rondures of scarlet blossom,
Weeping and smiling, strewn along my way.
Down to that plateau perfumed breezes wafted,[8]
Saddle and horse glittered in ornate splendour.
But I rode alone, in a hencoop of a cart,
Aware that I was clean out of the fashion.
Deep in my heart Substance held talk with Shadow.
Could I be happy journeying all alone?
Surely I could not lay aside my burden,
I'd tried to be a swan, but lost my luck.[9]
Under the gloomy shades of Mount T'ai-hua,[10]
Where ancient cypresses plant soldiers' banners,
I rode past dragons' hides strung out in lines,
And ever-fluttering wings of kingfisher-blue.[11]
Though faint and weary from my wayfaring,
The scenery still wrung a smile from me.
Flowering vines caught at my curving yoke,
Thin, silken mist shrouded the sunken trail.[12]
A fine, young man – a fine, young failure too –
I'm home to bring my aged mother shame.
Listening to a sutra, I pace beneath great trees,

---

[6]Mount Li lay east of Ch'ang-an.
[7]The terraces of the Ch'ing-hua palace, on the slopes of Mount Li.
[8]Wealthy travellers hasten down the road, their perfume scenting the breeze.
[9]Reading 鶪 for 鶴 with Suzuki.
[10]Mount T'ai-hua was famous for its cypresses, stretching in a row for eleven li.
[11]'Hides' and 'wings' – the bark and leaves of the cypress trees.
[12]Or: '. . . shrouded the distant borders'.

Reading a book, I walk by a winding pool.
I realize I'm no tiger loosed from cage,
Rejoice to be a panther veiled in cloud.[13]
Stringed arrows bring the birds of Han to earth,[14]
Fish-baskets catch the dace of the River Hsiang,[15]
This narrow path leads to no broad highway,[16]
Why must a man fret over petty things?

[13]The *Lieh-nü chuan* mentions a black panther who stayed up among the
rain and clouds of Mount South for seven days without coming down for
food, in order to soak its fur and pattern it. (. . . *erh ch'eng wen-chang*) – Ho is
punning on the expression *ch'eng wen-chang*, which can also mean 'compose
literary works'. He is no tiger fighting his way savagely through an official
career, but a literary panther, willing to suffer solitude and privation on his
Mount South (the hill near his family estate) for the sake of his verse.

[14]Read 繢 for 繪.

[15]Officials have to go north (like the bird of Han), or south (like the dace
in the Hsiang) during the course of their career. All of them are caught in the
snares of the world, from which Ho has escaped.

[16]Suzuki reads 落 for 路.

Ch'ang-ku[1]
(A Poem Written on the Twenty-seventh Day
of the Fifth Month)

5-character: 1 rhyme

PADDY fields at Ch'ang-ku, in the fifth month,
A shimmer of green just tops the level water.
Distant hills rise towering, crag on crag,
I grieve for their crumbling green, fearing they'll fall.[2]
Dazzling and pure, no thoughts of autumn yet,[3]
A cool wind from afar ruffles this beauty.
The bamboos' fragrance fills this lonely place,
Each powdered node is streaked with emerald.
The long-haired grass lets fall its mournful tresses,
A bright dew weeps, shedding its secret tears.
Tall trees form a bright and winding tunnel,[4]
A scented track where fading reds sway drunkenly.
Swarms of insects carve at the ancient willows,
Cicadas cry from high sequestered spots.
Long belts of yellow arrowroot are dangling,[5]
Purple rushes criss-cross narrow shores.
Stones coined with moss lie strewn about in heaps,
Plump leaves are growing in glossy clusters.
Level and white are the wave-washed sands,

---

[1]This poem was written two months after the previous poem, sometime in late June. Two editions lack the sub-title, which occurs in *Li Ch'ang-chi wen-chi*. Ho is describing the country around Ch'ang-ku (Fu-ch'ang county, Honan), where the Ch'ang-ku river flows past the foot of Mount Nü-chi (Maiden's Table).

[2]A reference to Mount Nü-chi.

[3]Arai reads 秋絲 for 秋思.

[4]An obscure line. Suzuki translates: 'Caves in the coign of the mountain rise up in stories around me.' I have followed Arai.

[5]'Yellow arrowroot': so called because it yields a yellow dye.

Where horses stand branded with green characters.[6]
At evening, fishes dart around joyfully,
A lone, lean crane stands stock-still in the dusk.
Down in their damp, mole-crickets chirp away.
A muted spring wells up with startled splash.
Crooked and winding, Jade Purity Road,
Where the Spirit Maiden dwells among orchid blossoms.[7]
Cotton-moss winds around the stones in the stream,
Crimson and purple, mountain fruits hang down.
Small cypresses with leaves like layers of fans,
Plump pines oozing essence of cinnabar.
A singing stream runs on melodiously,
Catalpas on its banks droop glowing grain.[8]
An oriole chants the song of a girl from Min,[9]
A waterfall unrolls like satin from Ch'u.
Wind and dew bring smiles or sorrow to flowers
That blossom or wither among the lines of caves.
Tangled branches leap from the stony heights,
Small-throated birds chatter by an island spring,[10]
The feet of the sun have swept away all shadows,
New-risen clouds open their ornate deeps.
Silent and still, these oppressive summer days,

[6]Government horses were all branded. Suzuki suggests the brands were green with age.

[7]Most commentators think this means the road to the Temple of the Spirit Maiden of Orchid Fragrance, the tutelary deity of Mount Nü-chi. Suzuki disagrees, believing that the road led to a shrine dedicated to Ch'ih-ying, Princess of Yü-chen (Jade Purity), daughter of Emperor Jui-tsung (*regnet* 662-90: 710-2), who was a well-known Taoist deity. In that case 'Spirit Maiden' would refer to Yü-chen, not to the tutelary deity of the mountain.

[8]Reading 楸 for 秋 with Suzuki. The seed-pods of the catalpa (*mallotus japonicus*) look like ears of grain. Yeh understands 秋 as 'ripe wheat'. 'The ripe wheat on the dike droops its glowing head.'

[9]Read 閩 for 関. Min is the old name for Fukien province, where the speech of the aborigines was thought to sound like the song of birds.

[10]Suzuki reads 鳥 for 島. This is not borne out by *Li Ch'ang-chi wen-chi* and seems forced.

Yet a west wind whispers of a cooling air.
His face, nurtured on jade, is stilled in sleep.[11]
Burns fragrant olive on the Heavenly Table.[12]
Her robes of mist are fluttering in the night,
He drowses on Her altar, pure of dreams.
The roosting simurghs grow old, awaiting the Emperor's carriage,
The pepper-walls of the ancient palace are ruined.[13]
Yet several of the bells still tinkle faintly,
Arousing this wandering courtier to desolate thoughts.
Dark creepers twine about the scarlet keys,
In dragon-curtains lurk the mountain trolls.
Flowering tamarisk clings to emerald brocades,[14]
These scented quilts served nobles long since dead.
No songs now stir the dust on wormy beams.
Where dancers' silk is festooned like long clouds,[15]
This precious land is cut in broidered pieces,
Our villagers prize truth and righteousness.
No sound of pestles is heard when calamity comes,
No evil rites are used to drive off plagues.
The fish-skinned oldsters, virtuous and kind,[16]
The horn-haired children, modest, quick to shame.[17]
The county justices have nothing to do,
No loud-mouthed tax collectors call on us,
In bamboo groves we find our writing paper,[18]

[11]Reading 服 with *Li Ch'ang-chi wen-chi*. Emendation is unnecessary. Taoists ate jade to ensure longevity.

[12]These lines describe the Taoist priest in charge of the shrine.

[13]A description of the Fu-ch'ang palace, originally built by the Sui (589–618) and rebuilt in 657, the ruins of which lay to the east of the valley.

[14]Probably *tamarix chinensis*. Suzuki calls it 'purple willow' and thinks the line refers to the patterns on the brocade quilts.

[15]Reading 絲 for 綠.

[16]The name 'globe-fish backs' was given to those over ninety, since their skin was like that of a globe-fish.

[17]The hair of young children was braided into horns.

[18]Bamboo-slips were an ancient writing material.

Our stony streams attract the hook and line.
Winding rivers girdle us with water,
Banana leaves curl round like paper from Shu,
Light from the peaks is a dazzling crepe collar.
Scenery savoured alone brushes away my cares.
Our fountains run with the wine of Governor T'ao,[19]
Our maids moon-browed, like Master Hsieh's singing-girl.[20]
Away in the distance booms a lonely bell,
High in the sky, wings a solitary bird.
Rose-mist pinnacles, blood-red towering peaks,
Perilous torrents roaring as they contend.
A pale moth floating in an emerald calm,[21]
A veiled moon saddened by a hint of shadow.
Its chilly light flows over streams and shores,
Among these hills, my thoughts grow infinite.
The fisherman's boy lowers his nets at night,
Frosty birds soar up on misty wings.
On the pool's mirror, slippery spittle of dragons,
And floating pearls spat out by fishes at play.
Wind in the jasper-cased lutes of t'ung trees,
Envoys of firefly-stars to the Brocade City.[22]
The willows let long, light green sashes fall,
Bamboos aquiver are short flutes playing.
Round the foot of the rocks, green mosses creep,

[19]The poet T'ao Ch'ien (365–427) was a renowned toper.
[20]The favourite concubine of Hsieh An (320–85).
[21]'A pale moth': the waning moon floating in the emerald calm of the water,
looks like 'moth-eyebrows'.
[22]During the reign of Emperor Ho of the Later Han (regnet 88–106) two
imperial messengers, travelling in disguise to Szechwan, stopped for the night
at the house of a certain Li Ho (not to be confused with our poet) and were
astonished to discover that he knew who they were. He explained that two
'messenger-stars' (shooting-stars) had just appeared in Szechwan, hence he was
expecting them. Ch'eng-tu, Szechwan, is called 'City of Brocade' because of
the beauty of its surroundings. Our line means: 'The fire-flies are darting to
and fro, round one of the messengers whom another Li Ho once saw.'

Reed-shoots are peering from the cinnabar pond.
While tossing whirlpools sport with the shadows of sky,
The hands of ancient junipers grasp the clouds.
The mournful moon is curtained with red roses,
Thorns of the fragrant creeper catch at the clouds.
The bearded wheat lies level for hundreds of leagues,[23]
Leisured carriages in front of a thousand shops.[24]
This man from Ch'eng-chi, now a servant of others,[25]
Would like to emulate Master Wine-sack's ways.[26]

[23]Literally: 'for hundreds of *ching*'. A *ching* is one square *li*.

[24]Suzuki reads 秉 for 乘. 'Leisurely handfuls of grain (left for the gleaners).' This seems forced.

[25]The Li family came from Ch'eng-chi county, Kansu.

[26]'Master Wine-sack skin' (Ch'ih-yi Tzu-p'i) was the name taken by the great statesman Fan Li (*floruit* 5th century B.C.) when he retired to Ch'i after helping Yüeh defeat Wu. *Ch'ih-yi* was the name given to a skin wine-sack carried in the attendant chariot of the emperor. Ho means he should like to retire to Ch'ang-ku – but only after achieving high office.

Lament of the Brazen Camels[1]

5-character: 3 rhymes

AT the end of the third month, out of office and poor,
I went to my eastern neighbour in search of flowers.[2]
Who was it wrote a farewell song to spring?
The brazen camels lament on the banks of the Lo.

South of the bridge are many riders on horseback,[3]
The northern mountain is girdled with ancient graves.[4]
While men are quaffing cups of wine,
The camels sit and mourn ten million springs.

Useless to toil away in this life of ours,
It's only a wind-blown candle in a bowl.[5]
Tired of seeing peach-trees smile again,[6]
The brazen camels weep as night comes on.

[1]Brazen Camel Street in Lo-yang derived its name from two small bronze
camels placed on either side of the street. Since these animals are mentioned
in a late third-century work, they must have been standing there for several
hundred years by Ho's time. The point of this poem, I think, is that while
men generally lament the shortness of life, conventionally symbolized by
spring blossoms, immortal beings like the camels find life intolerable because
it repeats itself endlessly. This is yet another of Ho's anti-Taoist poems. Another
layer of meaning may perhaps be uncovered beneath this. The *Chin-shu* relates
that So Ching (239–303), realizing that rebellion was about to overthrow the
dynasty at any moment, pointed to these camels and prophesied that they would
soon be overgrown with thorn-thickets. Ho may well be hinting that unless
the power of the eunuchs is checked the same fate will befall the camels once
more. This would be another reason for their weeping.

[2]An ambiguous phrase, since 'to hunt for flowers' generally means 'to go
looking for prostitutes'. This fits the ironic temper of the poem. For 'eastern
neighbour' see p. 32, note 4, above.

[3]The T'ien-chin bridge. A fashionable quarter.

[4]Actually Pei-mang, a hill north of Lo-yang, used as a burial ground.

[5]In Chinese temples today one sees candles set in bowls to protect them from
draughts.

[6]'Smile' was a conventional epithet for blossom during this period.

I Journey from Ch'ang-ku and Arrive at Lo-yang through the Rear Gate[1]

5-character: 1 rhyme

IN the ninth month, the great wilderness is white,
And azure peaks rear up their autumn portals.[2]
In the bitter cold of the tenth month's ending,
Snow and sleet confound both dawn and dusk.
The sky stays steely-grey throughout the day,
My heart feels like the clouds that clog the air.
Along the road, wind blows a thousand leagues,
The wild bamboos are scarred with snaky venom.[3]
From stony ravines, the sound of freezing waves,
A cock crows out in the cold of a clear dawn.
I keep pushing on till I reach my house in the east,[4]
Turn loose my horse, then rejoin my old neighbours.
My eastern neighbour's personal name is Liao,
In our district he carries on the line of Hsin.[5]
The money on my staff is not for wine,[6]
I need it for a visit to this fellow.
At first I wanted to go south to Ch'u,

[1]Ho must have written this poem in 811, while on his way to take up his post in Ch'ang-an. On his way there, he stopped for a while at his house in Lo-yang and consulted a fortune-teller.

[2]Earlier commentators believed this line referred to two gates in Lo-yang. I have adopted Wang's interpretation.

[3]The frost and ice on the bamboos look like congealed venom, drawn from the snakes by the cold.

[4]Could this have been his house in the Jen-ho quarter, near the Ch'ang-hsia gate?

[5]Hsin Liao was an officer of the state of Chin during the Spring and Autumn period, who prophesied good fortune for a man threatened with disaster. See *Shih-chi, XXXI.*

[6]An allusion to Juan Hsiu (270–311), an eccentric character whose biography in the *Chin-shu* states that he always carried a hundred cash tied to his staff when he went out, so that he could go and get drunk in any wine-shop.

Now once again I am heading west to Ch'in,
As for the king called Hsiang and Emperor Wu,[7]
Both of them wanted to stay young forever.
I have heard tell that to the Orchid Terrace,
Sung Yü's soul will never return again.
Among twin rows of characters in blue and light-yellow,
Torpid insects have eaten the autumn rue.[8]
What of my future among the towers of Ch'in?
Will it be my fate to carry firewood there?[9]

[7]Both King Hsiang of Ch'u and Emperor Wu of Han were noted for their love of literature.

[8]These four lines refer to Ch'u. Sung Yü was a famous writer of *fu*-poems, who had accompanied King Hsiang in his festivities at the Orchid Terrace. Now his works, bound in light yellow and placed in blue bags, have been eaten by bookworms, in spite of the rue placed there to drive them away. Ho is saying that the great literary tradition of the South has vanished.

[9]'Since literary merit no longer counts for much, what sort of menial position will I be given in Ch'ang-an?' 'To carry firewood' also means 'to suffer poverty'.

On the First Day of the Seventh Month
at Dawn I Enter the T'ai-hang Mountains[1]

5-character: 1 rhyme

IN just one night autumn invests the hills,
Fragrant dew bathes dodder and royal-grass.[2]
New bridges cling to cloud-hung slopes,[3]
Seasonal insects cry in dewy groves.
By now I'm far from the south of Lo-yang,[4]
How can I lie snug in my Yüeh quilt?[5]
The rock's breath chills me to the bones,[6]
The ageing sedge looks like short arrow-heads.

[1] This poem was probably written in 814, when Ho was on his way to Lu-chou. Autumn began on the first day of the seventh lunar month.

[2] A difficult line of which several interpretations have been put forward One commentator says it means: 'The reeds are suddenly wet with fragrant dew.' I follow Wang who says 蒙 is dodder and 葇 is 王芻. (arthraxon ciliaris, Beauv.).

[3] 'Bridges' – actually plank roads (棧道) laid up the side of a mountain. See the illustration in Dai Kanwa jiten, VI, p. 6115.

[4] Ch'ang-ku lay south-west of Lo-yang.

[5] One edition reads 禽 'bird' for 衾 'quilt'. Some commentators understand 禽 as 'bird-attracting fruit' 來禽果 (apple) and interpret it as meaning: 'For whom will the Yüeh apples (in my garden at home) ripen (since I am not there this autumn)?'

[6] 'Rock's breath': mist and clouds, believed to emanate from mountains.

Autumn Cold
A Poem Sent to My Twelfth Elder Cousin, the Collator[1]
5-character: 1 rhyme

SHUTTING the gates, I feel the autumn wind –
My loneliness is due to our long parting.
Beneath a white sky the great wilderness stretches,
A killing blast sweeps the wide heaven and earth.
Shining dew weeps over withered orchids,
Cry of insects sounds out night and day.
In my cold room the candle-stump burns dim,
My red silk curtains tattered by the wind.
I open my books to the old scent of rue,
Sing resentfully now your handsome face has gone.
For a hundred days we have not seen each other,
Bright flowers face in this bitter season.
Of all my brothers, who worries most about me?
I already have the letter you sent to me.
Clad in blue jacket, riding a white horse,[2]
You send your drafts up to the Eastern Gate-towers.
In my dream we are laughing together –
Then I wake to a half-moon over my bed.
Endless my thoughts, like a bracelet on my wrist,
My sorrows run wild like spreading arrowroot.[3]

[1]See p. 25, above.
[2]Officials below the ninth grade wore blue robes.
[3]*Song 2.*

Mowing Grass and Setting Our Nets[1]

Irregular: 4 rhymes

In cloak of brocade,
And broidered suit,
How busily you drink and peck,
Feeding your fledglings!

East of the dike, ripe grain lies flattened
By wind and rain,
Don't listen to the decoy bird
West of the dike![2]

Men of Ch'i have woven nets
Limpid as air,[3]
Strung them out in the wild fields'
Level emerald.[4]
Silken nets spread far and wide,
Without shape or shadow,
Run foul of them, your head will wear
A scarlet wound.

Who gathered this gay greenery
Of moxa leaves?[5]
You cannot guess at the cunning trap
Hidden within.

[1]This was the title of one of the eighteen *Drum, Flute and Bell Songs of Han*. Ho seems to have thought 艾 had its usual meaning of 'moxa' here. Actually it stands for 刈 'to mow'.

[2]Reading 逐 for 信 with Suzuki.

[3]Ch'i was famous for its silk.

[4]Reading 田 for 春 with Suzuki.

[5]The nets were camouflaged with leaves.

Music Rising to the Clouds[1]

Irregular: 2 rhymes

FLYING fragrance, running reds –
It seems spring fills the sky.
Flowery dragons coil and writhe,
Up to the purple clouds.[2]
Some three thousand palace girls,
Living in golden rooms,
Fifty-string zithers sounding out
To the shores of the sea.[3]

The Heavenly River is shattered –
A road of silver sand.
The Ying girls at their loom
Cut misty, white silk,[4]
Then sew their dancing gowns.
On the first day of the eighth month
They dance before their lord.

[1]Emperor Wu of Liang wrote seven *yüeh-fu* ballads under this generic title. This poem deals with a celebration in the palace on the first day of the eighth month.

[2] Presumably the smoke of incense rising to the clouds.

[3]The *se* had fifty strings.

[4]Ying was the clan name of the Ch'in royal house. The girls are likened to the Weaving Lady from the Milky Way (the Heavenly River).

Mo To Lou Tzu[1]

5-character: 3 rhymes

FROM Jade Pass to the Golden Man,[2]
Is twenty-four thousand leagues.
Wind swirls sudden clouds of sand
Over the waters of Liao.[3]

A white sky, water like raw silk,
Our armour's double thread broken.
'May no hardship mar your journey!'
A fading crescent over the Wall.

Northern mists rising in chill of dawn,
Nomad horses mincing on little hooves.
The travellers come to the sundering stream,
The river Lung parts them, stretching east and west.[4]

[1]The title is untranslatable. This was originally a non-Chinese *yüeh-fu*.

[2]From Jade Gate, Kansu, to the territory around Kara-nor, where in 120 B.C. the Han general Ho Ch'ü-ping (145–117 B.C.) captured the Golden Man, an image worshipped by the king of the Hsiu-ch'u. See *Han-shu*, LV, p. 7b. Suzuki understands 金人 as 'Brazen Immortal' – synechdoche for Ch'ang-an.

[3]The Liao river in Liao-tung.

[4]The Lung-t'ou river is in Shensi, nowhere near Liao-tung. The reference here is to the old ballad *Lung-t'ou Song*, which begins:

'The flowing waters of Lung-t'ou,
Come pouring down from the mountains,
I brood upon my loneliness,
Blown by the wind through this wilderness.'

Ballad of the Savage Tiger[1]
4-character: 1 rhyme

No one attacks it with a long lance,
No one plies a strong cross-bow.
Suckling its grandsons, rearing its cubs,
It trains them into savagery.
Its reared head becomes a wall
Its waving tail becomes a banner.
Even Huang from the Eastern Sea,[2]
Dreaded to see it after dark,
A Righteous Tiger, met on the road,[3]
Was quite enough to upset Niu Ai.
What good is it for that short sword
To hang on the wall, growling like thunder?
When from the foot of T'ai mountain
Comes the sound of a woman weeping,
Government regulations forbid
Any official to dare to listen.[4]

[1]A satire on oppressive government, of which the tiger was the symbol. See Margaret South, 'Li Ho and the New *Yüeh-fu* Movement', *Journal of the Oriental Society of Australia*, 4.2 (December 1966), pp. 49–61. Caught between the Central Government and the warlords, the people are harassed as though by tigers.

[2]Huang Kung, of Tung-hai, had magical powers which enabled him to control snakes and tigers. Unfortunately for him, he lost these powers through drinking to excess and was eventually killed by a tiger. See *Hsi-ching tsa-chi*, III, p. 1a, *Ssu-pu ts'ung-k'an* edition.

[3]The *chou-yü* was a white tiger with black markings. It appeared only when a state was perfectly governed. It would not tread on grain nor eat living things. Niu Ai was a duke turned were-tiger, who ate his own elder brother. Ho is pointing out that some tigers are worse than others.

[4]*Li-chi*, III, 2, tells how Confucius found a woman weeping at the foot of Mount T'ai. Though her whole family had been killed by tigers she refused to leave the district, because there was no oppressive government there. This caused Confucius to remark that an oppressive government was more savage than any tiger.

R

Ballad of the Rising Sun[1]

Irregular: 3 rhymes

THE white sun sets below the K'un-lun range,[2]
Its rays so many silken threads unravelled.
In vain it shines upon my sunflower heart,[3]
It never lightens up a traveller's sorrow.

To where the Yellow River curves and winds,
The sun comes wheeling down from its full height.
I've heard the sun comes out of Sunny Valley,[4]
But never seen it settle in the Jo-tree.[5]

Why do you smelt the rocks,
Melt men away?[6]
If Yi could bend his bow and shoot an arrow[7]
They why could he not hit the sun-crow's foot,
So that the crow would never fly again,
So that the fire would never move at all?[8]
Why must the flame of dawn grow dim at dusk?

[1]This *yüeh-fu* is akin to the ninth of the nineteen *Sacrificial Songs of Han* entitled *Jih ch'u ju* (*Rising and Setting of the Sun*).

[2]A mythical mountain in the extreme west of China, said to be the gateway to heaven.

[3]The sunflower, which follows the sun (a symbol for the emperor) in its course, is an emblem of loyalty.

[4]The valley where the sun rises.

[5]A mythical tree in the far west, whose branches give out a red glow in the evening.

[6]*Ch'u Tz'u, The Summons of the Soul* (*Chao Hun*), p. 104: 'And ten suns that come out together, melting metal, dissolving stone.'

[7]When the ten suns of the Fu-sang tree which the sun climbs as it rises, came out together during the reign of Yao, Yi, the Archer, shot down nine of them, so saving the earth from conflagration.

[8]Adopting the version found in *Wen-yüan ying-hua*, 13 vols. (Taipei, 1965), III, p. 1194. The usual text reads: 'Then why could he not hit the sun-crow's foot so that it would not stir for a long time. Why should the flame of dawn grow dim at dusk?'

Bitter Bamboos: A Tiao-hsiao Ballad[1]

Irregular: 2 rhymes

A WORD or two about the days
When Hsüan-yüan reigned.[2]
Ling Lun cut bamboos
Four-and-twenty of them.
Ling Lun gathered them
Upon the hill of K'un.
Hsüan-yüan ordered him
To halve them, making twelve.
Thus Ling Lun regulated
Musical pitch,
And with this Hsüan-yüan
Ordered the Primal Breaths.[3]

---

[1]Saitō emends the title to 調 嘯 引 on the grounds that Ho's ballad has nothing in common with the T'ang 調 笑 引. This latter form was composed of six lines (4–6–6–6–4–6 characters), with three rhymes in couplets, with the fifth line repeating and inverting the last two characters of the fourth line. The bitter bamboo (*phyllostachys bambusoides*) was used for making flutes.

[2]'Hsüan yüan' – the personal name of Kung-sun Hsüan-yüan, the legendary Yellow Emperor, supposed to have ascended the throne in 2697 B.C. and to have reigned for a century.

[3]*Lü-shih Ch'un-ch'iu, Ku-yüeh* (*Chu-tzu chi-ch'eng* edition, p. 51) says the Yellow Emperor sent his minister Ling Lun to a valley north of the K'un-lun mountains. Here he cut the bamboos from which the twelve pitch-pipes were made, thus creating music and regulating the cosmos.

When the Yellow Emperor
Ascended into heaven,
Three-and-twenty pitch-pipes
Followed in his train.
Only a single pipe remained
For men to play,
Yet since they lacked virtue
This pipe was not for them,
So it was buried deep
Within the shrine of Shun.[1]

Lyric for the Duster Dance[2]

Irregular: 5 rhymes

SONGS of Wu maidens rise to the heavens,
Across the sky unhurried clouds go drifting.
And yet one day the emerald moss must grow[3]
Outside these gates where horse and carriage throng.

This goblet brimmed with Wu-ch'eng wine,[4]
Will spur you on to live a million years.
Better than Emperor Wu in his ornate tower,[5]
Gazing at dawn on a clear, cold sky
And sipping dew from flowers.

[1]During the reign of Emperor Chang of the Later Han (*regnet* 75–88), a scholar named Chi Ching found a white jade pipe under the shrine of the legendary Emperor Shun in Leng-tao (east of Ning-yüan county, Hunan). See *Feng-su t'ung-yi*, VI, p. 5a, *Ssu-pu ts'ung-k'an* edition.

[2]The duster-dance, which originated in Wu during the period of the Three Kingdoms (220–80), was performed with a feather-duster or fly-whisk. Ho's lyric is another satire on Emperor Hsien-tsung's quest for immortality.

[3]Suzuki thinks the moss will grow on the graves of those who now throng the gates.

Suppose the sun stood always in the east,
Its heavenly radiance never in decline?
By eating cinnabar you may become
A serpent riding a white mist,
A thousand-year old turtle in a well of jade.[6]

Can't you see yourself transformed to snake or turtle
For twenty centuries,
Dragging your life out, year after year,
On the grass-green dikes of Wu?

Eight trigrams on your back,[7]
Blazoned 'Immortal'.
Your cunning scales,
Your stubborn armour,
Slimed with a fishy spittle!

[4]A famous wine from Wu-hsing county, Chekiang.
[5]The Shen-ming tower where the Brazen Immortal stood. See p. 65 above.
[6]The text is corrupt here. Read 龜 (turtle) for 土 (earth) in both cases with *Yüeh-fu shih-chi*.
[7]The shell of the turtle was supposed to have been the original source of the eight trigrams of *The Classic of Changes*.

Song: Sitting through the Night[1]

7-character: 2 rhymes

CLATTER and clatter of horses' hooves –
But who will visit me?
My eyes watch the Northern Dipper stand
In the River of Heaven.
The west wind ripples my awning of gauze,
Kingfisher-green.
As leaden flowers bloom on my face,
I knit blue brows.[2]

For you I rose and sang my song,
Long thoughts of love.
Outside the screens, in bitter frost,
All falls and flies.
The shining stars are glittering
On the eastern bounds.
Red mists of dawn come creeping forth
From the south-east shores.
Now Master Lu has ridden away
On his dappled horse.[3]

[1]Title of a *yüeh-fu* first written by the fifth-century poet, Pao Chao. A woman waits in vain through the night for her lover to come.

[2]'Leaden flowers'; face-powder. Read 蛾 for 娥.

[3]Lu Yü, style Kan-yü, was a well-known poet of the Ch'en dynasty (*regnet* 557–89). See p. 55, note 9, above.

Song for Vertical Harp[1]

Irregular: 1 rhyme

Oh, where are you off to sir, with your wine-jug?
Ch'ü P'ing drowned in the Hsiang,
Don't be like him![2]
Hsü Yen plunged into the sea –
He was really a fool![3]
There are mats of sedge upon your beds,
Fish in the bowls.
Your elder brother lives in North Village,
Your eastern neighbour has a young sister-in-law,
Millet and Indian rice grow thick
In the fields round the dike,
Flecked with light foam, the cloudy wine
Fills all your wine-jars.
Come eat the millet,
Drink the wine
Oh, what are you trying to do!
Why are you rushing wild-haired into the water?
Your brother and the girl are weeping bitter tears.

---

[1]This song is based on a ballad of depressing banality which runs as follows:
  'Sir, do not ford the river!
  Now you've gone and forded the river!
  Into the water you've sunk and drowned –
  What are we to do?'
Ho has improved on this considerably by using the device found in *The Summons of the Soul* (*Chao Hun*) in the *Ch'u Tz'u*, where a sick man is recalled to health by reminding him of the joys of life. Even so, our poem seems singularly uninspired. For the vertical harp, see p. 10, note 1, above.

[2]Ch'ü P'ing – Ch'ü Yüan, the reputed author of the *Li Sao*, is said to have drowned himself in the river Mi-lo, a tributary of the Hsiang, in 278 B.C.

[3]Mentioned in the *Hsin-hsü* of the Han writer Liu Hsiang (77–6 B.C.) as having drowned himself by walking into the sea carrying a stone towards the end of the Chou dynasty.

Mount Wu Is High[1]

Irregular: 1 rhyme

A CLUSTER of emeralds
Piercing high heaven!
Over the Great River's swelling waves
The goddess trails her mist.
The King of Ch'u's soul sought a dream
In a bitter wind.
In dawn wind and flying rain,
Grow coins of moss.
Jade Beauty has been gone
A thousand years,
Amid lilac and Szechwan bamboos
Old apes are wailing.[2]
Her ancient shrine is close to the moon's
Chill toad and cassia,
Pepper flowers shed scarlet petals
Among drenching clouds.[3]

---

[1]One of the eighteen *Drum, Flute and Bell Songs of Han* bears this title. Mount Wu, a famous twelve-peaked range, rises up on the northern banks of the Yangtze and stretches from Szechwan to Hupeh. It was on this mountain that Jade Beauty, daughter of the legendary Scarlet Emperor, was buried, thus becoming its tutelary deity. King Huai of Ch'u (*floruit* 3rd century B.C.) once spent the night with her, not knowing who she was. When she left him she told him that in the morning she took the form of clouds on Mount Wu, in the evening she marshalled the rain. Huai's son, King Hsiang, had the same experience.

[2]Literally: 'amid lilac and Ch'iung bamboos . . .' Lin-ch'iung is in Szechwan. Saitō understands 丁香 as 'cloves'.

[3]The pepper-tree is a native of Szechwan, a place Ho had never visited. Either he was unaware that its flowers are white, not red, or else the line means: 'Pepper-tree petals and scarlet fruit fall through drenching clouds.'

Down in P'ing-ch'eng[1]

5-character: 4 rhymes

HUNGRY and cold we stand here in P'ing-ch'eng,
Night after night, on guard by the shining moon.
Our keen-edged swords have lost their flowers of jade,[2]
Our hair is falling out in the Gobi wind.[3]

Where endless desert merges with white sky,
We see, far-off, red banners of the Han.
They sit and play short flutes in their green tents,
Mist soaks the painted dragons on their flags.

We climb up on the walls as dusk is falling –
Is something moving out there in the gloom?
A wind is blowing, stirring the dead weeds,[4]
Our half-starved horses whinny in their stalls.

We'd like to ask the brass who built this place
Just how many thousand miles from the Pass we are.[5]
We're sick of seeing men sent home dead in bundles,
Better die in battle and be planted under a lance.[6]

[1]P'ing-ch'eng was a northern border outpost in present Ta-t'ung county, Shansi, close to the Great Wall. The Han settlement of this name lay east of the T'ang fort. In 200 B.C. Emperor Kao-tsu of the Former Han was besieged in P'ing-ch'eng, which became the scene of a great battle.

[2]Reading 利 (sharp) for 別.

[3]*Hai* stands for *Han-hai* – the Gobi.

[4]The *p'eng* or tumbleweed.

[5]The Han-ku Pass was regarded as the gateway to China.

[6]The bodies of men who had died of cold, hunger or disease were sent back home for burial, wrapped in horse-hides. (This served the purpose of accounting for the skin of every horse that died; horses, as government property, being more valuable than men.) Those who died in battle were buried on the spot with their halberds stuck upside down on their graves.

Pleasures South of the Yangtze

7-character: 2 rhymes

GREEN mist over the River,
Cold waves rising
Skywards, crag is heaped on crag,
Jagged red rocks.[1]

Wind on water, clouds on shore,
Ancient bamboos.
From the darkening beach a rush-sail seems
Just a strip of cloth.
We have a thousand gobies,
A hundred kegs of wine.
Sprawled flat among the wine, we see
Green southern hills.
Catches of Wu, ballads of Yüeh –
Our songs never stop.
Over the River a cold jade is pasted,
Round as a ball.[2]

[1] Sunset clouds.
[2] The moon.

Joys of the Rich[1]

7-character: 10 rhymes

A YOUNG, owl-shouldered nobleman
Just turned twenty,[2]
Teeth like cowries,
Scarlet lips.

Rainbow-spirited,
Could drink like a rain-jar!
Galloping homewards at night
Past watchmen calling the hours.

He'd go straight to the Palace galleries,
Wander through the Pepper Apartments.[3]
Motley furs and golden rings
Gleaming with ornate patterns.[4]
Laughing and flirting in jade halls
With girls from gold houses,
Playing, mimicking under the stage
The Han-tan singing-girls,[5]
Singing and telling stories,
The perfect ladies' man.
All brocade sleeves and embroidered face
He came to the emperor
Who presented him with ten bushels of pearls
And a pair of white jade rings,
Bestowing on him a new, gold seal
Dangling from a purple sash.
Resplendent!

[1]Though actually directed at some contemporary of Ho's, this poem is
ostensibly a satire on the infamous Liang Chi (d. A.D. 159), one of the richest
and most powerful men in China during the closing decades of the Later Han.
Liang owed his rise largely to the fact that his sister was the Consort of Emperor
Shun (*regnet* 125–44). After Shun's death, Liang poisoned his successor and put

Horses flying past!
Rivers of people!
Nine Ministers, Six Officers,
Eyes fixed on his shoes.
Did he want the sun and moon to spin?
He turned his palm around.
Or did he want a river?
He drew a line on the ground.

His towering, high-cornered hat
Seemed to cut the clouds.
As he hurried along at dawn,
Rattling his sword,[6]
Cleaving the purple mist.
He would give mere lictors a thousand yards
Of embroidered silk,
And present a thousand pounds of gold
To household servants.

the government in the hands of his sister as Regent. Not until 159 did the young Emperor Huan (*regnet* 146–68) become powerful enough to overthrow Liang and his party in a coup that resulted in the execution of dozens of Liang's adherents and the dismissal from office of over three hundred high officials. Prior to this, Liang had been emperor in all but name for close on fourteen years. He and his wife, Sun Shou, lived in splendour in Lo-yang, vying with each other, so we are told, in vice and luxury. See Liang's biography in *Hou Han-shu*, XXXIV, pp. 14b–25a.

[2]Liang's biography described him as 'a man with an owl's shoulders and a wolf's eyes'. Both are symbols of cruelty and oppression.

[3]'Pepper Apartments' – the palace of the Empress, his sister.

[4]Highly unorthodox dress, especially when worn at court, indicating Liang's contempt for Confucian propriety.

[5]Han-tan (Hopeh), the capital of the ancient state of Chao, was famous for its singing-girls.

[6]The meaning of the expression 竦 劍 ('upright sword') is disputed by the commentators. I follow Saitō.

Around the twelve gates of Lo-yang
His mansions sprawled,
Through warm, spring air to the sapphire sky
The slow smoke crawled.
Golden door-rings threw back the sun's
Dazzling red light.
Brazen dragons, mouthing rings,
Writhed locked in fight.
On perfumed mats his jewelled girls
Lounged drunkenly,
Merman-pongee netted his casements
Invisibly.
He'd dine on a phoenix from Cinnabar Hill
When he wished to 'rough it',[7]
As for *potage aux petits macaques*,
He'd never touch it.[8]

Golden toads with gaping mouths
Burnt fragrant, orchid candles,
Singing-girls in battle-array,
With jangling armour.
Nobody knew if the blossom-rain
Had fallen at night,[9]
Only that spring grass grew more lush
By the terrace pools.

---

[7]'Cinnabar Hill' – a place mentioned in the compendium of travellers' tales, the *Shan-hai ching*, as the haunt of the phoenix. To eat one of these auspicious birds would be the height of barbarism and vulgar opulence. Compare the proverb: 'To burn a lute to cook a crane.'

[8]Literally: 'Macaques as big as a fist were not worth eating.' Macaques were a Szechwan delicacy.

[9]'Blossom-rain' – heavy downpours that strip the blossom from the trees at the end of spring. They were too busy carousing to notice the rain.

Clamour of strings and pipes encircled
The gaping heavens,
The sound of Hung Yai's flute came stealing
From the azure void,[10]
A single arrow shot at the welkin
Pierced two tigers,
They held the reins, let their steeds gallop on
Among the clouds,
Thunder from a rainless sky!

Wild sleeves criss-cross like bamboos,
Flute-girls were dancing,
Singers from Wu, like green parakeets
Just learning to talk.
He was wealthy enough to fill a cave
With purple gold,
Yet asked for presents of new costly rabbits
Burnt with his brand.[11]

Three empresses
Fifty colonels,
Seven noblemen,
A pair of generals –
All from his family.
Though these once gorgeous clouds dislimned
And flew away,
Translated to our capital
They brought us spring today.[12]

---

[10]Hung Yai hsien-sheng was an Immortal who had once been known as
Ling Lun. He was said to have cut the bamboos from which the Yellow Emper-
or made the twenty-four musical pitch-pipes. See p. 191, note 3, above.

[11]Hou Han-shu, XXXIV, p. 19a, recounts that Liang had a collection of
rabbits in his park which he guarded zealously. Over ten people were put to
death for having killed some of these animals, in ignorance of the prohibition.

[12]Throughout this poem Ho has followed Liangs' biography in the Hou
Han-shu. Only this last line makes it clear that this is not just an historical exercise but a satire.

Let's Drink Wine

Irregular: 3 rhymes

Hsi Ho gallops his six steeds,[1]
Days and nights leave us no leisure.
Chasing the crow to Mount Yen-tzu's bamboos,[2]
He flogs his horses with a Coiling Peach whip.[3]
Ju Shou no sooner breaks the kingfisher willows,
Then the Green Emperor creates red orchids again.[4]
Millions of years have rolled by
Since Yao and Shun,
And no king halted his chariot more than a moment.
Green coins, white jade-rings cannot buy time.
We should be merry, make the most of the present.
Turtle-soup and bears' paws – why bother with them?
Let's drink the North Sea out of flagons,
Cross-legged on South Mountain,
Sing loud and long
To the low lilt of flutes,
Bestowing gifts of tattoo gold[5]
For the amorous glances of singing-girls.
This is life at its best!
Why struggle to fathom the mind
Of the Creating Power?[6]

[1]Hsi Ho is the charioteer of the sun.

[2]A three-legged crow lived in the sun. Yen-tzu was a mountain where the sun set.

[3]Legend said that a peach-tree with roots 3,000 *li* long grew on the summit of Mount T'ao-tu. On top of the tree was a golden cock which sang when the sun shone on it.

[4]Ju Shou is the spirit of autumn. The Green Emperor is the spirit of spring.

[5]'Tattoo gold' – fine gold from the south where the tattooed aborigines lived.

[6]Why worry about the future?

Let's urge each other to drink,
Drink without stopping.
May the Emperor's great name
Endure without end!
His sons and grandsons spread abroad
Like arrowroot on rocks!

From Lo-yang to Ch'ang-an
Stretch lines of carriages.[7]
Liang Chi's ancient mansion![8]
The old gardens of Shih Ch'ung![9]

[7]I adopt the *Wen-yüan ying-hua* reading in preference to Wang's text which reads: 'Carriages come to Ch'ang-an in an endless stream.' Since both Liang Chi and Shih Ch'ung lived in Lo-yang, not Ch'ang-an, the *Wen-yüan ying-hua* text is clearly preferable.

[8]For Liang Chi, see p. 199, note 1, above.

[9]Shih Ch'ung (249–300) was a millionaire infamous for his extravagance and cruelty. His estate, Golden Valley Garden, lay just outside Lo-yang. Ho is obviously thrusting at some of his degenerate contemporaries, perhaps at officials and eunuchs notorious for their rapacity.

Delights of the Jasper Pool[1]

Irregular: 3 rhymes

HIGH-KING Mu
Urged on his dragon-decoys,[2]
Eight bridles jingling
As they drove round the world.[3]
Gods of five planets swept the earth for him,[4]
Thick clouds rolled back.

Upon the high gates left and right
Sun and moon were door-rings,
On all four sides rich carvings
Rose in blood-red tiers.
Dawn and dusk the mists kept dancing,
Drooping their tails.
Limpid as a river, pure as the sea,
The Mother Goddess's face,
Painted with red and brushed with green –
The Sunset Pool![5]
Clothed in clouds, adorned with jade,
She descended K'un-lun mountains,
Fluttering pennons like pine-trees,
Carriage-awnings like wheels.
The metal wind of autumn brought up the rear,[6]

[1] Reading 瑤 池 樂 with Wang. Suzuki and Saitō agree. Yeh prefers the original title 瑤 華 樂.

[2] 'Dragon-decoys' – heavenly horses, believed to be related to dragons, which their presence would attract.

[3] *Lieh-tzu*, III, recounts the story of High-king Mu of Chou, who drove his team of eight famous horses round the world. When he came to the K'un-lun mountains, the Mother who is Queen in the West feasted him by the Jasper Pool. See p. 71, *Twenty-three Poems about Horses*: No. 7; A. C. Graham, *The Book of Lieh-tzu*, p. 64.

[4] The Five Emperors who govern the Five Regions of the universe and reside in the Five Planets.

[5] Literally: 'The Pool of Yü', where the sun bathed after it had set.

[6] Metal was the element associated with autumn in the Han system of correspondences. Hence the 'metal wind' is the west wind.

The clear bright breeze of spring was in the van.
Eight horse-bells, ten carriages,[7]
Tall as gathering clouds.
Jade cups and jewelled mats
Degged with sweet dew,[8]
Black Frost and Scarlet Snow
Were not worth a mention.[9]
'I want to give you
Dyed Willow, Perfumed Plum,
And Lead-flower Water
To wash your very bones.[10]
Here I shall sit with you
While you grow immortal.'

[7]Since there were eight horses there should have been sixteen bells, not eight. Cf. *Song* 178, 2: 'The eight bit-bells tinkling', which refers to a team of four.

[8]The sweet dew sent down by Heaven to reward a king of great virtue (*te*).

[9]Second-class elixirs of life mentioned not in the *Han Wu Nei-chuan* (*Shuo-fu*, VII) as all the commentators assert, but in the *Han Wu-ti Nei-chuan* (*Tao-tsang*, 137, pp. 7a–b). The terms *hsüan* 玄, (black: mysterious) and *chiang* 絳 (scarlet) are not used to denote the colours of the pills but rather to hint at their astrological significance. *Hsüan* stood for the north and *chiang* for the south.

[10]The goddess is addressing the king. 'Perfumed Plums' and 'Dyed Willow' seem to be fanciful names for elixirs. Li Ho probably invented them himself since they do not occur in Taoist literature. Lead and cinnabar mixed in water formed an elixir known as 'Lead-flower Water'.

Cold up North[1]

1-character: 2 rhymes

ONE quarter lowers black while three turn purple,
Ice vaults the Yellow River, fish and dragons die.
Tree-bark three feet thick splits into patterns,[2]
Chariots of a ton or more travel on the flood.

Frost-flowers on the grass, big as silver pieces,
No brandished blade could penetrate this sombre sky.
Whirling in a raging sea the flying ice-floes roar,
Soundless hang mountain waterfalls, rainbows of jade.

[1]Yao believes this is a satire on the Armies of the Divine Plan, which had grown so used to soft living under their eunuch commanders that they had no chance of standing up to the Tibetan invasion of 812, when the barbarian armies staged a winter campaign in Kansu. All this seems rather far-fetched. Two old *yüeh-fu* bear the titles *Pei-shang hsing* and *Pei-shang p'ien*.

[2]Some commentators would amend 'three feet' to 'three inches', citing a passage from the *Han-shu* to support this.

Reflections on the Ancient Terrace of Liang[1]

7-character: 3 rhymes

TERRACE and pool of the Prince of Liang
Rear out of empty air.
The waters of the River of Heaven
Fly down to them at night.[2]
In front of the terrace, mortised jades
Form scaly dragons.
Green-powdered bamboos sweep the sky,
Grieving, damp with dew.

To the chime of bells he drank his wine,
Shot arrows at heaven.[3]
Golden tigers crowded his furs,
Dappled with spurted blood,[4]
Dawn after dawn, dusk after dusk,
He mourned that the seas spun round.
To a long rope he tethered the sun,
To fill his years with joy.

---

[1]The *Hsi-ching tsa-chi* says that during the Former Han Prince Hsiao of Liang constructed a magnificent palace and a park for his pleasure in Sui-yang, Honan. In the park, which extended for several hundred *li*, stood the Yao-hua palace and the Goose Pool. This poem is yet another example of Ho's obsession with the theme of the inexorability of time. The prince could not stay the course of the years for all his wealth. Now nothing is left of his palace but ruins; it has dissolved into air as suddenly as it seemed to spring out of it. The Wu edition reads 愁 for 意.

[2]The Milky Way seems to pour down on to the terrace, whose ruins stand out starkly against the night sky.

[3]A stock example of impious behaviour, taken from a legend about an early emperor who shot at a skin bag filled with blood and hung on high, claiming he was shooting at Heaven. There is, of course, no record of the Prince of Liang having behaved in this way. The bells were musical instruments.

[4]His fur robes were embroidered with golden tigers.

Lotus flowers' clotted crimson
Faded with fall.
Orchids' faces wept endless tears,
Parting from spring.
On reedy isles the migrant geese
Announced spring's return.
By the wild lands' desolate waters
Vast autumn gleamed white.[5]

[5] Read 湟 for 篁.

Do not Go out of Your Gate, Sir![1]

Irregular: 2 rhymes

HEAVEN dark,
Earth barred up.
Nine-headed serpents devouring our souls,[2]
Snow and frost snapping our bones.
Snarling dogs, barking
Hunt us down,[3]
Licking their paws, greedy for the flesh
Of the man with an orchid girdle.[4]
Once God sends a chariot to bear you away,
Your misfortune will end.
Your sword adorned with stars of jade,
Your yoke of yellow gold.

[1]An enigmatic poem. The point of the title, I think, is that the official career has become so dangerous that one is safest in retirement. Yao's guess that this poem may have something to do with Han Yü is probably correct, since Han's strict principles were always involving him in trouble. The difficulty is that it is impossible to translate the poem correctly without knowing what it is about. My very tentative interpretation is as follows: 'One of Ho's friends (Han Yü?) is menaced by vicious enemies. All his troubles will end with his death, which will paradoxically enough be his real reward. (This is a very un-Chinese idea, neither Confucian nor yet Taoist, which reveals Buddhist influence on Ho's thought.) Ho himself is in a similar plight, being menaced by dangers from every side. Like Yen Hui, his hair has turned white while he is still young. Is he to meet with the same fate as Pao Chiao, a man of strictest principles who came to a miserable end? Yet we must not despair at seeing virtue so shabbily treated. What looks to us like an undeserved death, is in fact Heaven's way of sparing the good from further suffering. If you doubt the truth of my words, think of Ch'ü Yüan, who found inspiration in his despair.'

[2]The 'bears and serpents' 熊 虺 of our text is almost certainly a variant of the 'nine-headed serpent' (雄 虺 九 首) of the *Ch'u Tz'u*, *Chao Hun*, p. 104:
'And the great Nine-headed Serpent who darts swiftly this way and that
And swallows men as a sweet relish.'

[3]*Ch'u Tz'u*, *The Nine Arguments* (*Chiu Pien*), p. 95:
'But ninefold are the gates of my lord,
And fierce, snarling dogs run out of them and bark...'

Though I have a horse to ride,
I cannot go home,
For the waves that drowned Li-yang.
Loom large as mountains.[5]
Poisonous, horned dragons glaring,
Rattling their brazen rings.[6]
Lions and griffons drooling
From slavering jaws.[7]
Pao Chiao spent his whole life
Sleeping under straw.[8]
Yen Hui's hair was mottled white
When he was twenty-nine.[9]
Yet Yen Hui's blood was not corrupt,
Nor had Pao Chiao offended Heaven.
Heaven was afraid the jaws would close on them,
So it treated them thus.
If you still doubt my discernment, sir,
Think of the man raving wildly by the wall,
As he wrote his 'Heavenly Questions'.[10]

[4] 'Orchid girdle' – symbol of the virtuous. See *Ch'u Tz'u*, *Li Sao*, p.22:
    'And twined autumn orchids to make a garland.'

[5] According to the *Huai-nan-tzu*, Li-yang commandery in Anhui (present day
Ho county) turned into a lake in one night. Is Ho referring to some sudden
calamity which had overtaken him?

[6] Suzuki thinks the roaring of the dragons sounds like brazen rings being
shaken.

[7] The *ya-yü* (loosely rendered 'griffon') was a fabulous beast with the head of
a dragon, tail of a horse and claws of a tiger. It ate only the wicked.

[8] Pao Chiao was a recluse of Chou times who set himself such exaggerated
standards of conduct that he starved himself to death. See the account of his
end in *Han-shih wai-chuan*, I. 27.

[9] Yen Hui, the favourite disciple of Confucius, had white hair before he was
thirty. Like Ho, he died young.

[10] Ch'ü Yüan was supposed to have been inspired to write *The Heavenly
Questions* by the frescoes that he saw in the ancestral temples of the kings of
Ch'u. Here again I do not understand why Ho should allude to the enigmatic
Heavenly Questions, rather than to some other work of Ch'ü Yüan's. This is a
poème à clef to which we do not have the key.

Song of the Magic Strings[1]

7-character: 2 rhymes

As the sun sets in the western hills
The eastern hills grow dark,
A whirlwind blows the horses along,
Steeds trampling the clouds.[2]
Painted zithers and plain flutes
Play soft, weird tunes,
To the rustle of embroidered skirts
She treads the autumn dust.[3]

Cassia leaves stripped by the wind,[4]
Cassia seeds fall,
Blue racoons are weeping blood
As shivering foxes die.[5]
On the ancient wall are painted dragons,[6]
Tails inlaid with gold,
Rain-elves are riding them away
To the autumn tarn.
Owls that have lived a hundred years,
Turned forest demons,[7]
Find emerald fire, laughing wildly,
Leaps from their nests.

[1]A female shaman exorcizes evil spirits. A ballad of this title existed as early as the 3rd century A.D. It originated in the south, long the home of shamanistic culture.
[2]The god arrives, riding the whirlwind.
[3]The shaman dances.
[4]The spirit brings the wind.
[5]Both animals were greatly feared by the Chinese.
[6]'Horned dragon': painted on the wall of the shrine.
[7]Owls were considered unlucky. Forest demons (*mu mei*) were four-legged beasts with human faces.

Magic Strings

7-character: 2 rhymes

THE witch pours out a libation of wine,
And clouds cover the sky,
In a jade brazier charcoal burns –
Perfumed boom of a drum.[1]
Gods of the sea and mountain demons
Flock to her seat,
Crackle of burning paper money[2]
As a whirlwind moans.

She plays a love-wood lute[3] adorned
With golden, dancing simurghs,
Knitting her brows, she plucks a note
For each word uttered.
She calls down stars and summons demons
To savour meat and drink,
When mountain-goblins come to eat,
Men are breathless and hushed.
Colours of sunset low in a coign
Of Chung-nan range,[4]
Long lingers the Spirit. Something or Nothing?
We cannot tell.[5]

[1]Wang suggests that the text is corrupt here since the last three characters (literally: 'perfumed drum-beats') do not make sense. I disagree. This is synaesthesia, sound and scenery blending into one.

[2]Paper money is burnt at Chinese funerals. Here it is used as an offering to the spirit.

[3]Wood of a tree mentioned in the *Chan-kuo ts'e*. Planted on the grave of a wife who had died while her husband was away on a campaign, its branches would turn towards the quarter where he happened to be. The lute here is the *p'i-p'a* or short lute, a short-necked circular instrument with four or five strings and twelve frets.

[4]A mountain range which stretches for over 800 *li* across Central China.

[5]Or perhaps: 'The Spirit lingers long between Something and Nothing.'

The Spirit's anger, the Spirit's delight
Shows in her face,
Ten thousand riders escort him back
To the emerald hills.

Farewell Song of Magic Strings

7-character: 2 rhymes

THE Maiden of Witch Mountain now departs
Behind a screen of clouds.[1]
In spring a breeze blows flowers of pine
Down from the mountain-side.
Alone beneath her emerald canopy she returns
Through fragrant paths,[2]
White horses and flower-decked poles,
Dazzle before her.

On the River in Shu blows a limpid wind,
Water like gauze.[3]
Who will float on a fallen orchid
To come to see her?[4]
A cassia tree on a southern hill
Is dying for her.[5]
Her robes of cloud are slightly stained
By its rouged petals.[6]

---

[1]For the goddess of Mount Wu, see p. 196 above. This is the shaman's farewell
song to the departing goddess.

[2]This must refer to the goddess and not to the shaman, as Wang points out.

[3]The Yangtze flows at the foot of Mount Wu.

[4]'Fallen orchid' – a boat.

[5]Suzuki says this means Mount Chung-nan, near Lo-yang. I think this highly
unlikely.

[6]The cassia (*olea fragrans*) flowers in spring and autumn. This is clearly the
red-flowered variety known as *tan-kuei*, 'cinnabar cassia'. The last line hints
that this may also be a love-poem. Suzuki thinks Li Ho is the cassia-tree of the
penultimate line.

Song of Green Water[1]

5-character: 2 rhymes

TONIGHT a pleasant wind and moon,
But where is poor Hou?
Because her beauty breaks men's hearts
She has her shame of pain and sadness.

Is she gathering lotus by east lake?
Or plucking cattails by south lake?
She has no little sister-in-law in mind,
They're but the tokens of her sorrow.[2]

---

[1]A poem of this title by Wang Yung 王融 of the Ch'i dynasty (479–502) is found in Ting Fu-pao, *Ch'üan Han San-kuo Chin Nan Pei Ch'ao Shih*, 2 vols. (Peking, 1959), vol. I, p. 778. A poem of Liang Wu-ti's (*regnet* 502–49) refers to A-hou ('poor Hou') as the child of the singing-girl Mo-ch'ou ('Never Sorrow'). Saitō, however, believes Ho was not referring to this story. We do not know whether A-hou was originally supposed to be a girl or a boy: but Late T'ang writers thought A-hou was a girl. The last four lines of this poem have produced endless speculation among the commentators. I have followed Saitō in the main.

[2]Presumably no one will marry her on account of her profession as a singing-girl.

Song: Sandy Road[1]

7-character: 3 rhymes

TAMARISK-FACES, half-asleep,
The Premier's trees.[2]
Jingle of bridle-bells, as horses
Tread the sandy road.
Lingering scent of burnt-out fires,
Emerald smoke swirling.[3]
Horseman with torches, on clattering hooves,
Riding to Heaven.[4]

Jade dragons in the emperor's home
Open nine gates.[5]
He writes on his tablet in the emperor's presence,
And Mount South trembles.
Alone, his weighty seal controls
A thousand officials,
On its golden face, red characters
Twirl and swirl.

---

[1]During T'ang, on the appointment of the new Prime Minister, sand was strewn along the road from his private residence to the eastern quarter of the city. Our poem celebrates the appointment of a Prime Minister, seen riding to audience at dawn. Saitō believes the Minister in question was Wu Yüan-heng (758–815), a friend of Po Chü-yi's, who became Prime Minister in the third month of 813. Other commentators have suggested Ho was referring to either Li Chiang (764–830) or Tu Huang-ch'ang (738–808). But Saitō argues cogently that these are unacceptable.

[2]The tamarisk (*tamarix chinensis*, Lour.), thought to bear a resemblance to a human figure, was called 'man-willow' (*jen-liu*). The trees look half-asleep at this early hour.

[3]Smoke from incense-burners.

[4]To the court of the Son of Heaven.

[5]Dragons were carved on the nine gates of the palace.

Going home along the sandy road,
He hears nothing but praise.
Drought fires are not blazing,
Rain falls everywhere.[6]

[6]Since the government is a good one, the macrocosm responds to the order displayed by the microcosm. So there are no droughts or other calamities. All this is due to the virtue (*te*) of the Prime Minister.

The Emperor Returns[1]

7-character: 3 rhymes

THE Emperor returns!
Great banners rejoice,
Hanging red clouds,
Fluttering phoenix tails.

Breaking from its case
His sword leaps like a dragon.[2]
Ch'ih Yu is dead![3]
The drums are rolling.

Heaven blesses us all,
Thunder falls to the earth.
Over ocean's thousand leagues
No wild waves fly.[4]

[1]The fourteenth of the *Han Cymbal Songs* bears this title (上之回). This originally referred to Han Wu-ti's visit to Hui-chung. Ho misunderstood this, taking 回 as a verb and 之 as a genitive particle. I have translated accordingly.

[2]Chuan Hsü, a legendary ruler, had a magic sword which could leap from its case to subdue his enemies.

[3]Ch'ih Yu – a rebel defeated by the Yellow Emperor.

[4]The text is very corrupt here. I have followed Suzuki who reads:

天齊慶　　雷墮地
無驚飛　　海千里

with the Wu edition.

The usual text reads: 'From high heaven auspicious clouds (thunder?) fall everywhere to earth. [Within] the [four] seas for a thousand leagues, earth displays no smoke [from warning beacons] to frighten us.' Saitō and Yeh adopt these two 7-character lines.

*The Tall Official Carriage Comes on a Visit
Written at the Command of Assistant Secretary Han Yü
and Censor Huang-fu Shih When They Visited Me*[1]

Irregular: 3 rhymes

ORNATE robes woven with kingfisher feathers,
Green as foliage,[2]
Gold rings weighing down their reins,
Shaking and jingling.
Drumming of hoofbeats in my ear,
Clopping and clattering,
In through my gates they come, alighting,
Auras like rainbows.

'Behold the geniuses from Lo-yang,
Lords of literature!'[3]
Eight-and-twenty constellations
Ranged within your hearts,
The Primal Essence, burning bright,
Pervades your inmost being.[4]
You write rime-prose by the Palace,
Renown reaching the sky,
Your brushes perfect creation,
Humiliating Heaven.

[1]We may safely discount the story that Ho wrote this poem when he was seven. Han Yü was appointed Assistant Secretary to the Board of Prisons in the sixth month of 809, becoming Magistrate of Honan the following year. Huang-fu Shih became Censor in the Court of General Affairs in 808. We may therefore conclude that this poem was written in 809, probably just before the examination held to select the doctoral candidates from Honan-fu.

[2]Arai points out that 蔥 here means 'green as foliage' and not 'onion-green'.

[3]One edition omits the characters 云是駏, thus making this a regular 7-character poem.

[4]Reading 元精耿耿, with Wang and Yeh, for 九精照耀 of the Wu edition.

This poet with bushy eyebrows,
Grieves for tumbleweed in the fall,
Yet may be even withered weeds
May wake in a blossoming wind.
With flagging pinions I fly after
You sky-soaring geese,
Yet some day, shamed no longer,
This snake shall rise a dragon.

Lady of the Cowrie Palace[1]

7-character: 1 rhyme

THE Sea-lady plays with her gold rings,
Jingling softly.[2]
Her sparrow-hairpin cocks its tail,
Both wings furled.
No voices sound through her six palaces,
She is idle for ever,[3]
High above her a silver sign
Reflecting green hills.
Long eyebrows of darkest green –
How many centuries have passed?
Cold and pure, ageless she seems
This mirrored simurgh.[4]
Soon her autumn flesh will feel
The chill of her jade robes.[5]
Under the heaven's calm, peaceful light
Water confounds with sky.

[1]We have no idea who this goddess was. The poem describes her image standing in her temple.

[2]Wind jangles the gold rings adorning the image.

[3]An empress traditionally possessed six palaces.

[4]Commentators quote the story of a king of Kashmir who caught a simurgh and caged it, only to find it would not sing. His wife pointed out that simurghs only sang when they saw their own kind, so he deceived the bird by putting a mirror in its cage. The bird then sang a mournful song and died. The goddess, rare and beautiful as a simurgh (and like this bird, mirrored in the silver sign above her) is unlike the simurgh in being immortal and free of all passions.

[5]An image reminiscent of that in Keats's *The Eve of St. Agnes:*
> 'The sculptured dead, on each side, seem to freeze,
> Imprison'd in black, purgatorial veils.'

T

The Temple of the Goddess of Orchid Fragrance[1]

5-character: 1 rhyme

YEAR after year the ancient spring endures,
An idle green caressed by the warm clouds.
Scent of pines and evening blossoms flying,
As willow islands swallow the darkling sun.
The pebbly sand is strewn with tumbled reds,
Round stony founts wild celery is growing.
Lonely bamboos are painted with new powder,
Moth-green mountains bar her gates at dawn.
Fragile orchids cannot bear the dew,
Hills soar on high, sad in their lonely spring.
Her dancer's gems are clipped from simurghs' wings,
The curtain sashes streaked with dainty silver.
Orchid and cassia breathe their heady perfume,
Water-chestnut, lotus-root, heaped as offerings.
Gazing at the rain, she meets Jade Lady,
Borne in her boat, encounters the River Lord.[2]
Playing her flute, a little drunk with wine,
She knots her girdle, smooths her gold lamé skirt.
Roaming the heavens, she chides at her white deer,
Wandering the waters, whips her bright-scaled steed.[3]
Thick hair has fallen now from her coiffure.
Petals stuck fast upon her glossy cheeks.
Spiders have wrought webs in her whorled tresses,

[1]For this goddess, see p. 177, note 7, above. This poem was written in the third month of the year in which he wrote the *Ch'ang-ku* poem. The first ten lines describe the exterior of the temple; the remainder the interior.

[2]The Jade Lady – traditionally associated with clouds and rain – was the tutelary spirit of Mount Wu. The River Lord was the husband of the Ladies of the Hsiang.

[3]The Fairy, Wei Shu-ch'ing, used to ride a white deer, while Ch'in Kao rode a red bream.

Spun toils about her eyebrows, her delicate lips.
Playing with butterflies, a gentle, graceful beauty,
Her slender body shrinks from wind and sun.[4]
Gold ducks shiver on the gloomy door-curtains,
A phoenix gathers dust in her vanity-box.[5]
Treading the mist, she's borne home on the breeze,
Her tinkling jades heard on the mountain-top.[6]

[4]Saitō understands as: '[The wind] plays with the butterflies, which go well
with the goddess's lightness and beauty. The surrounding scenery stands in awe
of her slender body.'
[5]The back of her mirror bore the pattern of a phoenix.
[6]Reading 聞 for 門. If we retain the original version, we must translate:
'By (on?) the gates on the hill top, a shaking of jade.'

I Escort Wei Jen-shih and His Brother to the Pass[1]

5-character: 1 rhyme

SEEING off my friends, I drink the wine of parting,
After a thousand goblets, no flushed faces.[2]
The most heart-rending sound I know?
Jingle of golden rings on horses' heads.
The coloured wilderness is vast, untamed,
Autumn bright under the boundless sky.
My courage ebbs from me all unawares,[3]
My straining eyes follow my friends in vain.[4]
Roadside pagoda-trees stretch away westwards,
Long, green branches thickly bunched together.
I've escorted these gentlemen to the waters of Ch'in,
Now I must go back to Lo-yang's mists again.[5]
The brothers Wei are both fine fellows,
Their brushes pour forth characters like jade,[6]
I live in a little hut on top of a hill,
Around it, a weed-grown patch of stony ground.
On rainy nights, the tax collector's shouts
Darkly mingle with thump of pestle on mortar.[7]
Who can understand my weary heart?
Only Mount South rears its green before me.[8]

---

[1]Wei Jen-shih is mentioned in *CTS*, CLXIV, biography of Wang Po, as addressing a remonstrance to the throne in A.D. 824. Apart from this, nothing is known of him. When Ho wrote this poem, Wei and his brother were probably going to Ch'ang-an to sit for their examinations.

[2]They are all too sorrowful to get drunk.

[3]Understanding 坐來 as 'without my knowing it' (*itsu-shika*), with Arai.

[4]*Wei-yüan ying-hua*, 341, reads 新月 for 斷目. 'Under the new moon, I cannot discern them.'

[5]These two lines, taken from *Wen-yüan ying-hua*, 341, are not found in other versions.

[6]Hinting at success in the coming examinations.

[7]Reading 舂 for 春.

[8]The hill south of Ho's house in Ch'ang-ku.

Outside the Walls of Lo-yang, I Take Leave of Huang-fu Shih[1]

5-character: 1 rhyme

THROUGH Lo-yang city blow the winds of parting,
At Dragon Gate rises estranging mist.[2]
Winter trees – bundles of bare, harsh branches,
Twilight purple freezes in the dappled sky.[3]
Alone through the frosty wilderness I go,
On a jaded horse, among the tumbleweed.
I lean on your carriage, shedding a tear or two[4]
That dare to fall on the front of your green robe.[5]

[1]Huang-fu Shih, a pupil of Han Yü's, was a patron of various writers of the time, among them Li Ho. Though rude, arrogant, bad-tempered and something of a drunkard, he enjoyed a great reputation for learning among his contemporaries. Since three other poems of Ho's are concerned with Huang-fu Shih, the two would appear to have been close friends. See pp. 90 and 219 above, and p. 227 below.

[2]Dragon Gate (Lung-men shan) was one of the two mountains that formed the Yi Pass, a few miles south of Lo-yang.

[3]Or perhaps, with Suzuki: '. . . the sky over Mount Hua', to the west.

[4]Or perhaps with Arai, 'I lean on the eaves . . .'

[5]During Ho's time, officials of the sixth and seventh grades wore green robes.

A Cold Gorge at Twilight

1-character: 1 rhyme

A WHITE fox barking at the moon
Calls out the mountain wind.[1]
Autumn chill sweeps off the clouds
Leaving an emerald void.
Jade mists over green damp,[2]
Like pennants of white.
The Silver Torrent winds its way[3]
To the eastern sky.
On the shores of the stream an egret sleeps,
Dreaming of migrant geese.[4]
Delicate ripples, unmurmuring,
Stir scarcely at all.
Storied crags and twisted peaks
Arched as a dragon's back.
The bitter bamboos this traveller sees
Are singing flutes.[5]

[1]Foxes had supernatural powers. Shrines to white foxes are common even today in Japan.
[2]Wang and Suzuki read 清 for 青. 'Jade mist, clear and damp . . .'
[3]Read 銀河 for 銀灣. 'Silver Torrent': the Milky Way.
[4]鴻 – the Eastern Bean Goose.
[5]The bitter bamboo (*phyllostachys bambusoides*) is generally used for making flutes.

The Official Has not Come
A Poem Written in the Office of My Senior, Huang-Fu Shih

Irregular: 1 rhyme

THE official has not come!
Autumn in his office courtyard.
Twisted trunks of kolanut trees –
Green dragons grieving.
Clerks and deputies
Milling like cattle.
I keep asking his assistants:
'Is he coming or not?'
The official is not coming,
His gateway darkens.[1]

[1]All commentators agree that this poem was probably written when Huang-fu Shih was Chief of Staff in Lü-hun.

Song of an Arrowhead from Ch'ang-p'ing[1]

7-character: 3 rhymes

FLAKES of lacquer, dust of bones,
Red cinnabar,
The ancient blood once spurted forth
And bore bronze flowers.
White feathers and its metal stem
Have rotted in the rain.
Only the three spines still remain,[2]
Broken teeth of a wolf.

I searched this plain of battle
With a pair of nags,
In stony fields east of the post-station,
On a weed-grown hill.
An endless wind, the day short,
Desolate stars,
Black banners of damp clouds
Hung in void-night.
Souls to the left, spirits to the right,
Gaunt with hunger, wailing.[3]
I poured curds from my tilted flask,
Offered roast mutton.[4]
Insects silent, the wild geese sick,
Reed shoots reddening.
A whirlwind came to see me off,
Blowing the ghost-fires.[5]

---

[1]Ch'ang-p'ing, 7 miles west of Kao-p'ing county, was the site of an ancient battlefield. Here, in 260 B.C., the forces of Ch'in were said to have captured and then buried alive 400,000 men of Chao. Farmers were still turning up relics of the massacre in Ho's day, over a thousand years later. Ho may have written this poem in 814, when he was on his way to Lu-chou, which is not far from Ch'ang-p'ing. The poem is faintly reminiscent of the *Kuo Shang* (*The Spirits of the Fallen*) of *The Nine Songs* in the *Ch'u Tz'u*, pp. 43-4.

In tears I sought this ancient field,
Picked up a broken arrow,
Its shattered point, scarlet and cracked,
Once drove through flesh.
In South Street, by the eastern wall,
A lad on horseback,
Urged me to exchange the metal
For a votive-basket.[6]

Song: The Mansion by the River[7]

7-character: 4 rhymes

BEFORE the mansion flows the water,
Road to Chiang-ling.
The carp-fish wind has risen,[8]
The lotus grows old.

At dawn she hastily pins her hair,
Talks to the south wind.
'To hoist his sail and come back home,
Is but one day's work.

[2]'Three spines': the triangular arrow-head.
[3]Read 飢 for 肌. The dead were crying out with hunger, since they had not been buried with proper rites nor offered libations.
[4]Curds and mutton are the food of the northern nomads, not of the Chinese.
[5]'Ghost-fires': will-o'-the-wisps.
[6]The money from the sale of the relic was to be used for buying a basket in which to offer sacrifices to appease the spirits of the fallen. Older commentators understood this line as meaning: 'Urged me to take my money and buy bamboo to make a new arrow-stem.' This is erroneous.
[7]A wife in thinking of her husband who has gone off to Chiang-ling, in Hupeh, a busy commercial centre.
[8]'Carp-wind' – the wind of late autumn.

Since the crocodile cried by the harbour
And the plum-rain flew,[3]
The blue linen wine-flag has been changed
Upon its pole.[4]
White waves roar and bluster,
Clouds scud wildly.
I sent a raincoat of yellow oil-cloth,
To my husband.

Splash of new wine into vats
Lonely and faint.[5]
Acres of South Lake have turned white
With water-chestnut.
Suddenly my mind's eye sees
A thousand leagues away.
Little Jade draws back the screen[6]
And I look at the coloured hills.'

[3]The crocodile's cry presaged rain. 'Plum-rain' fell in summer, when the plums were ripe. Her husband has been gone for several months already.

[4]Taverns flew linen flags which were changed when the season's new wine was made.

[5]Or perhaps: 'I regret that the new wine splashing into the vats has no power to dissipate my sorrow.'

[6]'Little Jade' – a name used for serving-girls during T'ang.

Song: Beyond the Frontiers

5-character: 3 rhymes

BARBARIAN horns have summoned the north wind,
Thistle Gate is whiter than a stream![1]
The road to Green Sea vanishes into the sky,[2]
Along the Wall, a thousand moonlit miles.

While dew falls drizzling on our flags,[3]
Cold metal clangs the watches of the night.[4]
Barbarian armour meshes serpents scales,
Horses whinny where Green Grave gleams white.[5]

In autumn stillness see the Banner Head,[6]
On the vast sands the mournful furze.[7]
North of our tents the sky itself must end,
Across the frontier comes the River's roar.[8]

[1]'Thistle Gate': another name for Su county, Hopeh, near present Peking.
The moonlit desert is dazzling white.
[2]'Green Sea': the Kokonor.
[3]The Korean edition reads 霧 for 露. 'Mist falls on drizzling banners.'
[4]Sentries beat metal drums to mark the night-watches.
[5]Green Grave is the name of the place in Central Asia where Wang Chao-
chün, the Chinese princess who married a Han chieftain, is buried. The horses
of the nomads who have massed for the attack have eaten all the grass round
the spot and stripped it white as the desert sands.
[6]'Banner Head': the constellation Mao, which roughly corresponds to the
Pleiades. The flickering of these stars was said to augur trouble on the northern
frontiers.
[7]Read 箕 for 器.
[8]The Yellow River.

Dyed Silk on the Loom in Spring

7-character: 4 rhymes

She draws water in jade jars
From the empress-tree petal well.
Silk dyed with madder, water-steeped,
Like a cloud's shadow.

This lively girl is tired,
Her rouged face looks sad.
In spring her shuttle clicks away,
Humming in the tall tower.

Bright-hued silk, knotted in
Double folds on the back –
A handsome man in a white-collared coat
Sent Peach-leaves this present.[1]

'Embroidered with simurghs
Is the belt I have made you.
I want you to roam round everywhere,
Drinking spring wine.'

[1]Peach-leaves (T'ao-yeh) was the name of a beautiful concubine of Wang Hsien-chih.

Song of the Young Five-grain Pine[1]

7-character: 2 rhymes

Bachelor Hsieh and Tu Yün-ch'ing once asked me to write a song for a young five-grain pine. I was very busy with my books at the time and could not write this lyric for them. Ten days later I composed these eight lines to fulfil their request.

> SNAKE'S son, snake's grandson,
> Scales coiled like a dragon's.
> My grains, new and fragrant,
> Were food for Hung Yai.[2]
> Leaves lapped in green wavelets,
> Glossy and rich.
> Neat bundles of dragons' whiskers,
> Trimmed off with scissors.[3]
>
> On my owner's wall
> Maps of the district.
> Round my owner's hall
> Mobs of uncouth scholars.[4]
> Bright moonlight, white dew,

[1]Several interpretations of this poem are proposed by the commentators. My translation is eclectic. The fruit of the five-grain pine (*pinus pentaphylla*, Mayr.) was said to be an elixir of longevity which drove off the Three Worms that attack one's life. In this poem the pine laments that its owners are too busy and their associates too uncouth for them to appreciate its rare qualities.

[2]A Fairy mentioned in the *Shen-hsien chuan*. See p. 202, note 10, above,

[3]Wang thinks this means the pine was a dwarf-tree (*bonsai*). It is more likely that the leaves were cut for eating.

[4]The maps indicate that the owners were busy local officials: the scholars were presumably their subordinates and their colleagues. The implication that Hsieh and Tu were unable to appreciate the pine is just a pleasantry among friends.

Autumn tears falling.
Pointed stones, stream clouds,
May I send you this letter?[1]

Song: By the Pool[2]

5-character: 1 rhyme

LOTUS flower degged with chill dew,
The petals ragged, the root grown harsh.
A lonely mandarin-duck comes winging down,[3]
With gentle splash in the waters of the pool.

[1]'Pointed stones' (*shih-sun*) – needle-like pieces of granite used for decorating gardens, but here metonymy for Ho's home in Ch'ang-ku.

[2]A poem of this title was written by one of the wives of Emperor Wen of Wei before her execution. Hence Yao believes that this quatrain of Ho's is a lament for a concubine of the Crown Prince, who was put to death in the eighth month of 809.

[3]'Duck' is the only reading that fits Yao's interpretation. There is no drake in the pool.

Song: General Lü[1]

Irregular: 7 rhymes

GENERAL Lü,
The valiant-hearted,
Riding alone on Scarlet Hare[2]
Out of the gates of Ch'in,[3]
To weep at Gold Grain Mound[4]
By funereal trees.

Rebellion in the north
Stains the blue sky.
His dragon-sword cries out at night –
But the general's left idle,

To shake his sleeves,
And stroke his cross-guard.
'Round the jade towers of Vermilion City,
A maze of gates and pavilions.'[5]

Slowly, the silver tortoise swings
To the gait of the white horse.[6]
A powdered lady-general rides
Under a fiery banner.[7]

[1]Lü Pu (d. A.D. 198), the great warrior of the Later Han, here stands for some T'ang general whom Ho admired, left idle at home while eunuchs mismanaged the imperial armies. This general probably bore the surname Lü.

[2]Lü Pu's famous steed.

[3]Ch'ang-an.

[4]The tomb of the T'ang Emperor Hsüan-tsung (regnet 712–56), 10 miles north-east of P'u-ch'eng. The general, who may have been Commander of the Guards of the Imperial Mausoleum, is weeping over the fallen glories of the dynasty.

[5]Eunuchs and women prevent the General from explaining the gravity of the situation to the emperor.

The iron horsemen of Mount Heng
Call for their metal lances,[8]
They can smell from afar the ornate arrows
In her perfumed quiver.

Cold weeds grow in the western suburbs,
With leaves like thorns,
High heaven has just now planted them,
To feed our thoroughbreds.
In tall-beamed stables, row on row
Of useless nags.[9]
Stuffing themselves on green grass,
Drinking white water.[10]

Inscrutable that vaulted azure,
Arching over earth,
This is the way the world wags
In our Nine Provinces.
Gleaming ore from Scarlet Hill![11]
Hero of our time!
Green-eyed general, you well know
The will of Heaven![12]

[6]During T'ang, the handles of official seals were shaped like fish. During Han times the seals had tortoise-shaped handles. Only high officials could wear silver seals.

[7]The commander is a eunuch, probably the hated T'u-t'u Ch'eng-ts'ui.

[8]Mount Heng, in Hopeh, was in territory controlled by the rebel general Wang Ch'eng-tsung.

[9]Read 排 for 挑 with Suzuki.

[10]Ho is once again using his favourite horse metaphor. Good men are left to starve while parasites prey on the court.

[11]At Scarlet Hill (Ch'ih-chin shan) in Kuei-chi, Chekiang, Ou-yeh Tzu once forged swords with copper from the Ho-yeh stream and tin from the mountains. See *Yüeh-chüeh shu*, XI, p. 16.

[12]The 'green-eyed general' was certainly not a Chinese. This fact disproves Saitō's theory that Ho was referring to T'ien Pu, son of T'ien Hung-cheng, who took part in the campaign against Wu Yüan-chi's forces in Huai-hsi in 815.

Don't Wash Red Cloth![1]

Irregular: 1 rhyme

DON'T wash red cloth!
For washed too often it will fade.
You are so full of youthful pride![2]
Yesterday we met at the bridge of Yin.[3]
Come home soon with a marquisate!
Don't be just another arrow from a bow!

---

[1] A wife laments her husband's absence at the wars. Her beauty will fade as quickly as red cloth which has been washed too often. The first two lines of our poem are almost identical with the opening lines of a Chin dynasty poem of the same title which Ho is imitating. See Ting Fu-pao, *Ch'üan Han San-kuo Chin Nan Pei Ch'ao Shih*, vol. 1, pp. 551-2.

[2] Suzuki reads 聘 for 騁. 'I was bought by this young man.'

[3] Place unidentifiable.

U

Song in the Wilds

7-character: 2 rhymes

ARROW plumed with duck-feathers,
Mountain-mulberry bow,[1]
Pointed skywards may bring down
A reed-bearing goose.[2]
In linen clothes, all black and greasy,
I brave the north wind.[3]
Drunk at twilight, I'm still singing
Down in the fields.

Bend my body though I may,
My heart's unyielding.[4]
Success and failure are both uncertain,
Why rail at the Creator?
This bitter wind will bring to life
The willows of spring,
These bare branches suddenly wear
A new, green mist.[5]

[1]Read 鵶 for 鴉 with Korean edition. The finest bows were made from mountain mulberry (*morus alba*).

[2]Geese were said to carry reeds in their beaks to defend themselves against arrows when they flew back north in spring, since they were too fat to be able to fly at a safe height.

[3]Earlier commentators understood these lines as referring to the goose or the hunter. I follow Wang, who points out that second-degree graduates (e.g. Li Ho) during T'ang had to wear linen clothes. Suzuki would read 肌 for 肥. '. . . skin blackened (by the sun).'

[4]Read 躬 for 窮.

[5]A man's lot in life may not be easy: but if he is talented enough he may yet bring good fortune for himself, as surely as a skilful hunter can shoot a goose. The winter of his poverty may yet turn to spring.

Let Wine Be Brought in![1]

Irregular: 2 rhymes

IN opaque, glass goblets
A viscous amber.[2]
From a little vat the wine drips down
True pearls of red.
From boiling dragons and roasting phoenix
Jade fat is weeping,
Gauzy screens, embroidered curtains.
Enclose these perfumed airs.[3]

Blow dragon flutes!
Beat alligator drums!
Dazzling teeth in song,
Slender waists in dance.
Especially now when green, spring days
Are turning to dusk,[4]
With peach-petals falling wildly
Like pink showers.
I beg you now to stay quite drunk
To the end of your days,
For on the earth of Liu Ling's grave
No one pours wine.[5]

[1]This is the title of one of the eighteen *Han Cymbal Songs*.

[2]*Liu-li*, opaque glass or glaze (sometimes glazed pottery) as contrasted with *po-li*, transparent glass.' Amber' is metonymy for wine.

[3]'Perfumed airs' – the singing girls and dancers. Some editions read 幃 for 屏.

[4]The line refers to the shortness of the season, not to the time of day.

[5]Liu Ling (221?–300?) a noted toper, was so fond of drink that he had flasks of wine buried with him. Yet his grave is now untended and no wine is ever poured on it as a libation.

Song: A Lovely Girl Combing Her Hair

7-character: 6 rhymes

HSI-SHIH dreaming at dawn,
In the cool of silken curtains.[1]
Scented coils of her falling chignon,
Half aloes, half sandalwood.[2]

The turning windlass of the well,
Creaking like singing jade,
Wakes with a start this lotus blossom,
That has newly slept its fill.

Twin simurghs appear on her mirror,
An autumn pool of light.[3]
She loosens her tresses before the mirror,
Stands on her ivory bed.

A single skein of perfumed silk,
Clouds cast on the floor,
Noiseless the jade comb tumbles down
From her lustrous hair.[4]

[1]Hsi-shih who came from Yüeh (Chekiang) during the Warring States period was the most renowned of all Chinese beauties. Her name stands for any beautiful woman.

[2]'To chi' here is short for 'to-ma chi' – 'falling-from-your-horse chignon', a chignon set on one side of the forehead, like a rider slipping from the saddle. This style, which originated during Han times, persisted well into the nineteenth century. Liu T'ieh-yün's novel, Lao Ts'an Yu-chi, describes a girl wearing her hair in this fashion. See Harold Shadick, The Travels of Lao Ts'an (Cornell, 1952) p. 11. For the expression 'ch'en t'an' see Dai kanwa jiten, VI. p. 6684. 17189. 286. Suzuki reads 氈 for 檀. 'Half as thick as a rug.' Arai thinks 沈檀 means 'deep pink lipstick and rouge'.

[3]The back of the mirror was decorated with simurghs.

[4]Even though she is standing on the bed, her hair covers the floor so thickly that the comb, falling on it, makes no sound.

Delicate fingers keep pushing back the coils –
Colour of an old rook's plumes,
Blue-black and sleek – the jewelled comb
And hairpin cannot hold.
Light-heartedly the spring breeze vexes
Her lovely disarray.
After tying eighteen knots or more,
Her strength has fled.[5]

Her toilet over, the well-dressed chignon
Sits firm and does not slip.
In cloudy skirts, she measures her step,
A goose treading the sand,
She turns away without speaking –
Where is she off to now?
Just down the steps to pick herself
A spray of cherry blossom.

[5]Suzuki interprets: 'At eighteen, she has so much hair that she lacks strength
to dress it.'

A Shining Wet Moon

Irregular: 3 rhymes

A SHINING wet moon,
Jade in misty waves,
Green sedge, a host of cassia flowers,
Lotuses drifting from riverside trees.

Powdered beauties cold in sendal robes,[1]
Goose-wings, brushing wet mist.[2]
Who can descry Stone Sail or ride
A boat upon the Mirror?[3]

White autumn, new reds dying,[4]
Sweet-scented water, lotus-seeds ripening,
Girls plucking water-chestnut part their dancer's sleeves,
Green thorns clinging to slime-silver gowns.[5]

The Capital

5-character: 1 rhyme

OUT of my gate I galloped, full of hope –
But now my heart is lonely in Ch'ang-an.
Since I have no one to confide in
I chant a poem alone with the autumn wind.

[1]Palace ladies, out in boats on a moonlit night, are picking water chestnuts.
[2]Geese are flying low, just above the autumn mist.
[3]Stone Sail is a mountain in Kuei-chi, Chekiang. Mirror Lake lies south of Shan-yin, Chekiang.
[4]'New reds': probably lotus flowers.
[5]'Slime-silver': a glistening material, colour of a snail's track.

Drums in the Street of the Officials[1]

7-character: 1 rhyme

DRUMS at dawn rumbling like thunder,
Hastening the sun,
Drums at dusk rumbling like thunder,
Calling out the moon.[2]
In the city of Han, yellow willows dazzle
On the new blinds,[3]
In a cypress mound lie the fragrant bones
Of Flying Swallow.[4]
Drums have pounded to pieces a thousand years
Of suns forever white,
Yet Emperor Wu and the Emperor of Ch'in
Are deaf to their call.
Our blue-black hair must turn to the hue
Of a flowering rush[5]
Only the drums and the Southern Hills
Can guard the Middle Kingdom.
How many times have Ethereal Immortals
Been buried in Heaven?
The drip of the water-clock, day after day,
Goes on without pause.

[1]During T'ang, drums sounded throughout Ch'ang-an to announce the closing of the city gates at dusk and their opening at dawn.

[2]Reading 呼 for 催.

[3]'City of Han' – the palace in Ch'ang-an. Suzuki says 'new blinds' refers to the empress's apartments.

[4]Flying Swallow – Chao Fei-yen, the notorious and beautiful consort of Emperor Ch'eng-ti of the Former Han (*regnet* 33–7 B.C.)

[5]Emperor Wu of the Former Han and the First Emperor of Ch'in were both known for their frenzied pursuit of immortality. Our poem is clearly another attack on Hsien-tsung's unavailing search for the elixir of life.

A Song for Hsü's Lady, Cheng[1]
(She Having Asked Me to Write This When I Was in Her Garden)

7-character: 6 rhymes

IMPERIAL relatives on the distaff side,
Generations of Hsüs and Shihs.
With a thousand yards of palace brocade
He bought his drinking-bouts.
By the Brazen Camels he mulled his wine,
Clear as warm glue,
On ancient banks, where emerald mist
Drapes the great willows.

A stranger came, a cassia-flower,
The renowned Cheng Hsiu.[2]
When she reached Lo, her fragrance wafted
From Tripod Gate.[3]
First he gave her a peony,[4]
Then a vanity-mirror,
And after this a nugget of gold,
Big as a bushel.

[1]Cheng was a singing-girl who had come to Lo-yang, found fame and fortune there and succeeded in establishing herself as the favourite of one of the scions of the Hsü family, maternal relatives of the T'ang emperors. The Hsü family and the Shih family had been maternal relatives of the Han emperors.

[2]Cheng Hsiu was the favourite of King Huai of Ch'u (Warring States period).

[3]The south-east gate of Lo-yang.

[4]Peonies were used to arrange assignations during T'ang.

[5]Never Sorrow, the famous courtesan from Shih-ch'eng, here stands for Miss Cheng.

As Never Sorrow let him dally
Behind the screen,[5]
She played her lute for his delight,
Fifty melodious strings.
Music sobbed on the wind of spring,
Stirring his soul,
Enraptured, he was moved to saddle
Both their horses.

Twin steeds pacing on twice four hooves
Through an orchid park!
Love clasped tight as knit bamboo –
No prying eyes.
Jade pillows gleaming in the dark,
Phoenix at rest,[6]
Heavy curtains shrouding the portals,
Silk passementerie.

On a long scroll of costly paper,
The ballad of Ming-chün.[7]
Gliding from note to note, her song
Pierced the sapphire clouds
Vanity-patches on her cheeks,
She trod the eastern road –
Now the long-browed girls of the gay quarters
See very few guests.

[6]The pillow was made of 'Night-shining Jade' (*yeh-kuang yü*), probably chlorophane, a luminescent variety of fluorite. See Schafer, *Golden Peaches*, p. 238.

[7]Wang Chao-chün (later known as Ming-chün to avoid the taboo name of Emperor Wen of Chin, 211–65) was the concubine of Emperor Yüan of the Former Han (*regnet* 48–33 B.C.). He gave her to the ruler of the Hsiung-nu as a bride. Wang interprets this line as meaning: 'A long piece of Shu paper with a portrait of Wang Chao-chün on it is rolled up into a scroll.' I follow Saitō and Suzuki, who believe this refers to a *yüeh-fu* ballad.

'On Hsiang-ju's tomb the autumn cypress
Flourishes still.
But who are the poets who sing of love
In the capital today?'
Hair piled high, eyes wild with wine,
She asked her friends,[8]
Then came to this scion of a royal house,
To entreat Ts'ao Chih.[9]

[8]Read 娥 for 蛾.

[9]Since Ssu-ma Hsiang-ju is dead, Li Ho is the only great poet of love remaining. Ts'ao Chih (192–232) was one of the finest poets of the pre-T'ang period. Like Ho, he was a scion of a royal house.

Song: A New Summer

7-character: 4 rhymes

At dawn, a thousand clumps of trees,
Glossy as wax,
Fading scent of fallen stamens
Lingering a little.

On shadowed branches, pale-green down
Of buds still furled,[1]
Summer breezes blow from afar,
Coaxing their verdure.

Villagers grow wheat on ridges,
High on new dikes,
Thick over long balks where I stroll,
Mulberry and silkworm-thorn,[2]

A piercing fragrance fills the earth
From the sweet-flag.
Swallows are chattering on rain-drenched beams,
Sad that I'm growing old,
Whirling petals of the third month,
Fly to River walks.[3]
Enriching heaven, enriching earth,
Willows sweep the ground.

[1]Reading 芽 for 牙 with Suzuki'
[2]The silkworm-thorn (cudrania triloba, Hce.) resembles the mulberry, its leaves being used to feed early silkworms.
[3]Reading 揭 for 楊 with Suzuki.

On the Theme of 'Dreaming I Was Back at Home'

5-character: 1 rhyme

BACK in Ch'ang-an, on a night of wind and rain,
A student who is dreaming of Ch'ang-ku,
Laughing and carefree in the sitting-room,
Cutting king-grass in the gorge with my young brother,
My whole family welcomes me with joy,
Counting on me to fill their empty bellies.
My inmost heart is faint and weary now.
A guttering lamp glimmers on a fish's eyes![1]

[1] A fish sleeps with its eyes open. Ho is studying so hard he has no time to sleep.

Passing through Sandy Park[1]

5-character: 1 rhyme

WHERE wild floods sail their watery waves,
Over the yamen the young madder grows.[2]
No one to see the willows turn to spring,
On grassy islands mandarin ducks are basking.[3]
 Horses lie on the sands, whinnying in the sun,
The old ones walk off, neighing piteously.[4]
Though spring has come, once again I have not gone home
On the frontier cries a goose with broken wings.[5]

[1]Sandy Park was a large imperial preserve of some 800 square miles in Shensi. It was used for rearing horses and other domestic animals needed for the palace. Yao believes that this poem refers to the floods which devastated the district around the capital in the spring of 812.

[2]Read 牙 not 芽 with Wang and Suzuki. I take it that the floods have ruined the official residence of the Superintendent of the Park. However, the line could refer to the ruins of the Hsing-te palace, which stood to the south of the park.

[3]The park is almost completely deserted, only a few animals having survived the floods.

[4]Suzuki reads 蹄 for 啼. '. . . sad that they cannot spread their hooves.'

[5]Like a goose which wants to return north in spring, Ho is unable to go home.

On Leaving the City and Parting from Chang Yu-hsin
I Pledge Li Han with Wine[1]

5-character: 5 rhymes

OUT of the capital I go as spring
Burgeons upon the peaks of the Southern Hill,
Tonight I cannot hear the drums [2]–
Some consolation to my aching heart.
Chao Yi wrote poems on his unhappy fate,[3]
And Ma-ch'ing's family lived in poverty.[4]
What news comes to me in letters from home?
'Clouds of purple bracken cover the rocks.'[5]

Ch'ang-an is a kingdom of jade and cassia,[6]
Halberd-pennants wave at noble gates.[7]
Even in winter's gloom the ground is shining,
Precious steeds prance by from dawn till dusk.
Winter and spring, they hunt in grassy parks,
Their fashionable carriages rumbling and clattering by.
Golden bells dangle from their green nets,
Coiling like mist round the clear pool's brink.
From loosened purses money flows like water,[8]
Just to buy ice to drive off summer flies.
At times the great quilts are split up,[9]
Among guests with swords, in cushioned carriages.

[1]Chang Yu-hsin, style K'ung-chao 孔 昭 (biography in *HTS*, CLXXV)
was a *chin-shih* of 814. Li Han, style Nan-chi 南 紀 (biography in *CTS*, CLXXI),
was a descendant of Li Tao-ming, Prince of Huai-yang, of the T'ang royal
house. He was a pupil of Han Yü, whose daughter he married. This poem was
written in 814, when Ho was leaving Ch'ang-an to return to Ch'ang-ku.

[2]The drums that announced the closing of the city gates at nightfall.

[3]Chao Yi, style Yüan-shu, was a talented man whose overbearing manner
frequently got him into serious trouble. See *Hou Han-shu*, CX. Ho was
obviously aware of the trouble his own haughtiness had brought on him.

[4]Ma-ch'ing: Ssu-ma Hsiang-ju, a poet to whom Ho frequently compares
himself.

I'm just a nobody, heart like dead ashes,[10]
Where only autumn thorn-bush grows.
The imperial sway governs the four seas,
And all our citizens are gentlemen.[11]
Yet shrouding mists obscure the emperor's radiance,
Tortoise-seals remain mere lumps of silver[12]
I wanted to noise Ritual and Music abroad,
Making sure the tunes were fresh and new,
So ordering things that for ten thousand years
The Imperial Way would be like a god on wing,
Nomenclature should match Reality,[13]
Glory pour out as from a tilted ewer.[14]
But hidden away unknown I bite my tongue,
Shed tears of blood and dare not say a word.

Now I am setting off down the eastern road,
With libations of wine I say farewell to Ch'in.
No brave men now in the six provinces,[15]
So who will wipe the dust from their long swords?
Yang and Wu-cheng are huddled deep in earth,[16]
And racehorses are yoked to carts of salt.

[5]Because the land was uncultivated.

[6]Su Ch'in, a character mentioned in the *Chan-kuo ts'e*, once remarked that in Ch'u food was dearer than jade and firewood more costly than cassia. Ho is complaining of the cost of living in Ch'ang-an.

[7]Halberds were set before the gates of noblemen and high officials, the number varying according to rank.

[8]Literally: 'pour out the water-beetle's mother.' An allusion to the belief that if the blood of the mother water-beetle is smeared on one string of eighty-one cash and the blood of its offspring on another string the two lots of money will always seek each other out. Hence the expression means 'to have an inexhaustible supply of money'. Suzuki understands it as meaning 'spend the interest on capital'.

[9]Meng Tsung of Wu studied under a certain Li Su. His mother made him a quilt twelve times as wide as normal so he could share it with other scholars who stayed overnight while visiting his master.

Since both of you are gallant gentlemen,
When it comes to Truth, you can tell black from white.[17]
After tonight, we shall laugh together no more,[18]
Bamboos are sprouting back in my garden at home.
At dawn a wind starts blowing from the west,[19]
A glimmering moon is hanging in the east,[20]
A man who finds the times are out of joint
Has written this poem he now presents to you.
Since partings always soak my breast with tears
I've brought my Yüeh handkerchief along.[21]

[10]The term 小人 here almost certainly refers to Ho himself. Wang and Yeh, however, believe Ho is referring to the noblemen of Ch'ang-an, whom he styles 'vulgar fellows'.

[11] Read 拖 for 施.

[12]During Han, official seals had knobs in the shape of tortoises. During T'ang, these knobs were shaped like fish. Once again Ho is using a Han symbol to refer to T'ang. The line means that the officials of the time were not doing their jobs properly.

[13]An allusion to the Confucian belief that name and thing must be in perfect accord if a state was to be properly governed.

[14] Reading 采 for 來 with Suzuki.

[15]The six commanderies of Lung-hsi, T'ien-shui, An-ting, Pei-ti, Shang-chün and Hsi-ho were noted for their brave men during Han times, according to Yen Shih-ku's commentary to Han-shu, LXIX, p. 1a.

[16]For Sun Yang (Po Lo) see p. 72 above, Twenty-three Poems about Horses, No. 11, note 3. Yu Wu-cheng was another famous judge of horses, the charioteer Wang Liang. Read 埋 for 理.

[17] Read: 講 道 調 清 渾 with Suzuki. Literally: 'In discussing the Way, you distinguish the clear from the muddy.'

[18] Read 今 for 冬 with Suzuki and Saitō.

[19] Read 西 for 四 with Wang and Suzuki.

[20] Read 耿 for 秋 with Suzuki and Saitō.

[21]Chekiang (Yüeh) had long been famous for its kerchiefs.

My Southern Garden[1]

7-character: 1 rhyme

I'm wearing straight collar, orchid belt,
And a bent-cornered hat,[2]
Pollia is withering,
Orchids flower in spring.
Southern hills rear up sharply[3] –
Blue jade fused,
A sudden shower dies away
Cool clouds wing past.
Apricots ripen in fragrant warmth,
Pear leaves grow old,
Grasses, twigs and a bamboo fence
Lock in the pond.[4]
Growing old in Cheng Kung's village
I open a flagon of wine,[5]
Sit drinking to strains of Ch'u music,
Humming 'Summoning the Soul'.[6]

[1]A description of late spring in Ch'ang-ku.
[2]He is wearing Confucian dress as he walks in his garden. Kuo T'ai (128–69) set the fashion for wearing hats with one corner bent, after his own got caught in the rain.
[3]Mount South in Ch'ang-ku.
[4]Reading 柵 with *Li Ch'ang-chi wen-chi* instead of 色 or 根.
[5]Cheng Hsüan (127–200) was one of the greatest commentators on the Confucian classics. Ho is complimenting the people of Ch'ang-ku by implying that they are as observant of the Confucian precepts as if they came from Cheng's own village in Shantung.
[6]*The Summons of the Soul (Chao Hun)* is one of the poems in the *Ch'u Tz'u*, pp. 101–9.

x

Song: Imitating the Singing of Dragons[1]

Irregular (4- and 7-character): 3 rhymes

STONE grating on a copper bowl,
The song is faint and forced.
Blood spattered from blue eagles!
Lungs ripped from a white phoenix![2]
Cassia seeds fall as clouds
Sway their carriage-awnings.[3]

Dead trees and crumbling sand,
A baleful valley-isle,
There the Western Mother, ageless now,
Once grew immortal.[4]
Grottoes washed clear of dragon's pure spittle,[5]
Gold claws buried in water-lapped coves.

[1]As a young man, Fang Kuan (697–763), who later became Prime Minister, was studying in a valley of Mount Chung-nan when he heard strange cries coming from the mountain. An old man told him that this was the singing of dragons, a sound always followed by rain. Later he came across a Buddhist monk who had succeeded in imitating a dragon's cry perfectly by striking a copper bowl in a certain way. In 778, the monk-poet Chiao-jan was visited by a monk from Ch'ang-an who could imitate a dragon in this way. Chiao-jan then wrote a poem called 'Striking the Copper Bowl to Imitate a Singing Dragon'. Ho is modelling himself on this. Our poem, however, is undoubtedly satirical. Men are frightened of real dragons (geniuses) and chase them away, but like to try to imitate their song nevertheless. This otherwise fine poem is marred by its rather precious diction.

[2]*Han Wu Nei-chuan* lists the lungs of a white phoenix and the blood of a blue simurgh as exotic drugs. The cry of the true dragon, here contrasted with the faint sound of the bowl, is as terrifying as the shriek of these slaughtered birds. So the cry of the true poet – that rarest of creatures – is one of agony.

[3]The dragon brought wind and rain, which made the cassia seeds fall.

[4]Like the Western Mother, the dragon has gained immortality.

[5] Read 洮 for 跳.

Green shrouds the hillside steps
Mourning in moss,[6]
The River Ladies, drying their tears,
Snapped off these giant bamboos.[7]
The Lotus Dragons left this land
A thousand years ago,[8]
Smell of fish lingers after rain –
And that of iron.[9]

[6] Read 蒼蒼 for 蒼苔.

[7] For the River Ladies, see p. 58 above, *The Ladies of the Hsiang*. Read 涕 for 帳 with Wu Ju-lun. The Ladies are weeping over the dragons' departure.

[8] A reference to the Blue (or White) Lotus-flower Dragon-king.

[9] Iron – a metal of which dragons were terrified – had been dropped into the water to drive them away.

Six Satires

All 5-character: 1 rhyme

No. 1

SPRING's rampant in the world!
Its fragrance wafts through sunlit curtains.
Darting sunbeams redden lonely flowers,
Enter her grottoed room to boast their beauty.
Pattern of golden snakes on her dancing-rug,
Zither and flute set out on ornate stands.
Her eyes are drunken with spring dusk,
Her tears yellow from her powder.
A prince arrives, gets off his horse,
On a winding pool, mandarin-ducks start singing.
How can he guess the carriage of her heart
Roaming the whole earth in a single night?[1]

---

[1]Another variant on the 'bird in a gilded cage'. A singing-girl, though patronized by princes, is desperately unhappy because her true love – who is presumably poor – is far away. The penultimate line reads literally: 'How can he know of the carriage rolling through her guts?' This alludes to an old love-song, which begins:

'I cannot tell of my heart's desires.
Within my guts the carriage wheels are turning.'

The girl's mind is not on the prince, but on her lost love.

No. 2[1]

A BITTER wind whistles up boreal cold,
Trees of Ch'in are snapped by bolting sand.
Dancing shadows reel through an empty sky,
Sharp beat of painted drums throbs in my ears.
No autumn letter comes to me from Shu,[2]
Only Black Waters' waves sobbing at dawn.[3]
A whirlwind will bear off my graceful ghost,
The moon of home hang over my lost grave.

[1]Yao interprets this poem as a satire on the marriage of a Chinese princess of the imperial house to the Uighur Khan. Such marriages had taken place on two occasions, in A.D. 758 and 788. Ho clearly resented Chinese subservience to the barbarians and pities the princesses who were sacrificed in the interests of diplomacy. But the poem need not refer to any specific occasion, as the reference to Wang Chao-chün (line 5) demonstrates.

[2]Wang Chao-chün came from Shu.

[3]There are at least three places of this name. The one referred to here is probably in Mongolia.

No. 3

Fog of dust from barbarian horses,
Forested halberds of frontier troops.
Heaven taught the nomad horseman how to fight,
At dawn the clouds are lowering blood-red.
A lady-general leads our Chinese soldiers,
A dainty kerchief tucked into her quiver.
She's not ashamed of her heavy, gold seal,
Lurching along with bow-case at her waist.
Simple old men, just honest villagers,
Tested the teeth of arrow-barbs last night,
But she sent her courier to cry victory –
Must powder and mascara blind us all![1]

[1]A deadly attack on a eunuch general – probably T'u-t'u Ch'eng-ts'ui himself – who was conducting the campaign against the rebel governor Wang
Ch'eng-tsung. The appointment of a 'lady-general' aroused such a storm of
criticism that the emperor was compelled to dismiss him. Ho's verses must have
played their part in this. The whole poem rings with a savage indignation
rarely found in Chinese verse.

No. 4

WHEN he hunts with crossbow at Green Gate,
His horses throng the empty suburbs.[1]
When did he get those presents from the palace?
Decked out with jade he swaggers in the saddle.
Off he goes, his hounds heading for home,
Back he comes to a banquet of boiled lamb.
A sack of gold couldn't buy such dishes,
He turns his nose up even at badgers' paws.
Dare we ask where this fellow springs from?
His father wears a sword hung at his belt.[2]
Yet in a white-thatched cottage on West Hill
A wise man lives in lonely poverty.

[1] A satire on a rich, young man, son of some general or other, who has risen to wealth and eminence through his father's influence. 'Green Gate': the eastern gates of Ch'ang-an.

[2] Suzuki objects to understanding 乃老 as 'your father'. He translates: 'Even when he is dead, he will be able to wear a sword at his belt.'

No. 5

DAWN chrysanthemums wet with cold dew,
Seem sad as the wind from her round fan.[1]
Chill of autumn creeps through the Han palace,
Pan-tzu wept for her fading beauty.
I would never refuse to ride in the royal sedan-chair,[2]
Nor think of entering an empty palace.
The pearl belt at her waist is broken now,
Ash butterflies flutter by gloomy pines.[3]

---

[1]Pan Chieh-yü (*floruit* 48–6 B.C.) was for many years the favourite of Han
Ch'eng-ti (*regnet* 33–7 B.C.). Towards the end of her life, seeing herself ousted
by a younger favourite, she withdrew to the Palace of Eternal Trust, where she
lived out the rest of her days. She is best known for a poem supposed to have
been written on a round fan which she sent to the Emperor after her loss of
favour. (See J. D. Frodsham, *An Anthology of Chinese Verse*, pp. 21–2). In our
poem Ho contrasts himself with Pan Chieh-yü, who relinquished her position as
imperial favourite much too readily. If he had the chance of gaining such
favours, he would not be hampered by such scruples. Yet even if he did gain
fame and fortune, like Pan herself he must eventually come to dust.

[2]As Pan did, when invited to ride with the Emperor. She refused on the
grounds that only degenerate rulers allowed women to accompany them on
their outings.

[3]Paper money, burnt at funerals, flutters around the graveyard pines.

No. 6

PRETTY girls on a terrace where butterflies flit,
A willow-swept road where harmonicas play.[1]
Ten suns are hanging in the entrance court,[2]
Through ninety days of fall no flowers fade.
Sound of singing borne afar on the breeze,
Cup-like ponds where little white fishes play.[3]
Feasting by the pool, they sup on fragrant meats,
Water-chestnut gleams in green fish-baskets.
Pear-blossoms cover luxuriant grass,
Long whistles sound through vernal dark,[4]
They only grieve that fragrant blossoms fall,[5]
Not realizing their whole world must decay.
Brooding on the past has fettered my spirit,
Mount South's unchanging peaks have made me sad.[6]

[1]A party is going on in a wealthy household.
[2]A reference to the legend about ten suns once appearing on the Fu-sang tree. The line means: (a) the entrance court was bright with candles, (b) the sun never set on their merrymaking.
[3]'White fishes': culters. The fish are attracted by the music.
[4]Whistling was a form of entertainment.
[5]Text reads 苦. One edition reads 晚. Suzuki and Saito suggest 芳, which I adopt.
[6]Because Mount South is eternal, while man's life is ephemeral.

Song: Never Sorrow[1]

5-character: 2 rhymes

BELOW the Pool of Dragons grasses grow,[2]
Up on the city battlements crows are cawing.
Who is it dwells within the city walls,
By pomegranates planted in their corner?
With emerald silk her horses five are bound,
With yellow gold her oxen two are haltered.
White fishes harnessed to her lotus boat[3]
Carry her full ten leagues in a single night.

Then she returns, unknown to everyone,
Unheeded climbs her aloes-scented tower.[4]
She sings to a jewelled lute on her silk-hung couch,[5]
A sliver of moon wanes on the curtain-hooks.[6]
Today the hibiscus must cast down its petals,
Next dawn, the plane-trees feel the autumn come.
It seems her life is one of thwarted love.
Why ever she was known as 'Never Sorrow'?[7]

[1]Songs about a singing-girl called Mo-ch'ou (whose name means 'Never Sorrow') date back to the Six Dynasties period, probably to the early fifth century or so. They belong to that rather languid yet passionate tradition of southern love-songs which was later to assert itself anew in that genre known as the *tz'u*.

[2]A pool near Chiang-ling. North of it stood the Fishing Tower of King Chuang of Ch'u.

[3]The fishes were painted on the prow of the boat, which she needed for gathering lotuses.

[4]For aloeswood, see above, p. 26, note 5.

[5]She was playing a *se*, a half-tube zither with twenty-six strings of silk-gut.

[6]Or possibly: 'A sliver of waning moon, like a curtain-hook.'

[7]Yeh and Suzuki follow the version given in *Yüeh-fu shih-chi*, reading 若 for 莫 and 作 for 何. Saitō retains the original reading:

> 'Since she never worries about anything,
> She has taken the name "Never Sorrow".'

Joy Comes at Night[1]

7-character: 2 rhymes

LINED curtains of red sendal,
Gold-tufted tassels,
Nine-branched candelabra,
Hanging carp.[2]
This lovely girl, by the shining moon,
Opens her ringed door,
Pours out wine in a spring flood
From a gibbon jar.[3]
Her price is high: ten incense-sticks
In costly caskets,
Ingots of red-melon gold
And bran-cake flakes,
A green jade duck in wrappings
Of five-coloured silk –
Over such costly presents
A-hou laughs with delight.[4]

The Milky Way wheels past southern eaves,
Screen shadows fade,
In the kolanut woods, crows are crying,
Nestling their young.
Hill-hafted sword, sectioned whip,
Green stones and pearls,
His piebald horse is flecked with foam,
Frost stiffening its coat.[5]

[1] A fashionable singing-girl, with a wealthy clientele, entertains her guest.
[2] A pattern of carp was carved onto the candelabra.
[3] Gibbons were so fond of wine that they were generally captured by making them drunk. Hence wine-jars were often shaped like gibbons.
[4] Reading 笑 此 for 此 笑 with Suzuki. A-hou was a name used for singing-girls, deriving from a poem of Emperor Wu of Liang. See p. 215, note 1, above, and p. 265, note 5, below.
[5] Dawn has come and her guest is departing for the court.

She speeds her guest to Ch'eng-ming lodge,[1]
At dawn by the water-clock.
Then back to her tall mansion,
And a bright, lonely moon.
Another guest is just dismounting
As the first one leaves,
Once more she combs her 'green cicadas',[2]
Brushes on her brows.

Deriding the Snow[3]

5-character: 1 rhyme

YESTERDAY it left the Ts'ung-ling ranges,[4]
Today it's fluttering down on our orchid isles.[5]
Delighted to have come a thousand miles,
It's laughing wildly, promising the spring.
On the Dragon Sands it drenches our Han banners,
Phoenix-wing fans welcome its Chinese white.[6]
'My Liao-tung crane left me so long ago,
By now his feather-robe must have grown sere.'[7]

[1]Where high officials stayed while awaiting audience with the emperor.

[2]'Green cicadas': a type of hair style.

[3]A girl is deriding the snow because its promise of the joy of spring is false, since her soldier husband is still away from home.

[4]Ts'ung-ling mountains – mountains in the Himalayas, north of Nepal.

[5]'Orchid isles' – perhaps gardens of rich families in Ch'ang-an.

[6]'Dragon Sands': the desert beyond the Great Wall.

[7]Ting Ling-wei, from Liao-tung (on the Korean border), was a Taoist who could change himself into a crane. He returned home after an absence of a thousand years to find all his friends long dead. The girl is comparing her husband, now feathered white with the snow that is falling beyond the Great Wall, to an ageing crane that has flown off to Liao-tung never to return. Yeh believes these lines describe the snow-flakes and would presumably translate thus: 'It's been long since the snow parted from the crane on the walls of Liao. The feather-robe by now must have grown sere.'

Ballad: Spring Longings[1]

7-character: 1 rhyme

DEEP in shadows, this fragrant path
Is a flower-hung cave,
Tangled willows wreathed in mist,
Fragrant sashes heavy.
The moon-toad rolls its jade along,
Hangs out a bright bow.
A girl is striking fairies and phoenix
With a golden plectrum.[2]
Clouds tumbling over her jewelled pillow[3]
She seeks a spring dream,
In caskets cold with inlaid sapphires,
The dragon-brain grows chill.[4]
A-hou ties her brocade girdle
And looks for Chou Yü,[5]
She has to rely on the east wind
To waft her to him.

[1]A courtesan, alone at night, is dreaming of her lover.

[2]She is playing her *p'i-p'a*, which is decorated with a pattern of phoenixes and fairies with a plectrum, whose guard (*han-po*) was made of gold. Suzuki, following Wang, understands 'fairies and phoenixes' as referring to an air called 'Fiery Phoenix'. Hence they render: 'Strumming with a plectrum tipped with gold, she plays "Fiery Phoenix".'

[3]'Clouds': her hair, Wu edition reads 誰 云 for 垂 雲.

[4]Dragon-brain was a name given to Borneo camphor (*dryobalanops aromatica*), a highly prized aromatic.

[5]'A-hou': a name for a singing-girl. Chou Yü (175–210) was noted for his bravery and good looks.

Ballad of the White Tiger[1]

7-character: 6 rhymes

THE fire-bird's sun sank into shadow,[2]
Surging clouds dislimned.
The King of Ch'in glared like a tiger
On all the people.
He burnt the books, wiped out the states,
Not wasting a day,[3]
Forging swords, he bawled to his generals,
Rings on his belt.[4]

Libations poured on a jade altar –
Thoughts soared to heaven,
One generation, two generations –
Surely ten thousand years!
Burning cinnabar could not bring him
The immortal drug,
So he sent a fleet to scour the ocean,
Searching for fairies.[5]

---

[1]Wu Cheng-tzu believed that this poem was not by Li Ho but by some later imitator. Yeh agrees, insisting that the poem is too prolix and commonplace to have been written by Ho. While agreeing that this poem is markedly inferior in style to the rest of Ho's work, I feel that since arguments based on stylistic grounds alone are rather dubious, its exclusion from this collection would be unjustifiable. The white tiger stands for the Ch'in dynasty, which conquered the last of the old feudal kingdoms in 221 B.C., thus bringing about the formation of a centralized state. White was the symbolic colour assigned to Ch'in; the tiger was the symbol of oppressive government. The King of Ch'in, who reigned as First Emperor of Ch'in (Ch'in Shih Huang-ti) from 221 to 210 was a ruthless innovator, a great destroyer of tradition, who earned for himself the undying execration of the Confucian literati.

[2]The fire-bird was the symbol of Chou. When King Wu of Chou was on his way to destroy the Shang dynasty, fire fell from heaven upon his house and then took on the form of a red crow with a melodius song. See *Shih-chi*, IV.

Leviathans whipped sea-waves to foam
With flailing flukes,
Half our peasants vanished, turned to
Soldiers' ghosts.
Fierce and cruel as savage fire
He flamed to the heavens,[6]
Never a man who could unlock
The Sky River's waves.[7]

Some who suffered would not suffer
Such suffering,[8]
Righteous men vowed to each other
To help their fellows.
Chien-li sat and strummed his lute
While Ching K'o sang.
Ching Ch'ing held his wine,
Prince Tan of Yen spoke out.[9]

---

[3]Li Ssu, Ch'in Shih Huang-ti's minister, persuaded his master to order that all histories of the feudal states (with the exception of those of Ch'in) should be burnt, as well as *The Classic of Poetry*, *The Classic of History* and the philosophical works of the hundred schools.

[4]The expression *p'ei chüeh* 佩 玦 'to wear a jade ring at the belt', also means by a play on words, 'to act decisively'. The government was militaristic and ruthless.

[5]Ch'in Shih Huang-ti is said to have sent the magician Hsü Shih on an expedition to search for the three magic islands of the Immortals which were supposed to lie in the eastern sea. On his return, Hsü Shih excused his failure by claiming that a great fish had prevented him from reaching the islands. He went on to ask that an archer with a multiple-firing crossbow should accompany him on his next trip to deal with the fish. The Emperor then ordered that all fishermen and sailors should take arms against this fish.

[6] Reading 猛 焰 烈 燒 空 with Suzuki and *Li Ch'ang-chi wen-chi*.

[7]Nobody could enlist the aid of Heaven to destroy Ch'in. 'Sky River': the Milky Way.

[8]Literally: 'Who suffered most, who suffered most?'

Sword like frost!
Gall like iron!
Out of the walls of Yen he went,
Gazed at the moon of Ch'in,
Heaven had given Ch'in its seal,
Its sway was not yet over,
So the dragon robes were drenched
With Ching Ch'ing's blood.

When scarlet banners were planted in earth,
The white tiger died.
Then we knew the true Son of Heaven –
The king of Han![10]

[9]Ching K'o, also known as Ching Ch'ing, was a man from Wei who eventually became a retainer of Prince Tan, the Heir-apparent of the state of Yen. He was something of a drunkard, spending his days sprawled in the marketplace with his friend Kao Chien-li, who was a skilled performer on the five stringed *chu*-lute 筑, singing and drinking wine. In 227 B.C., when Yen was menaced by Ch'in, he volunteered to set off on a suicidal mission to assassinate the King of Ch'in. The attempt failed and Ching was cut to pieces. Kao Chien-li then tried to avenge Ching's death by filling his lute with lead and attacking the King of Ch'in with it. This attempt was also unsuccessful.

[10]Liu Pang, the founder of Han, called himself the son of the Scarlet Emperor. Hence the Han banners were scarlet.

Someone I Love[1]

Irregular: 5 rhymes

LAST year, by the wayside we sang
A song of parting.
Today you have sent me a letter
From far-off Shu.[2]
Outside my screens, the flowers are opening
In the April wind.[3]
In front of the terrace, a thousand tears
Bathe the bamboos.[4]
My heart and the lute's are breaking tonight,
Yet will mend again.

My thoughts are with you, astride a white horse,
Carved bow at your side.
No place on earth where the winds of spring
Are not blowing now.
You were not willing to make your heart
As firm as stone.
The beauty of my face will fade
Like the pink of petals.

[1] *Someone I Love* is the title of one of the eighteen *Han Cymbal Songs*. Here the poet is speaking through the person of Wen-chün, wife of the poet Ssu-ma Hsiang-ju. She is waiting for him to return from his journey to Shu.

[2] Szechwan.

[3] Literally: 'the wind of the second month'. This can fall any time between the end of February and mid-April.

[4] As did the tears of the two wives of Shun, which fell upon the bamboos near the river Hsiang and made them speckled.

[5] The Milky Way.

[6] Ming edition reads 自 for 白. Suzuki follows this.

[7] The *Yi-yüan*, a fifth-century collection of tales of the supernatural, carries the story of a certain T'ao K'an, who pulled up a shuttle while out fishing. After he had taken this home and hung it up on a wall, it changed into a red dragon and flew away. Presumably shuttles were sometimes carved in the shape of dragons to commemorate this story.

Y

High in its sapphire, as night wears on,
The Long River glides.[5]
Across that River there is no bridge,
Lonely white waves.[6]
Sadly, before the west wind stirs,
She plies her Dragon-shuttle.[7]
Year after year, she spins her plain silk
Knitting her brows.[8]

Mountains and rivers stretch into the distance,
Endless, unbroken.
My tear-filled eyes gaze at the taper,
Flaring, then dying.
Since I hid myself in my lonely mansion,
Windows firmly barred,
How many times has the Cassia Flower[9]
Waxed and then waned?

Crow after crow, as dawn draws near,
Cries in the grove,
A wind blows from the banks of the pool,
Tinkling musical-jades.[10]
Bleak and lonely breaks the white day
Ending my dreams.
South of the bridge, I ask the Immortal
To tell me our fortunes.[11]

[8]The Weaving Lady and the Herd-boy, lovers separated by the river of the
Milky Way, are fated only to meet on the seventh day of the seventh month,
when the wings of magpies form a bridge for them to cross the waters which
divide them. Since the west wind, harbinger of autumn, has not yet risen, the
seventh month is a long way off.

[9]The moon.

[10]Pieces of jade arranged so that they would tinkle musically when the wind
blew, were hung by the windows of well-to-do houses. Suzuki, however,
thinks this means 'groves of bamboo'.

[11]To consult the omens so that she might know when her husband would
return. One version reads 'south of the Wall . . .'

Ridiculing a Young Man

7-character: 6 rhymes

SADDLES of his well-fed greys
Gleaming with gold,
Silken jacket really reeking
Of dragon-brain,
Lovely girls all over him,[1]
Jade goblets flying –
'He's a real swell, isn't he!'
The poor exclaim.

In a tall tower that he's built
By green bamboo-grass,
He hauls red fish from a deep pool
On silken lines.
Sometimes he sprawls – half drunk, of course –
Among his flowers,
Or brings the birds down on the wing
With golden bolts.[2]

'I've never been any man's guest!' he brags,
'In my born days.[3]
Three hundred gorgeous girls I've got,
Or maybe more.'
How can *he* know that among the farmers
Tilling our fields,[4]
No girls are left to weave the cloth
For dunning tax-collectors![5]

---

[1] Read 狹 for 挾.

[2] As Han Yen, companion of Emperor Wu, did during the Former Han dynasty, losing a dozen a day.

[3] '. . . been anyone's guest.' Arai takes this to mean 'been under obligation to anyone'. Suzuki understands as 'never travelled'.

Piling up gold, heaping up jade,
He boasts his noble blood,
Bowing to strangers as he goes,
Puffed up with pride.
He hasn't read more than half a line,
Since he was born.
But bought high office for himself
With gleaming gold.

How can a young man hope to stay
Forever young,
When even ocean waves must change
To mulberry fields?
Quick as an arrow, fortune turns,
To misery,
Will the Creator shower his favours
Only on you?

Don't think the sunny days of spring
Will last till late –
For white hair and a haggard face
Are lying in wait![6]

4 Read 田 for 苗 with Suzuki.
5 Read 没 for 勿 with Suzuki.
[6]An allusion to a passage in the *Saddharmapuṇḍarīka-sūtra* (*Fa-hua ching*) which warns: 'When the hair grows white and the face turns haggard, death is near.'
Yeh points out – rightly, perhaps – that this poem is too superficial and vulgar to be anything but a forgery.

A Private Road in Eastern Kao-p'ing County[1]

5-character: 1 rhyme

FRAGRANT and thick the leaves of the scarlet-seed,[2]
Trees and flowers dripping with cold rain.
This evening – autumn on the mountains –
Forgotten forever they blossom in lonely places.
Long, stony path overgrown with rank grass,[3]
Bitter fruit of the wild pear dangles down.
Surely long ago a hermit sought this spot
And asked you to construct this private road.

Ballad of the Immortals

7-character: 2 rhymes

WHERE sapphire peaks rise from the sea
Magic books are stored.[4]
The Creating Power chose this place
As a dwelling for Immortals.[5]
On clear, bright days their laughter echoes
Round the empty sky,
As they strive to ride enormous waves,
On the backs of whales.

[1]This poem was probably written when Ho was visiting Chang Ch'e in Lu-chou. Kao-p'ing county is in Shanshi.

[2]*Ternstroemia japonica.*

[3] Reading 蹊 for 谿.

[4]On the magic islands of the Immortals in the Eastern Sea.

[5]Wu edition reads 神 仙 for 仙 入.

With words of welcome on spring silk
To greet the Western Mother,
They will feast together in the Red Tower's
Deepest recess.
Wings of a crane, beating the wind,
Too slow to cross the sea,
Far better despatch a messenger
Riding a blue dragon.
Still doubtful whether the Western Mother
Will accept the invitation,
They send a mist-haired beauty
Off with the message.[1]

Song: Dragons at Midnight

7-character: 5 rhymes

A CURLY-HAIRED nomad boy
With eyes of green,
By a tall mansion, in the still of the night
Is playing his flute.
Every note seems to have come
Down from heaven.[2]
Under the moon a lovely girl weeping,
Sick for home.

[1]Reading 娃 for 妖 with Wu edition.
[2] Reading 自 for 向.

Deftly he fingers the seven holes,
Hiding their stars,
Kung and *chih* secretly harmonize
With the pure breeze.[3]
Deep autumn on the roads of Shu,
A cloud-filled forest.
From the Hsiang river at midnight
Startled dragons rise.[4]

A lovely girl in her jade room
Broods on the frontier.
Bright moonshine on her sapphire window –
Sadly she hears the flute.

A hundred feet of glossed silk beaten
On the cold fulling-block[5]
Tears congeal as pearls in her powder,
Soak her red gown.

Play no more the Lung-t'ou tune,
Nomad boy!
No one knows a girl's heart is breaking
Beyond that casement.

[3]*Kung* and *chih* are the first and fourth notes of the pentatonic scale.
[4]Images evoked by the music.
[5]The sound of silk being beaten on the fulling-blocks in autumn, to make winter clothes, is a familiar symbol of parting and sorrow.

The K'un-lun Envoy[1]

7-character: 2 rhymes

OF THE K'un-lun envoy
No news at all,
Mist dyes the trees of Mao-ling tomb
With mournful hues.[2]
Drop after drop of jade dew trickled
In brazen bowls,
But Primal Humours proved too vast
For him to gather.[3]

Backs of stone unicorns by the grave
Crack into patterns,
Red limbs of little dragons break
Beneath their scales.[4]
Where is the restless heart that yearned
For ten thousand kingdoms?
High in the heavens, a brilliant moon
Lights the long nights.

[1]Emperor Wu of Han sent Chang Ch'ien as an envoy to the far west, where he came upon the source of the Yellow River, in a range of mountains he dubbed 'K'un-lun'. Though this poem appears to be a satire on the insatiable ambitions of Emperor Wu, who was always eager to enlarge his empire, it is actually an attack on Emperor Hsien-tsung.

[2]Emperor Wu was already buried in the Mao-ling tomb before Chang Ch'ien returned.

[3]No Taoist recipes could give the Emperor the secret of eternal life. For the brazen bowls, see p. 65, note 2, above.

[4]Stone unicorns (*ch'i-lin*) and carved dragons around the mausoleum are weathering with time.

T'ang-chi of Han Sings as the Wine Is Drunk[1]

5-character: 2 rhymes

THE emperor's clothes were drenched with frosty dew,
The palace roads all overgrown with thorns.[2]
When gold is sullied over with autumn dust,
No one will wear it as an ornate belt.
All songs were stilled within those halls of jade,
Mist cloaked the fragrant forest trees.
A song came from the tower of Yün-yang,
Wail of a ghost, and all to no avail.[3]
Swords of iron, gleaming and glittering,
Threatened the emperor with their vile intent.[4]
Savage owls gnawing their mother's skulls!
Evil demons slavering for souls of the dead!
Emperor and lady wept as they gazed at each other,
Their tears falling in an endless stream.
'Why do you have to drink this crystal wine
Must plunge you deep within the Yellow Spring?
No question of a toppling hill of jade,[5]
But swallow this, death's pallor stamps your face.
Only the Lord of Heaven will hear your plaint,
At least in Heaven you will be safe from harm.
No ornate curtain will be hung for you,
And neither pine nor cypress mark your grave.[6]

---

[1] In the ninth month of A.D. 189 Tung Cho forced the boy-emperor, Liu Pien (Shao-ti), to abdicate after a reign of only a few months. In the first month of the following year Cho ordered Li Ju, one of his officers, to force the Emperor to drink a poisoned draught. The Emperor then held a farewell banquet at which his wife, T'ang-chi, sang and danced for him. When this was over, he drank the poison and died. Afterwards T'ang-chi returned to her native town to live in seclusion, refusing to marry. See *TCTC*, pp. 1894, 1904 and 1909; *Hou Han-shu*, 10(B), pp. 17b–18b (*Po-na* ed.)

[2] Read 榛 for 蓁 with Suzuki.

I shall drag out my life through weary days,
Your spirit must roam lonely in its night,
No longer will I tend my moth-like eyebrows,
Who'll gaze with love on my white-powdered neck?
Proudly I'll treasure memories of Chao-yang,[7]
Nor turn my eyes towards the southern road.[8]

[3]Since the Emperor was not imprisoned at Yün-yang (Shensi), Suzuki believes this is an allusion to Ch'eng Miao, who was said to have invented the form of writing known as *li-shü* (clerk script) while in prison at Yün-yang. Hence Yün-yang here is simply a literary term for 'gaol'. Since the Emperor was on the verge of death he is styled 'a ghost'.

[4]Following Suzuki, who adopts the Wu edition's reading. The usual text, which Saitō and Yeh prefer, reads:
           'Grasping swords as bright as autumn water,
           Evil powers often threatened the emperor.'

[5]The expression 'a mountain of jade about to topple' was used to describe the poet Hsi K'ang (223–62) when drunk.

[6]The Emperor will not be buried with imperial honours.

[7]'Chao-yang': the name of the palace of the Han Empress Chao Fei-yen. Here it means the palace where T'ang-chi had lived.

[8]'Southern road': the busy road to the south. T'ang-chi will live in seclusion.

Song: Listening to Master Ying Playing the Lute[1]

7-character: 4 rhymes

CLOUDS of the Shores of Parting home
From the isle of cassia flowers,[2]
Through strings of a lute from Shu
Two phoenixes talk.[3]
Lotus leaves falling in autumn
As simurghs part,
A king of Yüeh wandering at night
On Mount T'ien-mu.[4]

Hidden girdle-gems of an honest minister,
Tinkling crystals,[5]
Fairy maidens crossing the sea,
Leading white deer.
What vision is going to Long Bridge,
Sword in hand?[6]
What vision is writing on spring bamboo
With ink-soaked hair?[7]

[1]Ying was evidently a celebrated performer on the *ch'in*. Han Yü also wrote a poem to him, with the same title.

[2]The clouds drift towards the Milky Way leaving the moon ('the isle of cassia flowers') shining serenely.

[3]'Two phoenixes': Ying's hands.

[4]The lute sounds like the singing of the goddess of Mount T'ien-mu (in Hsin-ch'ang county, Chekiang), which was once heard by a King of Yüeh.

[5]'Hidden' because worn inside the garments.

[6]See p. 25, note 7, for the story of Chou Ch'u.

[7]Chang Hsü, a contemporary of Li Ho's, was famous for his calligraphy in the draft script. When drunk he would rush wildly around shouting, then soak his long hair in ink and use it to write huge characters. When sober, he could remember nothing of this, swearing he must have been possessed by a spirit.

An Indian monk is standing here,
Right at my gate,
An arhat with venerable eyebrows
In a Buddhist temple.[8]
His antique lute, full eight feet long,
Has massive stops,[9]
An ancient tree-trunk from Mount Yi-yang,
Not a puny branch.[10]

Sound of strings through the cold room
Rouses me from my sick-bed,
Leaving my potions for a while
I sit on the dragon's beard.[11]
If you want a song, you ought to ask
A cabinet-minister,
Maestro, do not demean yourself
With a mere clerk.

[8]Master Ying must have resembled a Buddhist monk.

[9]This was the great lute (*ta ch'in*) which was eight feet one inch in length.

[10]Literally: 'Not the grandson of a kolanut tree.' Mount Yi-yang, in Kiangsu, was renowned for its kolanut trees, which were prized for lute-making. The small branches which were generally used, were called 'grandsons'. Ho remarks that this particular lute is so big it must have taken a whole tree to make it, not just a branch.

[11]A mat of dragon's-beard or Baltic rush (*juncus balticus*, Willa).

Ballad of the World[1]

5-character: 1 rhyme

A LITTLE butterfly in Shang-lin park
Trying to accompany the Emperor of Han.[2]
It flew away towards South Wall,
Alighting, by mistake, on a pomegranate skirt.[3]
Purposeful blossom masses on the trees,
Darting swallows wheel around the clouds.
'Outside the gates, I did not know the way,
Yet felt ashamed to ask the passers-by.'

[1]A young girl, brought up in the Imperial palace, leaves it to become a singing-girl.
[2]'Shang-lin park' – the Imperial park.
[3]'Pomegranate skirt' – the pomegranate-coloured skirt of a singing-girl.

Song: A Modest Maiden in the Spring Sunshine[1]

7-character: 1 rhyme

YOUNG butterflies in love with fragrance
Cling to new petals,
Branch after branch is weeping dew,
Shedding heaven-born tears.
Powdered windows choked with perfume,
Tumbling clouds of dawn.[2]
Hills of brocade, strewn with petals,
Hide her spring dreams.[3]
Peacocks shaking their golden tails
Embrace the screen,
Her oriole's silver tongue is calling
Her serving-maids.
Cold dragons in an icy cave[4] –
Ewers of water,
This white simurgh, rising, drives away
The mists of sleep.

---

[1]This poem and the next one were not found in the earliest edition of Ho's work, but are attributed to him in the Sung anthology, the *Yüeh-fu shih-chi* of Kuo Mao-ch'ien. (See *Yüeh-fu shih-chi*, LXVI, p. 3b: XCVI, p. 9b, *Wen-hsüeh ku-chi* edition, Peking, 1955.) On this account, the commentators have been wary about assigning authorship of these works to Ho. I can see no reason why these should not be from Ho's own hand.

[2]'Clouds of dawn' – her hair.

[3]'Hills of brocade' – the quilts.

[4]'Icy cave' – the girl's room.

Joys of Youth

7-characters: 1 rhyme

SCENTED flowers, falling petals,
Earth like brocade,
A youth of twenty roaming
In the Land of Drunkenness.[1]
Red ribbons never stirring
On his proud, white horse,
Weeping willows golden silk
Brush the perfumed water.
The girl from Wu unsmiling,
Flowers folded still,[2]
Green tresses tower and topple,
Orchid clouds arise.
Master Lu, drunk and reeling,
Tugs her gauze sleeve.[3]
Pulls out a jewelled hairpin,
A kingfisher of gold.

[1]Wang Chi (Sui dynasty) wrote the *Record of the Land of Drunkenness* (*Tsui-hsiang chi* 醉鄉記). This is quoted by Han Yü in his *Preface When Seeing off Bachelor Wang* (*Sung Wang Hsiu-ts'ai Hsü* 送王秀才序 in *Han Ch'ang-li ch'üan-chi*, XX, p. 7a). Since Yü had read this work, it would seem very likely that Ho was familiar with it too.

[2]'The girl from Wu' – a conventional expression for a beautiful woman.

[3]'Master Lu' – see above, p. 54-55, *Pearl – A Lo-yang Beauty*, note 9.

APPENDIX I

Major Extant Editions of Li Ho's Works

Our earliest record of Ho's poems occurs in Tu Mu's *Preface* (A.D. 831) which mentions 233 poems divided into four sections. Early bibliographical notices are:

T'ang-shu yi-wen chih 唐書藝文志: *Li Ho chi* 李賀集, 5 *chüan;*

Sung-shih yi-wen chih 宋史藝文志: *Li Ho chi* 李賀集 5 *chüan;*

Wen-hsien t'ung-k'ao 文献通考: *Li Ch'ang-chi chi* 李長吉集 4 *chüan; wai-chi* 外集 1 *chüan.*

   This indicates that the *wai-chi* was composed of poems discovered later. There are at present some 36 editions of Li Ho's poems extant, with or without commentaries. Only the major editions are listed below. Of the Sung editions, the 京本蜀本 and 會稽本 each contains 219 poems; while the 宣城本 and 鮑氏本 both contain 242 poems.

Sung   1. *Ko-shih pien* 歌詩編 Northern Sung edition.
   2. *Li Ch'ang-chi wen-chi* 李長吉文集 From the Chu 朱 family library.

Chin   3. *Ko-shih pien* 歌詩編 From the Ch'ü 瞿 family library.
   4. *Ko-shih pien* 歌詩編 From the Ch'ü family library. *Chi wai shih* 集外詩 added from a Northern Sung edition. In *Ssu-pu ts'ung-k'an.*

Yüan   5. *Li Ch'ang-chi ko-shih* 李長吉歌詩 by Wu Cheng-tzu 吳正子 and Liu Ch'en-weng 劉辰翁 (*Fu-ku t'ang* edition of 1337. Reprinted in Japan, 1819). This work combines the *Li Ch'ang-chi shih p'ing* 李長吉詩評 of Liu with the *Li Ch'ang-chi shih* 李長吉詩 of Wu.
   6. *Chin-nang chi* 錦囊集 *Fu-ku t'ang* edition (Reprinted 1922).

Ming   7. *Ch'ang-ku shih-chu* 昌谷詩註 by Hsü Wei 徐渭 and Tung Mao-ts'e 董懋策. This edition was put together from two separate works of this title.
   8. *T'ang Li Ch'ang-chi shih chi* 唐李長吉詩集 Version of no. 7 above in *Tung-shih ts'ung-shu* 董氏叢書.

9. *Ch'ang-ku shih-chu* 昌谷詩注 by Tseng Yi 曾益.

10. *Ko-shih pien* 歌詩編 in *T'ang ssu ming-chia chi* 唐四名家集.

11. *Ch'ang-ku shih-chu* 昌谷詩註 by Hsü Kuang 徐光.

12. *Li Ch'ang-chi Ch'ang-ku chi-chü chieh ting-pen* 李長吉昌谷集句解定本 by Yao Ch'üan 姚佺 and Ch'iu Hsiang-sui 丘象隨. Incorporates the *Ch'ang-ku shih-chien* 昌谷詩箋 of Yao Ch'üan, along with the comments of thirteen other scholiasts.

Ch'ing 13. *Li Ch'ang-chi chi* 李長吉集 by Huang Ch'un-yao 黃淳耀 (1731).

14. *Li Ch'ang-chi chi* 李長吉集 by Huang Ch'un-yao and Li Chien 黎簡 (1773: Reprinted 1892, 1909).

15. *Li Ch'ang-chi ko-shih pu-chu* 李長吉歌詩補註 by Shih Jung 史榮. MS copy.

16. *Ch'ang-ku shih-chu* 昌谷詩註 by Yao Wen-hsieh 姚文燮 (1657).

17. *Li Ch'ang-chi shih-chi* 李長吉詩集 by Fang Fu-nan 方扶南 (1751).

18. *Li Ch'ang-chi ko-shih* 李長吉歌詩 by Wang Ch'i 王琦 (1760: 1908: 1959).

19. *Hsieh-lü kou-hsüan* 協律鉤玄 by Ch'en Pen-li 陳本禮 (1808).

20. *Li Ch'ang-chi shih p'ing-chu* 李長吉詩評註 by Wu Ju-lun (1921).

21. *Li Ch'ang-chi ko-shih* 李長吉歌詩 by Ho Yang-ling 賀揚靈 (Shanghai, 1933).

22. *Li Ho shih-chi* 李賀詩集 by Yeh Ts'ung-ch'i 葉蔥奇 (Peking, 1959).

Japanese editions:

23. *Yakuchū Ri Chō-kichi shishū* 譯註李長吉詩集 by Urushiyama Matashirō 漆山又四郎 (Tōkyō, 1933).

24. *Ri Ga* 李賀 by Arai Ken 荒井健 (Tōkyō, 1959).

25. *Ri Chō-kichi kashi-shū* 李長吉歌詩集 by Suzuki Torao 鈴木虎雄 (Tōkyō, 1951).

26. *Ri Ga* 李賀 by Saitō Shō 齋藤响 (Tōkyō, 1966).

z

APPENDIX II

Possible Forgeries

Li Ho's poems now number 241, made up as follows:

Chüan 1	58 poems
Chüan 2	55 poems
Chüan 3	56 poems
Chüan 4	50 poems
Wai-chi	22 poems
	241 poems

The original collection, for which Tu Mu wrote his *Preface*, numbered 233 poems. Wu Cheng-tzu's edition of 1337, however, contained 241 poems. To this we must add the two poems generally included in Ho's collected works under the rubric 'Appendix' (*pu-yi*). The presence of eight more poems in the Sung and Yüan editions than in the T'ang manuscript has led commentators to assert that certain poems in the 'Exoteric Collection' (*Wai-chi*) are forgeries. A list of these queries is appended below:

Commentator	Alleged Forgeries
Wu Cheng-tzu	*Joy Comes at Night* (p. 263) *Ballad of the White Tiger* (p. 266) *Ridiculing a Young Man* (p. 271) *Ballad of the Immortals* (p. 273)
Ch'ien Yin-kuang	*Ballad of the White Tiger* *Someone I Love* (p. 269) *Ridiculing a Young Man*
Fang Shih-chü	The whole of the *Wai-chi* except: *My Southern Garden* (p. 253) *The K'un-lun Envoy* (p. 276) *Song: Listening to Master Ying Playing the Lute* (p. 279) Also: *A Song for Hsü's Lady, Cheng* (p. 244) *Song: A New Summer* (p. 247)

Wang Ch'i	None, except the two poems in the Appendix.
Yeh Ts'ung-ch'i	*Ballad of the White Tiger:*
	Ridiculing a Young Man

All commentators reject the two poems in the Appendix on the grounds that they come from the *Yüeh-fu shih-chi* and are not found in the earliest editions. The other poems are excluded on stylistic grounds. But this, of course, is very treacherous terrain indeed. At the best our scholiasts are only making informed guesses. My own opinion – if I may join in this game – is that all the poems are genuine, including those in the Appendix, except for *Ballad of the White Tiger* and *Ridiculing a Young Man*, these being the only two poems in the *Wai-chi* which every critic would exclude. It is possible, however, that even these rather clumsy pieces are from Ho's brush for they may well be among his earliest poems.

BIBLIOGRAPHY

Sources

The following editions of Li Ho's poems have been consulted:

1. *Li Chʻang-chi wen chi* 李長吉文集 photolithographic reproduction of Sung edition in *Ku-yi tsʻung-shu* (Taipei, 1967).

2. *Li Ho ko-shih pien* 李賀歌詩編 *Ssu-pu tsʻung-kʻan* edition.

3. *Tʻang Li Chʻang-chi ko-shih* 唐李長吉歌詩 reprint of *Fu-ku tʻang* ed. of 1337 (Kyoto, 1952). Commentaries by Wu Cheng-tzu 吳正子 and Liu Chʻen-weng 劉辰翁.

4. *San-chia pʻing-chu Li Chʻang-chi ko-shih* 三家評註李長吉歌詩 (Shanghai, 1959). This includes works by Wang Chʻi 王琦 (preface dated 1760); by Fang Shih-chü 方世舉 (1675–1759: preface dated 1751); by Yao Wen-hsieh 姚文燮 (preface dated 1657). Fang's commentary is re-edited from an MS copy of Yao's edition with marginal notes. This commentary, hitherto unknown, was supplied by Hsü Sheng-yüeh 徐聲越 from his family library.

5. *Li Ho shih-chi* 李賀詩集 ed. with commentary by Yeh Tsʻung-chʻi 葉葱奇 (Peking, 1959).

6. *Ri Ga* 李賀 ed. with commentary by Arai Ken 荒井健, *Chūgoku shijin senshū*, vol. XIV (Tōkyō, 1959). This work is especially valuable, since Arai has utilized a rare Korean edition in movable type of *Li Ho ko-shih pien*.

7. *Ri Chōkichi kashishū* 李長吉歌詩集 ed. with commentary by Suzuki Torao 鈴木虎雄, 2 vols. (Tōkyō, 1961).

8. *Ri Ga* 李賀 ed. with commentary by Saitō Shō 薺藤晌 (Tōkyō, 1967).

Books and Articles on Li Ho

1. Arai Ken 荒井健, 'Ri Chō-kichi no shi: toku ni sono shikisai ni tsuite'. 李長吉の詩: 特にその色彩について *Chūgoku bungaku hō* 中國文學報, 3 (1955), pp. 61–90.

2. Chʻen Yi-hsin 陳貽焮, 'Lun Li Ho ti shih', *Wen-hsüeh yi-chʻan tseng-kʻan* 文學遺産增刊 (Peking, 1957), pp. 110–30.

3. Chou Lang-feng 周閬風 *Shih-jen Li Ho* 詩人李賀 (Shanghai, n.d.)

4. Chu Tzu-ch'ing 朱自清, 'Li Ho nien-p'u' 李賀年譜 Ch'ing-hua hsüeh-pao 清華學報, 10.4 (1935), pp. 46–85.
5. Harada Norio 原田憲雄:
  (1) 'Hakugyokurō chū no hito – Ri Chō-kichi o megutte', 白玉樓中の人李長吉をめぐつて Hōkō 方向 6 (1953–6).
  (2) Kindō sennin jikan ka: Ri Ga shōki', 金銅仙人辭漢歌 李賀小記 Jimbun ronsō 人文論叢 8 (September, 1963), pp. 1–56.
6. Ishikawa Kazunari 石川一成, 'Ri Chō-kichi no shikisai kankaku' 李長吉の色彩感覺, Chūgoku bunka kenkyūkai kaihō 中国文化研究會會報 (1955), pp. 18–22.
7. Li Chia-yen 李嘉言, 'Li Ho' 李賀, Ku-shih ch'u-t'an 古詩初探 (Shanghai, 1957).
8. Wada Toshio 和田利男, 'Ri Ga no kishi to sono keisei' 李賀の鬼詩とその形成 Gumma daigaku kiyō jimbun kagaku hen 群馬大學紀要 人文科學篇 5.8, (1956), pp. 88–102.
9. M. T. South
  (1) 'Li Ho – a Scholar-Official of the Yüan-ho Period (806–21)', Journal of the Oriental Society of Australia 2.2 (June 1964), pp. 64–81.
  (2) 'Li Ho and the New Yüeh-fu Movement', ibid., 4.2 (December 1966), pp. 49–61.
10. Ch'ien Chung-shu 錢鍾書 T'an-yi-lu 談藝錄 pp. 53–71.
11. E. G. Pulleyblank: 'The Rhyming Categories of Li Ho (791–817)', Tsing Hua Journal of Chinese Studies, New Series VII, No. 1 (August 1968), pp. 1–22.

INDEX

300   INDEX

Imperial Sacrifices, Court of, xvin, xxiv, xxvi, 14n, 111n, 122n.
Imperial Son-in-law, see Shen Tzu-ming.
Imperial Temple, 32n.
Imperial Travelling Lodge, 6, 119.
Imperial Way, 251.
Incense-burner Peak, 96.
India, 75; Indian monk, 280; Indian rice, 147n, 195; Indian unit of measure, 52n.
Indigo-field (Lan-t'ien), 26, 26n, 79n.
Indigo river, 79.
Introduction to Chinese Literature, An, ln.
Introduction to Sung Poetry, An (Sōshi gaisetsu, Chūgoku *shijin senshu*), xxxviiin, lxivn.
Ishida Mikinosuke: modern Japanese scholar, xxviin.
Ishikawa Kazunari: modern Japanese scholar, lviiin.

Jade Beauty: daughter of the legendary Scarlet Emperor, 196, 196n.
Jade Dog (Dog of Jade), xxxvii, 33, 33n.
Jade Dragon (Dragons of Jade): name for a sword during T'ang, 27, 27n.
Jade Gate, Kansu, 122, 122n, 188n.
Jade Grass: mythical plant, 45, 45n.
Jade Hill, 69.
Jade Lady: tutelary spirit of Mount Wu, 222, 222n.
Jade Lake, 71n.
Jade Pass, Kansu, 188.
Jade Purity Road, 177.
Jade Toad: toad-shaped clepsydra, 56, 56n.
Jade Towers: cloud towers, 31n.
Japan, 226; Japanese critic, xxxviii, lvn; editions, 285; people, 36n; tree, 24n.
Jasper Pool, 8, 205, 205n.
Jaxartes: the river Syr Daria, 76n.
Jen: surname, xxii.
Jen-ho: quarter of Lo-yang, 5, 90, 90n, 182n.
Jen Kung-tzu, xlvii, 171, 171n.
Jih ch'u ju, see *Rising and Setting of the Sun*.
Jo-hsia, 25n.
Jo tree: mythical tree, 170, 170n, 190.
Jo-yeh: river, xxx, 62.
Journal of the Oriental Studies of Australia, xxiin, xlvii, 189n, 289.
Juan Hsiu (270–311): an eccentric, 182n.
Jui-tsung, Emperor of T'ang (r. 662–90: 710–2), 177n.

juncus balticus: Baltic rush, 280n.
Jung-chou (Jung county), Kwangsi, 83, 83n.
Ju Shou: spirit of autumn, 203, 203n.

K'ang, King of Sung, 109n.
K'ang-pai, see Han Pai.
K'ang Ping: T'ang writer, xxin.
Kansu: province, 88n, 122n, 180n, 188n, 207n.
Kan-yü, see Lu Yü.
Kao Chien-li (Chien-li): skilled lute performer of the third-century B.C., 267, 268n.
Kao-chou: region in Kwangtung, 76, 76n.
Kao-lien: Bachelor Hsieh's concubine, 6, 126, 129n.
Kao-p'ing: county in Shansi, 9, 228n, 273, 273n.
Kao T'ang fu: poem, 123n.
Kao-tsu, Emperor of the Former Han (206–195 B.C.), see also Liu Pang, 197n.
Kao-tsu, Emperor of T'ang (r. 618–26), xiiin.
Kao-yao: county in Kwangtung, 167n.
Kara-nor, 188n.
Kashmir, king of, 221n.
Keats, John (1795–1821): English poet, xxxviii, xlivn, lxiv, 221n; Keatsian, xliv.
'Keats's style: Evolution towards Qualities of Permanent Value', xlivn.
Kenyon Review, lvn.
Kiangsu: province, 94n, 96n, 102n, 280n.
King's son, see Wang Tzu Ch'iao.
Kokonor, the, see Green Sea, the.
Kuan Chung (d. 645 B.C.): Ch'i prime minister, 22n.
Kuang-lu ssu, see Imperial Banquets, Office of.
Kuan-wa palace, Wu, 158n.
Ku-chin chu, 57n.
Kuei-chi (present day Shao-hsing), Cheki-ang, 3, 13, 13n, 236n, 242n.
K'uei-chou, Szechwan, 29n.
Kung-an: place-name, xiii.
K'ung-chao, see Chang Yu-hsin.
Kung Kung: demon, 11n.
Kung-lü, see Chia Chung.
K'ung-t'ung hills, 92, 107.
K'un-lun envoy, 9, 276.
K'un-lun mountain range (Mount K'un,

'Night-shining Jade' (*yeh-kuang yü*): luminescent variety of fluorite, 245n.
Nine Arguments, The, (*Chiu Pien*): ex *Ch'u Tz'u,* 106n, 210n.
Nine Doubts Mountain, *see* Mount Ts'ang-wu.
Nine-headed Serpent, 210n.
Nine Longings, The, (*Chiu, Ssu*): ex *Ch'u Tz'u,* 13n.
Nine Ministers, 200.
Nine Mountains, *see* Mount Tsang-wu.
Nine Palaces, *see* Great Purity, Nine Palaces of the.
Nine Provinces, 236.
Nine Songs, The, (*Chiu Ko*): ex *Ch'u Tz'u,* 46n, 50n, 51n, 68n, 137n, 228n.
Ning-yüan: county in Hunan, 192n.
Nirvana, lxiii.
Niu Ai: a duke turned were-tiger, 189, 189n.
Niu Seng-ju, 90n.
Nomenclature, 251.
North, the, 6, 8, 121, 207.
North Sea, 203.
North Village, 195.
'Note on Ink Cakes, A', 167n.
Nothing, 213, 213n.
Nü Kua (or Wa): snake-bodied goddess, consort of Fu Hsi, lxii, 11, 11n.

olea fragrans: cassia, 214n.
On First Taking up My Post as Supervisor of Ceremonies: Li Ho's poem, xxvin.
'On the Semantics of Poetry', lvn.
Old Man of the North Mountain, *see* Master Simple of the North Mountain.
Orchid Terrace, 89, 89n, 183, 183n.
Orion, *see* the Three Stars.
Outing among Blossoms, An: Li Ho's poem, xxvii.
Ou-yeh Tzu: semi-legendary metallurgist 62n, 236n.
Ox: constellation, 146.

Pa: ancient state located in the present-day Pa county, Szechwan, 6, 107, 130, 130n.
Pa: river in Shensi, 65n, 121n.
Pai-hsiu, *see* Han K'ang.
Palace(s), 199, 219; Southern, xxvi, 143; Triple, 111.
Palace Affairs, Court of, 87.
Palace of Eternal Trust, 260n.

Palace of Jade: in the moon, 45, 45n.
Palace Poetry, 2.
Palace Spirits: in Shang-ch'ing's palace, xxxvii, 33.
Pan Chieh-yü (Pan-tzu; Pan, *fl.* 48–6 B.C.) favourite of Emperor Ch'eng-ti of the Former Han, 260, 260n.
P'an Yüeh, Governor, (*hsiao-tzu* T'an-nu; Master T'an; Governor P'an): poet and official, 139, 139n, 160, 160n; Ho-yang Magistrate, 155n.
'*P'ang-mei hao-fa*', *see* 'Beetling eyebrows and white hair'.
Pan Ku (32–92): historian, 65n.
Pao Chao (Pao): fifth-century poet, xxxvii, 49, 49n, 194n.
Pao Chiao: Chou recluse, 210n, 211, 211n.
parafiliara multipapillosa: parasite, 76n.
Parnassians, the, xliv.
Pass(es), 155n, 166, 171, 224.
paulownia imperialis: t'ung trees, 10n.
Peach Blossom Banquet, 71n.
Peaches of Immortality, 10n.
Peach-leaves (T'ao-yeh): Wang Hsien-chih's concubine, 110n, 232, 232n.
'Peaceful and Slow', 78.
Pear-garden School: school of music, 10n.
Pearl (Lady Pearl): a Lo-yang beauty, 4, 54, 283n.
Pearl Game, 107n.
Pearl – A Lo-yang Beauty: Li Ho's poem, 283n.
P'ei: place-name, 101n, 102n.
Pei-kuo Sao, xxv, 151.
Pei-mang: a hill north of Lo-yang, 181n.
Pei-shang hsing: title of old *yüeh-fu,* 207n.
Pei-shang p'ien: title of old *yüeh-fu,* 207n.
Pei-ti: commandery, 252n.
P'eng, Grandfather (the Chinese Methus-aleh), 46, 46n.
Pen-ts'ao, 82n.
Perfect Peace: flute, 78.
Perfumed Plum(s): fanciful name for elexir, 206, 206n.
Persian rug(s), 93, 164.
Pepper Apartments: palace of Han Emperor Shun's wife, 199, 200n.
phellodendron amurense: Siberian cork-tree, 24n.
Phoenix Park, 69.
phyllostachys bambusoides: bitter bamboo 191n, 226n.